China Fast Forward

China Fast Forward

The Technologies, Green Industries and Innovations Driving the Mainland's Future

Bill Dodson

WILEY

John Wiley & Sons Singapore Pte. Ltd.

Other Wiley Editorial Offices
John Wiley & Sons, 111 River Street, Hoboken, NJ 07030, USA
John Wiley & Sons, The Atrium, Southern Gate, Chichester, West Sussex, P019 8SQ, United Kingdom
John Wiley & Sons (Canada) Ltd., 5353 Dundas Street West, Suite 400, Toronto, Ontario, M9B 6HB, Canada
John Wiley & Sons Australia Ltd., 42 McDougall Street, Milton, Queensland 4064, Australia
Wiley-VCH, Boschstrasse 12, D-69469 Weinheim, Germany

ISBN 978-1-118-17632-0 (Cloth)
ISBN 978-1-118-17634-4 (ePDF)
ISBN 978-1-118-17633-7 (Mobi)
ISBN 978-1-118-17635-1 (ePub)

Typeset in 11.5/14 point Bembo by MPS Limited, Chennai, India.
Printed in Singapore by Markono Print Media.

10 9 8 7 6 5 4 3 2 1

For my son,
Ashley Xavier "Si Cheng" Dodson

Contents

Acknowledgments

Nearly every ambitious effort an individual concludes is couched in collaboration. *China Fast Forward* is an attempt to survey a wide range of industries, technologies, and social developments in China that are as disparate as they are fast-moving. The effort required me to extend my shallow perceptions of trends with which I had little experience to a depth that would provide readers informative and engaging insights. None of the revelations could have happened without the extensive rounds of conversations with the experts, analysts, and practitioners who live the developments every day in China. Any errors or omissions readers may find are solely mine.

Practitioners who have shared for years the insights and experiences they've gained from their hands-on work in their industries include Peter Holmes, Michael "Mickey" Duff, Mark "Six" Kissner, Robert Kong, and Fulvio Hernandez. The continued jovial support and industry-specific banter of the Blue Marlin "Think Tank" over the years in the China-Singapore Suzhou Industrial Park also contributed to insights in the book. Through the accretion of countless conversations during our gatherings I have gained a great appreciation for the efforts involved in cultivating approaches to innovation in manufacturing in China.

I owe a debt of gratitude to my friend Andrew Hupert for sharing his thinking and wisdom about industry trends and government involvement in China. Andrew was an adjunct professor at the Shanghai campus of New York University while I worked on this project. He always made the time to discuss major developments with me and to review drafts of articles and chapters that came to make up the final publication of *China Fast Forward*.

I talked with countless professionals involved in one way or another with China's energy sector. Some of those who offered me their valuable time without reservation included Franz Lang, Poul Kristensen, Hans Suo, Johann Wiebe, and Torben Jorgensen. Bhavesh Mistry and Basile Waite also contributed insights into some of the articles I published, that eventually made their way into the final manuscript. Staff members of the Daoda Heavy Industry Company were great hosts who enlightened me to the special challenges confronting the shipping and wind power industries in China.

I reserve a special note of thanks for the *China Economic Review*, based in Shanghai, for its support and encouragement of the China energy and environment column I produced for their publication. In particular, great thanks to the publisher, Graham Earnshaw; Pete Sweeny, who while chief editor suggested I contribute to the column; and Ana Swanson, Pete's successor, who encouraged me to dig under the surface of China's cleantech sector. Author and China industry analyst Paul French was as always supportive and informative about the publication process throughout the project.

The chapter on services outsourcing trends was several years in the making. Pivotal in its development were the generous introductions that the operations directors gave me to their facilities in Shanghai. Sushil Asar and Michael Su were warm and informative hosts at Mahindra Satyam, as were Cai Jieru and her colleagues at Shanghai SAFE Software. Local government officials in China were also helpful and supportive of my interests in the development of the services outsourcing industry. Daisy Gao in the Suzhou Industrial Park, Juliet Zhu in the Suzhou New District, and Cara Long at the Chengdu Tianfu Software Park were particularly helpful and gracious hosts in explaining to me their operations. The energetic staff at the economic development zone of the Jiangning district of Nanjing was always a pleasure to visit, and the efficient staff of the Hangzhou New and High Technology Park was especially informative. Sustainability should be such a well-defined sector.

Richard Brubaker, professor of Corporate Social Responsibility at the China-Europe International Business School (CEIBS), was exceptional in helping me frame sustainability within the context of China's modernization drive. Bambu owners Rachel Speth and Jeff Delkin are tireless business people whose housewares company should be a model for many businesses to emulate. For a decade they have thought deeply about the practicality of sustainable manufacturing within an Industrial Revolution context and have met implementation challenges with grit and honesty. Despite their busy lives in Shanghai, southeast Asia and the United States, they took considerable time in educating me about sustainability issues in business. My greatest thanks to Brubaker, Speth, and Delkin for the time they spent reviewing portions of the manuscript.

Even before *China Fast Forward* became a manuscript Grace Lu was a most charming and forthcoming guide to charity work in China and the promise of social entrepreneurship. My deep gratitude, as well, to Linda Hou for the sort of unselfish support that helped me reach the finish line of the project.

My publisher, Nick Wallwork, and Jules Yap, the editorial executive at the Singapore division of John Wiley & Sons, were instrumental in accepting the initial proposal for *China Fast Forward* and in shaping its momentum. I deeply appreciate their patience with this author during the writing and editorial process. Despite her hectic schedule, Emilie Herman in the Hoboken, New Jersey office of Wiley, was always positive, considerate, and patient in taking the manuscript from rough to refined.

In no small measure has the unwavering support of my friends Doug Wack, Franziska Gloeckner, and Palle Linde enabled this project to come to completion. Their help defined for me the true meaning of friendship.

My wife, Jessica Zhou, was not always clear about what I was on about with the project and why I found it important to invest so much of my time and attention to it. Still, she hung with me during the entire birthing process, for which I am grateful.

The true inspiration for *China Fast Forward* was my son, Ashley Xavier "Si Cheng," who was just a few months old while I was writing the book. Throughout the writing process I considered just what sort of world he would be living in when he reached adulthood. Both of American and Chinese ancestry, he will be confronted with choices and challenges I can scant imagine. If he one day reads this book and excavates even a single nugget of insight that helps inform his decisions, I will have considered *China Fast Forward* a success.

Introduction

China today is a train traveling through a lightning storm.
None of us are spectators; all of us are passengers.
                              —*A Chinese user of Sina.com's Weibo, a Twitter-like*
                                         Internet application, July 24th, 2011

On the night of July 23, 2011, China's perceptions about its society, its leadership, and the direction in which the country was developing shattered like a mirror under a hammer blow. Even the Chinese Communist Party (CCP) was forced to recognize its own disjointed reflection in the glare of the frightful lightning strike that changed the course of the central government's momentum for global leadership status. A high-speed train traveling nearly 400 kilometers per hour (240 miles per hour) came to a crawl and then a full-stop when lightning struck the high-tension wire that had lured it through the mountainous countryside. Night poured into the disabled train, black as pitch. Suddenly great sparks sprayed from the tail-end of the marooned vessel as another express train smashed into it like the hammer of a gun firing its load into the gully below. Forty people died that night. Two hundred more were injured.

Just three weeks before the incident, CCP officials were extolling the virtues of their super-fast trains to the international community. They charmed the Americans with the promise of cheap high-speed rail to lace together its far-flung cities. They told the Germans "finder's keepers" in reference to the train technology the Chinese had acquired from the Europeans and now exported to other countries. They extended, too, a metaphorical middle finger to their arch-enemies, the Japanese, who had warned the world months before that the Chinese leadership was driving trains too hard, too fast, and using Japanese technologies not thoroughly tested on Chinese rails.

Within hours of the accident, the Ministry of Railways buried the damaged coaches in heaps of earth not far from the bridge where they had cascaded. Some Chinese who viewed the video of the cover-up claimed to have seen unrecovered bodies still flopping around in the cars. Nevertheless, one little girl named Yiyi was discovered still alive nearly a day after the accident as officials prepared to bury what would have become her coffin. She was wedged between her parents, both dead.

Millions of Weibo "tweets" had already been aflame with news and views of the accident. The sheer number of text messages proved to expose the crisis of confidence citizens had in its leadership and the direction in which the country was developing. With Twitter blocked in China, Weibo had become the default microblogger of choice for hundreds of millions of Internet users in the country. During a prime-time slot Central China Television (CCTV) broadcaster Qiu Qiming echoed Internet calls for accountability from central government authorities:

"If nobody can be safe, do we still want this speed?" he said. ". . . Can the roads we travel on in our cities not collapse? Can we travel in safe trains? And if and when a major accident does happen, can we not be in a hurry to bury the trains? China, please slow down. If you're too fast, you may leave the souls of your people behind."

The short message encapsulated the times in which 1.5 billion people—including my family and I—were living in the country: Economic growth and modernization had morphed dangerously out of control. The event itself and the government's response to public excoriation were truly historic.

Conventional media grilled the CCP and the Ministry of Railways. Traditional Party mouthpieces like the national television network CCTV, the *China Daily* and the sensationalist *Global Times* roasted the highest levels of authority. Weibo and blogs authored by millions of Chinese Internet users continued the flow of vitriol for weeks. Beijing then did the most unexpected thing.

It did not shut down the media channels. Any of them.

Some high-profile media commentators were censured, according to sources, while others were suspended or may have been fired. However, none of the popular, unofficial Internet sources of news suffered wholesale censorship. The armies of censors at first tried to filter out messages with keywords deemed inflammatory, and, initially, some blogs were pulled down. The central government, however, did not block the most sensitive parts of the incident from the public. Apparatchiks understood that they would have to act quickly, decisively, to keep the populace from massing against them.

Another completely unexpected—and, for the central government, a highly embarrassing—move was to slow trains with a top design speed of 350 km/h to 300 km/h. Trains designed to run up to 250 km/h were not allowed to exceed 200 km/h. The CSR Corporation Ltd., makers of the trains for the highly publicized Beijing-Shanghai line, recalled over 40 coaches built specifically for the line, the crown jewel of China's high-speed rail. Authorities reverted to the older equipment of the traditional overnight train between Beijing and Shanghai, which resulted in a dramatic change in travel time from 6 hours by high-speed rail to 11 hours with conventional rolling stock and locomotives. In addition, all newly built high-speed rail lines were to undergo a thorough inspection. By the end of 2011, all new construction on the rail lines had come to an abrupt stop. Innovation with Chinese characteristics—what the central government called "indigenous innovation"—was in for a serious review.

■　■　■

In 2006 Beijing implemented a national initiative that required foreign companies with proprietary technologies to share those technologies with local partners. The policy applied for the most part to industries the country deemed strategic to its economic preeminence, like information technology, aerospace, biotechnology, and cleantech. Joint cooperation meant Chinese interests having access to product blueprints, in some product categories. The Chinese would then localize the technology to meet conditions within the country's borders, and patent the remake in international markets as China's own. Beijing called the policy "indigenous innovation." The innovation policy failed, however, in the critical signaling technology the Japanese had passed over to the Chinese to build the Beijing-Shanghai high-speed rail line.

The Japanese had placed their technology in a black box the Chinese were unable to reverse-engineer. Their best railway technicians set about replicating the contents of the black box without fully understanding the design. The misunderstanding in how signaling works within a Japanese context and how it needed to be adjusted in Mainland China was a major contributor in the Hangzhou-Wenzhou train crash. The ripple effects of the innovation misstep touched on every major aspect of modern Chinese society's vision of the perfect future its leadership had been molding for its people and promoting to the world. *China Fast Forward* explores the critical juncture at which the society then found its development and the choices remaining open to it in the near future.

China Fast Forward is a survey of some the many technologies, industries, and innovations China is adopting from the West, modifying in many instances, and applying to build and consolidate its position in the world as a global leader. To be a superpower in modern terms implies the highest level of social development any country can attain in an epoch, as well as the greatest capacity the nation has to sustain the lofty heights it has attained. *China Fast Forward* explores the nature of innovation in the manner in which China understands it and the nation's interpretation of the mechanism by which discoveries are made and integrated with the world in which we live. The book also explores whether the society's innovation priorities will assist it—and the rest of the world—in overcoming the energy, resource, and environmental constraints against which it is already pressing.

In 2011 China's central planners understood they had reached a tipping point in the nation's economic and social development. The quality of the innovations central planners intended for mass consumption was becoming more important to citizens than the quantity and the speed with which products were offered up for consumption. This included infrastructure projects. Whether high-speed trains, bridges, roadways, residential property, or a plethora of other government and commercial interests, Chinese were beginning to fatigue under the constant stress of not knowing whether the cars they drove in, the airplanes they flew in, or the trains in which they commuted were going to disintegrate mid-operation. For instance, six months before the bullet train accident, central authorities had placed a moratorium on any further development of wind power farms. Half the wind turbines manufacturers had built were off-line and the half that were online were having constant maintenance problems. Three months later, the nuclear power plant disaster at the Fukushima-Daiichi facility in north Japan forced Chinese central authorities to place a moratorium on the approval of new projects. Nuclear power promoters within the government had slated 77 new nuclear power plants to be built in the nine years leading up to 2020—the most any country in history had attempted to build in such a short time span. Before the end of 2011 the central government had announced it would be paring down the number of nuclear power projects that would actually be built and that the new facilities would use safer third-generation technology, imported from Europe. Re-innovation, the central authorities were beginning to admit, had its limitations in building a modern, digital society.

The public shortcomings of re-innovation impacted the credibility of Chinese scientists and researchers filing the second most patents in the world by 2010. Critics charged that if the patents were simply adaptations and localizations of technologies copied from designs implemented elsewhere, were those real innovations? And what was so earth-shattering about them? Ultimately, did answers to these questions matter to us in the West, or to other developing nations?

The answers, it seemed, did matter to any nation that had been or was building its society on outmoded paradigms of the Industrial Revolution. How China in particular adapted imported technologies to develop its high-speed rail system and other critical projects reflected on China's understanding of the nature of innovation. The integrity of its undertakings illustrated how it was spending its creative capital to meet the challenges of modernization, overpopulation, and aging demographics.

For instance, just over half the country's population lived in cities by 2012. By 2020 China's urban centers will support a migration of 100 million people from rural to urban life. By 2025 China will have more than 220 cities with populations greater than 1 million. The country will have paved 5 billion square meters of road and built 5 million buildings, including 50,000 high rises.[1]

The leadership will have to find jobs for its newly urbanized. It will have to ensure ample water and food for the new city dwellers. It will also have to provide constant supplies of electricity, quadruple the amount their rural cousins require. Governments at every level will also be responsible for moderating air, water, and land pollution to ensure the spaces are livable for residents. The high-speed rail was one of the country's most important components in reducing its carbon emissions. Still, bullet trains require their electricity to come from somewhere. The fount of energy will likely be one of the thousands of coal-burning power stations pock-marking the Chinese landscape. The ways, means, and will with which the country ameliorates its dependency on fossil fuels—especially coal—matters greatly. Climate change will dramatically affect the degree to which China will be able to build and sustain a post-industrial society—its digital dynasty. However, just as China fully realizes its vision mid-century it will meet a "hard ceiling" of social development similar to what it has hit several times before in its long history. The Industrial Revolution paradigms upon which it has careened into modernity have exposed resource, environmental, and energy constraints on a global scale. Modernization has created new problems and conditions the country must resolve to maintain living standards.

Ian Morris, in his thought-provoking book *Why the West Rules—For Now: The Patterns of History and What They Reveal About the Future*, defines social development as a society's ability to get things done, to shape its physical, economic, social, and intellectual environments to its own end. Morris relates four essential measures of social development: energy capture, urbanism, information processing, and a society's capacity to make war. Energy capture is a society's ability to harness energy, as in burning coal to heat water into motive steam that drives turbines. Urbanism represents a society's ability to organize its resources—like energy, people, and matériel—into rational drivers that facilitate the society's efforts to achieve its goals. Information processing reflects the sophistication, the rapidity with which information travels, and the capture rates of the transmissions. The Internet has proven a much more effective means of communications than the telegraph, for instance. And a society's wherewithal to make war on others or to defend itself is critical in some instances to preservation of the society. The hard ceiling, as Morris defines it, is the point in a society's lifetime when it can no longer sustain current levels of complexity in its society. Joseph Tainter, in his book *The Collapse of Complex Societies*, places the base of the pyramid of social measures squarely on the ability of a society to find and integrate ever-greater sources of energy; or, even more effective, energy sources with greater bangs for the buck than those previously used.

China and the Western core—today's European Union—have hit their hard ceilings three other times in history, almost in synchrony, with equally disheartening results: in the 1st century CE (Common Era), when the Han Dynasty and Roman Empire disintegrated; in the 13th century with the Mongol invasions and black plague that brought the Song Dynasty and medieval Europe low; and then again in the 17th century, when the populations in both Eastern and Western cores doubled in size in a matter of decades and adequately feeding, clothing, and housing citizens became a very real concern for the governments of both regions. The Europeans, on the other hand, realized in the 17th century that technology had cleared an avenue to a new way of negotiating with the limitations of social development.

The philosophical antecedents of the Industrial Revolution can be found in the thought of Francis Bacon, the English philosopher, scientist, and statesman who looked to the mechanical nature of the clock rather than the natural philosophy of the ancient Greeks. In France, Rene Descartes, another philosopher and a mathematician, wrote, "It is not less natural for a clock, made of the requisite number of wheels, to indicate the hours, than for a tree which has sprung from this or that seed, to produce a particular fruit." Bacon and Descartes and other thinkers intuitively understood that Europe, together with the colonies in the New World, could transform the cycles of war, famine, and pestilence that characterized Western history for millennia.

The Chinese core, however, cloistered from influences from the West, allowed the Industrial Revolution to pass it by in favor of reviving the ancient Chinese classics to consolidate the political power of its new foreign rulers, the Manchus. Chinese society fell into ruin and chaos 200 years later, in the 1800s. Morris called the dynamics behind the rise and fall and rise again of societies "The Paradox of Development." He writes, "rising social development generates the very forces that undermine further social development." Or, as Albert Einstein so plainly put it, "We can't solve problems by using the same kind of thinking we used when we created them."

■ ■ ■

I open *China Fast Forward* with a chapter on the nature of modern Chinese scientific research, and the ways in which the nation is going about innovation in industry to frame the ensuing discussion. Chapter 2 discusses the intersection between government and business in Chinese cyberspace as domestic Internet companies struggle to be free of the ideology that dictates the boundaries of innovation. Chapter 3 conveys my exploration of an aspect of the services sector that is dependent on digital technologies and that the central government considers vital to the country's continued growth: services outsourcing. Chapter 4 details how China is developing heavy industries to pull the country up the value-chain of sophisticated export products. Chapter 5 investigates the "soft" innovations China and its corporations need to make to re-image themselves in the eyes of the world and become truly incomparable international brands. Chapters 6 through 9 reflect my belief that energy generation and mobilization and the sector's relationship with the environment are fundamental to the society's viability in the long run. The last chapter addresses perhaps the most important innovation China must undertake to remain a viable modern society. It is incumbent on its leadership to create a safe and supportive context for the assembly of individuals with social interests that lie beyond the solely commercial and political. Charities, non-governmental organizations (NGOs), and eldercare will become increasingly important in China's future. By 2050 about 30 percent of the population will be over the age of 60, while drought, climate change, and energy constraints will force open a floodgate of rural refugees into the cities.

A China at the leading edge of history is meeting global challenges ahead of most countries. Its huge population, its dearth of energy and mineral resources, and its concentrated pollution issues are mobilizing the country for dramatic change. The approach the country takes to resolve these issues and the level of success it attains in building a sustainable society will hold important lessons for all of us, no matter where we live on this fast-shrinking planet.

Chapter 1

Innovation Nation

The interview with the reporters from Liaoning province had been an easy one, Fang Shimin considered; a simple case of fraud. He had exposed the self-anointed Taoist "Supreme Master" Li Yi as a fake. Li and his 30,000 adherents had claimed throughout 2010 that he could sit underwater for two hours while holding his breath in a lotus position and could withstand 220 volts shot throughout his body, as well as other impossible feats. Fang simply laid the facts out before the reporters: Li had practiced the underwater stunt in front of cameras in Chongqing ten years before while encased in glass, insulated from the water; and there was no objective evidence of Li ever surviving electrification.[1]

Fang stepped out of the hotel onto the wide Beijing sidewalk into a hot, mid-afternoon August day filled with the cacophony of traffic noise, blaring horns, pedestrians talking on their cell phones, and street vendors hawking fruit, vegetables, sunglasses, hair clips, and the like. Sometimes he missed the blandness and isolation of his life back in California, when he simply went to his biochemistry lab at the Salk Institute, put in long but fruitful hours, and then went home. When royalties from patents began to flow in, he decided to return to China to pursue work that would benefit his society, making it a better place for the country's countless millions who had not been as fortunate as he. Applying the scientific method used in Western institutions and combining it with his hatred of bullies and fraudsters, he took on the mantle of China's "Science Cop." His pen name was Fang Zhouzi, a name millions came to know throughout China for his forthright approach to the lies and inequalities that permeated his beloved country.

Nearly home, he grew excited at the thought of the evening ahead, filled with further research into the medical fraudster Xiao Chuanguo. Xiao Chuanguo claimed that he cured the urinary incontinence of many children by operating on certain nerves.[2] Fang Shimin was sure Xiao had falsified the data. To Fang Shimin, Xiao Chuanguo was a public menace.

He turned down a side street. The neighborhood was quieter now, and he felt more relaxed. As he rounded the corner a big man stepped in his way. Fang Shimin saw a shadow, a blur, and then a bottle held up to his face. His friend Fang Xuancheng had been attacked on the street just two months before in just such a manner. Fang Xuancheng had been badly beaten and hospitalized. Fang Xuancheng was a correspondent for *Caijing*, a Chinese financial journal that took controversial stances against companies and institutions in China. This was no time to wonder if this was a similar sort of attack, though.

Fang Shimin ducked, instinctively. Still, part of his face was caught in the mist of pepper spray. His cheek stung, then numbed. He blindly sprinted into the street to escape the assault. Fang Shimin heard an iron bar clamber to the ground, and two men cursing behind him. "Goddamn it, Xu! You sprayed me in the face instead! You turtle's egg!" one of them shouted.

"Shut up!" Fang Shimin heard a second voice shout, "Catch him!"

"Your mother and father! I can't f—king see!" Xu screamed.

Xu leaped over his comrade, who lay crumpled on the sidewalk, and dashed into the street after Fang Shimin. He pounded the air with the hammer in his hand to know its heft, to feel how hard he would have to wield it to crack Fang Shimin's skull.

Fang Shimin knew if he hesitated for even a second the thug would kill him. He laced his way through traffic and was nearly run over twice by irate drivers who honked their horns at him. Meanwhile, the assassin had closed the distance between them. As Fang Shimin changed direction once more, he saw out of the corner of his eye his assailant lobbing something long and heavy at him. Again Fang Shimin's instincts took hold and he ducked his wiry frame to protect his head. When he looked up he saw a hammer coming at him. He ran faster. A moment later he felt a stab of pain in one of his shoulder blades. Fang Shimin dared not slow his pace. He rounded the next corner and sprinted through the gate of his apartment complex.

Xu stopped his pursuit a hundred meters before the gate of Fang Shimin's residence. He glared at the guards gaping at him. After a time, he realized others were staring at him, too. He had failed. He would have to return the ¥50,000 yuan[3] ($7,000) advance to Big Brother Dai. Dai Jianxiang had trusted Xu and Long Guangxing to teach that turtle's egg a lesson. Xu cursed again and then set off to bring back Long. It was turning out to be a very bad day.

Actually, it turned out to be a bad week for "brothers" Dai Jianxiang, Xu, and Long Guangxing. Days later police picked up Xu, who had been recorded on closed-circuit television cameras stalking Fang just before the incident. Xu led the authorities to Long Guangxing and both confessed that they had been paid to teach Fang Shimin a lesson by Dai Jianxiang. With little pressure applied, Dai Jianxiang admitted Dr. Xiao Chuanguo—Fang's arch enemy—had paid Dai Jianxiang, a distant cousin of Xiao Chuanguo's, ¥100,000 to make all the arrangements. So informed, the Police picked up Xiao Chuanguo at the Beijing airport after he had just returned from a trip abroad.[4] Xiao Chuanguo confessed to the crime within hours of incarceration. He also confessed to having arranged for the attack on Fang Xuancheng, the financial news reporter at *Caijing*. Both Fang Xuancheng's media assault on Xiao Chuanguo's background, credibility, and research work had caused the Chinese Academy of Sciences to deny his application. Years of Xiao Chuanguo's work was held in ill-repute in China, though Western scientists found some of his research promising. His endless defamation suits against Fang Shimin had only brought more attention to him, instead of absolving him.

Dr. Xiao Chuanguo pleaded not guilty, despite having already confessed his crime to the police. The court passed judgment down in less than a day, without Fang Shimin, Fang Xuancheng, and their lawyers present in the court room. The court found Dr. Xiao merely guilty of creating a public nuisance. The triumvirate of judges fined Xiao Chuanguo several thousand dollars and sentenced him to five and a half months in prison. Immediately both Fangs and their attorneys accused the court of backroom dealings that denied them justice. They filed an appeal to a higher court, the outcome of which would take years to finalize.[5] The case, however, did not deter the Science Cop from his mission to continue uncovering fakery in the fields of science and technology.

Impure Research

Fake permeates Chinese society. For many without the connections or money, making up one's past is the only way to achieve the social and economic status one seeks. The walls of alleyways in some cities are littered with the phone numbers of agents who can get you a technical certificate or university diploma, or even PhD. In August 2010 authorities discovered that several dozen pilots had faked their flying histories. It took a plane crash in northeast China and the death of 42 passengers to begin an investigation into the mass deception.[6]

In 2010, Science Cop Fang Shimin revealed that the former head of Microsoft China, Tang Jun, had falsified his resume. He had presented to his employers that he had received his doctorate from the California Institute of Technology. The deception had facilitated his rise to become a millionaire and a sort of modern-day Chinese folk hero, who with grit and determination had overcome adversity.[7]

Zhang Ming, a professor of international relations at Renmin University in Beijing admitted that a great many Chinese academics prefer to serve a more economically practical cause than seeking the truth through research. "We need to focus on seeking truth, not serving the agenda of some bureaucrat or satisfying the desire for personal profit," he said.[8] However, the plea fell on the deaf ears of 55 percent of his colleagues surveyed by the China Association for Science and

Technology, who claimed to know someone who had falsified research findings or plagiarized papers for publication. Six of the country's top research institutions admitted in a government report that they had falsified data or copied research results from other researchers. In December of 2009 a British scientific journal had to withdraw more than 70 papers after editors discovered findings of questionable veracity.[9] A bit of software called CrossCheck, which checks for plagiarism, flagged nearly a third of the papers submitted for testing as highly suspicious. In some instances, the software found 80 percent of some papers had been copied from elsewhere.[10]

The sort of veracity and transparency Western scientific research institutions take to with religious zeal is far from affecting the agendas of the political leaders who have been appointed to manage Chinese research organizations. The Communist Party appointees who direct daily affairs at the departments dole out budgets, housing, and reputations. Nepotism is rife. *The Party ultimately defines the meanings of discovery and invention in China.*

The Patronage Party

The public accusations against Dr. Xiao Chuanguo, his confessed attacks on his accusers, and the court's light sentences for his crimes point to a fundamental flaw in China's plan to surpass the United States as a preeminent innovation nation. The country lacks checks and balances within its own scientific community and society. Science prides itself on its scientific method of repeatable results rigorously tested and approved by a group of peers. As Thomas Kuhn wrote in his seminal study of the work of scientists, *The Structure of Scientific Revolutions*, most often discoveries are resisted by peers who have vested interests, yet eventually the community of scientists adapts—typically in nonviolent ways—as the discovery becomes a fact that expands on previous understanding. The scientific method is supposed to weed out wrong or misleading results and researchers contribute to a base of standing knowledge upon which others may continue to build. The court systems in a civil society function similarly, with judgments passed based on a body of evidence that is indisputable in its objectivity and certainty. Both science and society in China are based on patronage, though.

Patrons are typically political appointees with ties to the Chinese Communist Party (CCP), who are made department heads, school directors, and research presidents. Often, political appointees have little or no experience in the fields they are charged to manage. Subsequently, patrons themselves dole out positions of responsibility to scientists, funding for projects, even living quarters for the families of researchers. Consequently, researchers learn not to "bite the hand that feeds" if one wants to advance his or her career.

Judges on the bench are also political appointees with little training or experience in the complexities of litigation and judgment. As a Beijing lawyer once told me, she practiced "fake law." For most cases, she told me, she was expected to take the judges out to dinner and treat them well. Sometimes she would have to play drinking games with a judge to decide the outcome of a case.

In other words, the two most important systems supporting innovation in a society are woefully skewed to meeting the demands and vanity of CCP sponsorship. Ultimately, Chinese business and industry is beholden to the same kind of patronage; and the larger the enterprise and more closely aligned with national industrial policy, the fewer degrees of freedom of research and development (R&D) interests and commercial viability the entity has—the State directs the former and decides the latter, as Richard McGregor so engagingly wrote in his penetrating expose *The Party: The Secret World of China's Communist Rulers*. Yigong Shi and Yi Rao, deans of Life Sciences at Tsinghua and Peking Universities respectively, noted in an editorial in *Science Magazine*, "it is an open secret that doing good research is not as important as schmoozing with powerful bureaucrats and their favorite experts. China's current research culture . . . wastes resources, corrupts the spirit, and stymies innovation."[11]

The network of patronage that laces China's R&D efforts affects the objectivity, quality, and veracity of efforts to push back the frontiers of science and to address some of the most profound challenges humankind has ever faced. Issues such as meeting burgeoning energy requirements; growing pollution hazards to the earth's ecosystem; and consumption of nonrenewable resources such as land and water require a clear-eyed, apoliticized approach that will ensure the habitability of the country. Britain's National Endowment for Science, Technology and the Arts offered that China's economic rise and new-found geopolitical heft make the country hugely important in working with other countries to resolve such sustainability issues.[12]

Chinese patronage also affects the efforts of organizations that are attempting to blaze trails beyond a stultifying domestic environment into a world bristling with ideas and applications. Fields such as services outsourcing and Internet applications risk being smothered for fear that devolution of creative energy destabilizes the country. The gravity well of patronage also pulls on and warps genuine efforts of Chinese companies to become innovative global players that can go toe-to-toe against titans such as IBM, General Electric, Procter & Gamble, and others. Whatever plans the country has to become a global innovation powerhouse, it first has to surmount huge, self-inflicted challenges. Some of the challenges are based in historic patterns that have become habits of thinking and actions that run counter to international norms of transparency and reportage, and to the scientific method itself. Other hurdles the nation needs to overcome are socio-political. The leadership will need to learn how to balance the will to survive, and maintain control over the society and economy, with the very real expediencies of creating safe environments in which creativity, enquiry, and impassioned dialog can ensue. With so many conflicts of interest throughout China's government, educational, and research institutions, it is little wonder that so much of the country's innovation should be constrained to the inconsequential.

Gimme a Big "I"!

In November 2010 the State Intellectual Property Office of China published its *National Patent Development Strategy*, which outlined the country's plans for innovation ascendance. China planned to register patents at a rate of two million per year by 2015. In 2009 Chinese would-be inventors filed 600,000 patents with its patent office. By September 2010 Americans had filed 480,000 patents in the United

States patent office. China also planned to double the number of patent examiners by 2015, to 9,000. The United States in 2010 had 6,300
inspectors.[13] China was able to accelerate the manufacture of patents at
such an astounding rate because of its growing R&D budget in relation to its Gross Domestic Product (GDP).

China's R&D expenditure increased to 1.5 percent of GDP in
2010 from about 1 percent in 2002. The government aimed in 2010
to have its R&D budget at 2.5 percent of its GDP by 2020. Its share
of the world's total R&D expenditure was a little more than 12 percent in 2010, while the United States' contribution was around
35 percent.[14]

Some of the other metrics the original strategy cites include, "The
quantity of patents for inventions [made in China] for every one million citizens and the quantity of patent applications in foreign countries will quadruple." And, "The proportion of patent applications in
industrial enterprises above [a] designated size will reach 10%." The
paper, though, does not designate the size of said enterprises. However,
the plan does include designating 10 "model cities" that will be patent
examination hubs.

A closer look at the kinds of patents China is encouraging reveals a
skew in the numbers. The patent goals breakdown into 1 million patents for each of China's patent types: utility-model patents and invention patents. Utility-model patents are incremental improvements or
lateral changes to products and invention patents are true patents for
new inventions.

Most of the patent applications were expected at the time to be in
what the central government called "pillar" industries, areas the government considered of vital interest to the country's economy and
social stability. These industries included solar and wind energy, information technology and telecommunications, and battery and manufacturing technologies for automobiles, according to David J. Kappos,
director of the United States Patent and Trademark Office (USPTO).[15]
John Kao, an innovation consultant, described the central government
plan as "a brute-force approach at this stage, emphasizing the quantity
of innovation assets more than the quality."[16]

Research by Anil Gupta and Haiyan Wang into the complexion
of Chinese patents revealed Chinese institutions were nowhere near

as creative as they would have the world believe. Based on more than 95 percent of the patents filed with China's own patent office, Gupta and Wang found that the vast majority of these patents are "tweaks" to current developments. A more telling number of Chinese patents filed with three of the world's leading patent offices in the United States, Japan, and the European Union revealed a different story. The "triadic" international patent standard involves approval by each of these patent offices. In 2008, the Organization for Economic Cooperation and Development (OECD) cited only 473 triadic patent filings from China versus 14,399 from the United States, 14,525 from Europe, and 13,446 from Japan.[17] The Chinese were actually far behind other countries in meeting international standards for invention patents. The statistics did not dissuade China's leadership from centrally planning innovation, however.

China, in its efforts to become the "workshop" of the world, has never let the emphasis on quantity ahead of quality deter its efforts. In late 2010, Wang Yong, chairman of the state-owned Assets Supervision and Administration Commission of the State Council (SASAC), announced the Council would develop 50 state-owned enterprises (SOEs) to become top-ranking global companies before 2015. The key to moving into this top tier entailed upgrading their innovative capacities to meet international competition head-on.[18] The move came as regulators called for the upgrading of innovative capacities to strengthen the international competitiveness of the SOEs. Thirty-five of the companies had already pledged before the announcement to develop into global industrial giants possessing advanced technology in line with international standards.

The technocrats who run the Chinese Communist Party (CCP) seem to believe that innovation can be constructed in much the same way as a bridge or a dam or a highway. The approach runs in the same vein as the way in which the leadership has carved up its ecology in favor of economic growth over environmental sustainability. China's leadership anoints cities throughout the country as being innovation centers of services outsourcing, animation, information technology research, aviation, and so forth. Entire cities in the country also have the unfortunate reputation as centers of counterfeiting products, designs, and innovations.

What's a Little Intellectual Property Theft between Friends?

If there is any aspect of "Brand China" that is well-known to foreigners, it is the extent to which Chinese businesses play fast and loose with the intellectual property of original inventors and artists. Chinese counterfeiting of American products alone cost American businesses at least $60 billion.[19]

Chinese merchants have considered everything from consumer products, industrial equipment, vehicles, music, movies, and art as fair game in the hunt for profits. A walk through nearly any emporium in any Chinese city will leave visitors breathless from the extent of copied products for sale at steep discounts. Many of these malls—indoor and outdoor—have booths or small alcoves where energetic sales staff call out to passersby to entice them to browse what's on sale. In the summer, indoor corridors are not air-conditioned, leaving visitors gasping for breath and relief from the incessant heat and din. In the winter, the corridors are often freezing cold. The only real protection the display tables have from the rain at outdoor emporia are tarpaulins drawn down with clothes line.

The markets sell all manner of brands, typically within a single industry, such as textiles, shoes, or lady's bags. One visit to the Hongqiao Pearl Market in Shanghai revealed warrens chock full of Louis Vuitton hands bags, Tommy Hilfiger shirts, and Gucci shoes. In some instances—such as the alligator shirt a German tourist may be fingering—the merchandise is actually a genuine article that has "fallen off the truck during shipping" and made its way to the fake market. The item was actually commissioned by a brand-name company to be manufactured in China. Factory owners make a few extra sets of the product, matching the same specifications the factory's corporate buyer had laid down for operators. Employees ship the extra sets out of the factory to middlemen to find retail shelf space in some emporium, where they'll be sold for 20 to 50 percent of the original retail price.

The phenomenon reaches into industrial components and equipment. One Danish manufacturer of parts for heating, ventilation and air conditioning (HVAC) systems took a phone call while we were having lunch near his factory in the Yangtze River Delta. It was a Western customer. The conversation was about how the customer could be a great help to my friend by visiting a competing Chinese HVAC-parts manufacturer, taking photos of the knock-off parts to pass on to my friend. Then, my friend would have his lawyer in China send the offending party a warning letter about the course my friend's company would be taking if the Chinese maker continued to copy my friend's HVAC parts.

I myself have visited Chinese manufacturers with my own Western clients to have my customers whisper to me, "Those are our products in their display case!" Either the manufacturer was nonchalant about the rip-off, and felt safe enough that they did not have to protect themselves, or they had simply forgotten they had copied a potential foreigner partner's part and left it in the display case for all to see. Entire cities in China are devoted to copying products from abroad and selling them to gray markets or even exporting them to developing countries as originals. Putian, in Fujian province, on the coast across from Taiwan, is well-known as a knock-off capital for sneakers. Dongguan, in Guangdong province, is famous for knock-offs of shoes, golf clubs, furniture, you name it (and your price).

The culture of IPR infringement, mass copying, and outright fakery has its roots in China's history and has carried forward into the 21st century through the trunk and branches of its education system. The copy culture has such a strong hold on China's modernizing society that its grip sometimes makes for actual casualties.

Education

Jo Jo (a pseudonym) was 11-years old when he took his own life. His mother discovered him at their home, just after lunchtime one wintry January school day in Yunnan province. The boy had been starving. Teacher Tang, who was close to retirement, had kept Jo Jo after class to copy by hand pages from a Language Training Materials textbook. Old Tang was disciplining the boy, though for what, in the end, no one was quite sure. Jo Jo had had to copy in his neatest handwriting four chapters from the textbook, a total of seven densely-filled pages of Chinese characters. Jo Jo complained to his mother he was sure he wouldn't be able to finish the assignment by the end of the day. She assured him he would be able to, as he was a clever boy, and served him a bowl of sweet, glutinous rice balls filled with black sesame paste—a favorite of Chinese children. She returned to work, and assured him she would call to remind him he had to go back to school an hour before his scheduled return. Later, when she called, no one answered the phone. As only a parent's intuition would have it, she returned home, concerned something might be the matter.

Jo Jo had hung himself with his Red Pioneer's scarf tied to the door knob. He sat listless on the floor when his mother discovered him, the scarf still strangling what life may have remained in the limp body. The little red scarf, worn by hundreds of millions of children in classrooms during the school year, is the symbol of the sacrifice every citizen of the country must make to promote the welfare of the People. In this case, Jo Jo's sacrifice presented to the society the rigidness, insularity, and soul-crushing weight of its conformist approach to education and socialization. His mother stated her son was ashamed he would not be able to finish the copying exercise by the end of the day, and was not up to facing further punishment. Teacher Tang checked himself into a hospital and made himself unavailable for comment on the matter. By his and the school's reckoning, Jo Jo had stayed after class for some extra help on his schoolwork, but Chinese parents and students know the system works otherwise. The system will survive such sacrifices as little Jo Jo's, however.

Chen Zhiwu, a finance professor at Yale University, tweeted in response to an online public discussion in China about why China could not produce a Steve Jobs. Chen felt that in Chinese schools, "the first thing the teachers do is to rub down the edges of those students who are different from the crowd."[20]

The modern Chinese education system has its roots in the sort of study required to pass the imperial examination for entry into China's government. During the Sui Dynasty in 605 AD the country found itself with too many people and too few routes to prosperity. Nepotism for plum government positions was rife. The emperor commanded administrators to build a meritocratic bureaucracy. They developed a rigid examination system that would filter the best educated for government seats. Passing the imperial system for nearly 1500 years also assured that the backgrounds, thinking, philosophies, and initiative of bureaucrats were near harmonious, no matter where in China they were from. Since then, the Chinese examinations at all levels of education emphasize regurgitation of memorized treatises over individual displays of creativity, personal insight, and hands-on experience.

China—or rather, specifically, Shanghai—was quite proud when in 2010 its students placed first in the world in scoring on an international math examination, ahead of South Korea, Singapore, and Hong Kong. Finland finished very strongly, with America coming in 25th out of 34 countries. Many infer—including Americans—that the Chinese approach—or, at least, the Shanghai approach—to education is superior to the American system. They further infer that, *ipso facto*, China is able to produce superior engineers and scientists who will file more patents and publish more research papers than the United States. The line of thought concludes that China, then, will be a first-rate innovation nation. Chinese ascribe their success on such examinations, as well as in business, to "Confucian values."

Confucian theory is basically one of maintaining harmony within a family, a community, and in greater society. A society will remain stable through constant, self-referential study of social and historical phenomena, and by following those in authority. It is, at its most simplistic, a philosophy of follow-the-leader: the wife follows the husband (and the husband's mother); the husband follows his boss; the boss follows local government officials and so on, all the way to the seat of central authority, in Beijing. A Chinese middle-aged mother of a ten-year-old boy explained to me, "Chinese people at an individual level do not really know what they want. Their entire lives they are told what to think, what to say, what to desire." The culture of following and copying makes it difficult for multinationals invested in China to find educated and creative professionals with initiative to make breakthroughs in invention. Instead, foreign companies and their local hires find themselves constrained to adapting tried-and-true technologies for the country's domestic market.

Grafting Innovation

It was during a flight from Shanghai to Chicago that I realized Western-style innovation for China would be a transplant conception, not something indigenous to Chinese society (despite the Chinese leadership's promotion of its efforts at "indigenous innovation"). I sat next to a charming Chinese engineer who was, for much of the trip, engrossed in an American patent for AC-electric motors. Applications for such motors include the paper industry and the steel industry, in which extremely thin sheets of material need to be manufactured at exacting thicknesses without interruption and at the same rotational speed. Though shy at first about speaking English, the technologist quickly warmed up to chatting with me when I offered her (and her husband) sticks of gum near the end of the long flight.

It turned out she was indeed a rocket scientist, or nearly so; she specialized in the research and design of electric motors that would be efficient and steady. Surnamed Wang, she had been working for an American aerospace manufacturer since 2000. She was the first of the three researchers hired into the Shanghai R&D center years before. The R&D center was the first of its kind for the company in China. She was fairly certain that only IBM, at the time, had already established an R&D center in China.

When we spoke, the engineer's R&D center had thirty researchers. It was one of the few in the world that was at "headquarters level"; that is, most of the R&D done for the company was at the product or department level. The Shanghai R&D center reported directly to HQ in the States for projects for current, high-profile customers.

I noted that it was impressive the American company had established a China R&D center given that China-market conditions and product requirements could be quite different from America's. The engineer responded in PhD-speak (for I think she would have struggled to use English nouns and adjectives of less than three syllables) that most of the R&D work the Shanghai Center was doing was for Western customers, though they were receiving more projects from China-based companies. "I was just in Suzhou at a manufacturer's factory to hear their voice." Suzhou is a manufacturing hub little more than an hour's drive west of Shanghai. What she meant was that they had told her what they needed from the motors she designs.

She noted that the American company was extremely conservative in setting up the R&D center eight years before. Not only in the number of researchers they hired, but also in the size and kind of projects they gave the Shanghai group. "They watched us very closely," she said, "to see the kind of work we did, the quality, how we solved the problems . . . At first we had to listen to everything they said. There seemed to be only one way . . . But China is very old, and has some good things to contribute. Now they listen to us to help solve the problems." I did not mention anything to her about the level of discomfort with intellectual property rights (IPR) issues the company must have initially had; no need in making the kindly and talkative engineer squirm in her too-narrow seat. IPR concerns, however, seemed to deter foreign investors from setting up R&D operations in China.

By 2010 China became host to more than 1,000 foreign-owned R&D centers. Nearly all those centers, however, focused on adapting technologies developed in other countries to local market conditions in China. A culture of copying, weak intellectual property rights (IPR) enforcement and Beijing's expressed policy of "indigenous innovation" forced foreign multinationals to keep their leading technologies in countries in which they felt their IPR was protected. Anil Gupta and Haiyan Wang identified that half of the top 10 U.S.-based technology giants that received the most patents from the U.S. Patent and Trademark Office (USPTO) between 2006 and 2010 were not doing any significant R&D work in China. During the same years the USPTO did not award a single patent to any China-based units for 5 out of the 10 companies. However, 9 out of 10 centers in India *did* receive patents from the USPTO. *India does not have a policy of indigenous innovation, nor does it force foreign technology companies into joint ventures with domestic companies with the sole aim of transferring technology.* Seven out of 10 of the Indian units of the multinationals received more patents from the USPTO than their Chinese labs, with a tally of 978 versus 164.[21]

As Gupta and Wang wrote, "Yet Beijing is standing in the way, because it's looking at the problem from the wrong angle. Instead of trying to extract technology from foreign firms today, it should be creating a hospitable environment for these firms to create and train world-class innovators."[22]

The probability, in other words, of the charming Ms. Wang working on state-of-the-art R&D projects for a foreign lab in China was remote. She would have to move to a country that did not force investors to transfer their technologies to local champions, nor local champions to give up their spoils to the government.

A Cautionary Tale

An indicator of how a country's government may treat foreign-invested companies—especially in the worst of times—is to look at how its domestic champions fare. Multinational corporations with R&D operations in China have much with which to be concerned in light of the legal case of Cathay Industrial Biotech (Cathay).

Cathay produced a chemical building block of nylon—called a diacid—through a process of fermentation. It produced about half the world's inventory of the polymer-grade diacids, and counted the chemical giant DuPont among its customers. Manufacturers use nylon ingredients to make some lubricants, while pharmaceutical companies produce diabetes drugs with the nylon components. Liu Xiucai established Cathay in 1997 in Shangdong province, near the Korean peninsula, when he was 40 years old.[23]

Born and raised in China he was a victim of the purges of the Cultural Revolution in the 1970s. He was amongst the first graduates of universities that had reopened in 1977 after a decade of being shuttered. Afterward, he went to the United States to receive his Masters and PhD in Chemistry. He returned to China in 1989 with the idea of finding Chinese investors to commercialize projects based on outdated patents in the West. Liu Xiucai became a darling of the Chinese Academy of Sciences and of the Beijing elite after he helped China become the largest export manufacturer of industrially produced Vitamin C in the world, with 80 percent of the market in 2010. Cathay was to be his defining moment as an entrepreneur and innovator. From its inception the central government lavished subsidies and tax breaks on the investment to ensure its success. Government largesse ended, however, when patrons found another, less willful supplicant than Liu Xiucai.[24]

In 2011 Cathay filed a patent infringement suit against Hilead Biotech, another private Chinese company in Shandong province. Liu Xiucai accused his former plant manager, Wang Zhizhou, of infringing on patents and stealing trade secrets from his former employer and setting up Hilead in 2009 with six other former employees of Cathay. Hilead received direct assistance from the highest levels of the Shandong provincial government, where the company was being set up. The CCP's Party Secretary for Shandong province accelerated government approvals and financing for the project. The Chinese Academy of Sciences also did its part to sponsor and promote the company and its technologies as national priorities. The state-run China Development Bank gave Hilead a US$300 million loan to get up and running. Hilead captured a tenth of the global market for the nylon components a year after it had started up. The irony of the cut-throat competitor that Cathay had spawned was not to be lost on Liu Xiucai.[25]

He used his own patrons at local and national levels of government to hobble Hilead. Liu Xiucai, though, had made enemies during his rise to national glory. Liu Xiucai had been going public for years about the corruption, nepotism, and fraud in state-run institutions. He had also complained about the official interference in the private sector, crippling the competitiveness of potential national champions. The accusations had weakened Liu Xiucai's political base considerably.[26]

Wang Zhizhou's patronage, meanwhile, had only grown stronger once he left Cathay. The central government listed Hilead's diacids as national security interests. Neither foreign nor domestic challengers were allowed to impede the commercial success of Hilead without severe repercussions. Beijing stripped Cathay of one of its top patents when the company began its suit against Hilead. Hilead filed a countersuit that accused Cathay of stealing patents from the Chinese Academy of Sciences. Liu Xiucai again took the offensive.[27]

The American-trained researcher convinced a local Shandong court to send officials to Hilead's manufacturing operation about 400-kilometers away to document that Hilead was using the same technologies and fermenting processes to produce diacids. Guards at Hilead's company gate turned the officials away with the proclamation that Beijing authorities had designated Hilead a national security interest. That meant that further intrusion into the factory compound would be tantamount to espionage. Indirectly, Beijing could construe continued pursuit of a patent infringement case against Hilead as treason.[28]

Undeterred, Liu Xiucai told the *New York Times*, "Personally, I will not give up on this dream. I'm Chinese, you know, so the Chinese government should want me to contribute. We're pioneers. If the Chinese government does not allow me to do this, I will find another place."[29] Sentiments like these from the country's leading lights only make it more difficult for the nation to realize historic heights of scientific discovery and genuine invention.

The Glory That Was Ours

China has imposed on itself several limitations to fostering innovation such as: a culture of copying, falsification, corruption and IP theft, and an education system that intentionally seeks to rub out individual initiative and creativity. Nonetheless, the Chinese leadership seems convinced it will regain the era of invention it enjoyed from about 1500 BCE to 1500 CE. Chinese are rightfully proud of their contributions to the world, which include paper, printing, gunpowder, the compass, porcelain, the clock, and much more. Invention ground to a halt in the Middle Kingdom after the voyages of Zheng He, the Muslim eunuch who several times took armadas of the largest ships to ever ply the oceans of the time from southeast Asia to India and Africa in the mid-1400s. At the end of the 15th century infighting in the imperial palace resulted in the country's breaking up the ships, "losing" the records of the amazing discoveries the armadas must have made, and shutting itself off from the rest of the world. China was content that economically, militarily, and technologically it was paramount in the world.

The throne did not see at the time that its society had hit a ceiling. To break through the barrier to further social development China required radical innovations on the order of an Industrial Revolution. The Europeans took to the new energy sources and machines the Revolution offered with a gusto that allowed the social development of the Western countries to blow past China's. China spent the next 500 years in decline, periodically convulsed by war, famine, plague, and flooding. China—and most Chinese, really—believe it is their birthright to be the most technologically astute and socially advanced society on earth, because they had already several times in history held the mantle. Many countries at various levels of publicity harbor a vision of the restoration of their former glory. There is the Glory that was

Rome; the Glory that was Greece; the Glory that was the British Empire and so on. Citizens and politicians that rally their countries around their nation's past glories ignore the critical technological and demographic trends constrained by geography.

Jared Diamond's *Guns, Germs and Steel* illustrates how China had been blessed with two rich river plains and a geography that permitted a union of states that a peninsular and fratricidal Europe could only dream of. Linking the economies and foodstuffs of the northern and southern plains allowed populations to mushroom to the extent that the societies needed to innovate or devolve into simpler states—which happened at the end of several dynasties. Now, technology has made geography matter even less, especially in the world of the Internet. Consumer societies are tightly linked through global supply chains and knitted together through international financial markets. With the low-hanging fruit of geographic advantage nearly picked clean and the Industrial Revolution model bringing the earth's resources and ecosystem to near-exhaustion, regaining past glories hardly seems germane. Instead, it's in the virtual world of digital communications that the next empires rise—and former glories are made irrelevant.

Chapter 2

The Fractured Web

A young girl with the Weibo microblog moniker Smm Miao "tweeted" in the early evening of July 23, 2011, "After all the wind and storm, what's going on with the high-speed train? It's crawling slower than a snail. I hope nothing happens to it." Minutes later, during a torrential downpour punctuated by thunder and lightning, the country girl watched as another bullet train rammed the stalled locomotive from behind, killing 40 passengers and injuring hundreds more. The message was the first of 26 million that would be posted and echoed throughout Chinese Internet space. Most of the microblogs were scathing about the country's government, the quality of the railway infrastructure and its handling of the tragedy. Representative messages included:

"We have the right to know the truth. That's our basic right!"
"In the eyes of the authorities, regular people will always be gullible three-year-old children."

"When a country is corrupt to the point that a single lightning strike can cause a train crash, the passing of a truck can collapse a bridge, and drinking a few bags of milk powder can cause kidney stones, none of us are exempted."

"They [the CCP] think: 'We built this. We built that. You don't need to care what happens along the way, or who gets the benefits, as long as you get to use it,'" Han Han, a famous blogger in China, wrote. "Why aren't you grateful? Why all the questions?"

The high-speed train accident and the scores of fatalities resulting from the incident proved to be a tipping point in China's hurried modernization. The contract between citizens, the leadership of the country, and domestic commercial interests on the Internet was coming undone.

The last time the tacit agreement between the leadership and citizens had come under such strain because of a tragedy was in the spring of 2008, during the aftershocks of the Sichuan earthquake just outside the provincial capital, Chengdu. More than 90,000 people died in a matter of minutes. Bloggers and the media blamed the corruption of local government agencies and property developers for the poor quality construction of schools and apartment buildings, and for the death of so many. Commercial Internet operators in China like the search engine Baidu.com and news and entertainment portals like Sina.com and Netease.com quickly fell into line behind government directives to only report on stories of heroism in the face of a natural disaster.

The bullet train incident nearly three years after the Sichuan earthquake was significant in China's modern history to the extent that citizens and professional media outlets ignored government directives to avoid unofficial investigations and commentary about the incident. The railway incident was also significant in terms of the extraordinary leniency with which the government treated the media outlets—especially the Internet. And finally, the incident exposed the degree to which the CCP's fortunes had become bound up in the Western-inspired innovations upon which e-commerce in China is based. China had less than 10 million Internet users at the start of 2000[1] and no sellers or buyers doing business through the Internet.

In 2008, China's commercial interests totaled only US$7 billion and Internet users numbered 200 million, according to the China Internet Network Information Center (CINNIC). By 2011, the number of Internet users in China was nearing half a billion and e-commerce revenues were close to US$80 billion, growing 87 percent year-on-year. IDC, a technology market research company, reported the number of Chinese sellers on the Internet had reached nearly 50 million at the start of 2011. Analysts expect the number of online merchants to reach 100 million by 2012.[2]

China's online shopping industry saw revenues of $80 billion in 2010, and grew 87 percent from the year before.[3] Deutsche Bank projected that e-commerce, instead of detracting from brick-and-mortar retail sales in China, would actually increase overall retail sales by more than 1.5 trillion yuan (about US$100 billion) by 2014, or about 7 percent of all domestic retail sales.[4] In 2010 Chinese Internet users invested a billion hours each day online. Out of a total of 420 million users at the time, 185 million made at least one online purchase. The Boston Consulting Group expected volume to increase fourfold by 2015.[5] Seemingly overnight, the balance of power between the CCP and Chinese netizens had tipped in favor of consumer advocacy.

The Chinese government had to tread lightly on Internet channels after the train disaster of 2011, for great wealth derived from China's Internet was at stake, with thousands of companies creating millions of jobs for Chinese who based their livelihoods on the World Wide Web: web designers, games makers, customer service representatives, marketing mavens, administrators, sales staff, executives, investors, State Owned Enterprises (SOEs), online shopkeepers, and more. Meanwhile, without CCP authorization, shopping on the Internet had become a right—not a privilege—for hundreds of millions of Chinese netizens. Innovation for the sake of commercial gain on the Internet had outstripped the CCP's ability to control the medium as strictly as it had in the past. Developments in information technology had left the Party with little choice but to curb innovation in Chinese cyberspace to fit its political expediencies while at the same time motivating the leadership to cultivate its own state-owned digital champions. In the meantime, the CCP put privately owned Internet companies in China on notice that their implementation of innovation with Western characteristics had begun to run counter to national interests as the CCP defined them.

Finger on the Button

The private company whose fate hung most on the auspices of the central government after the 2011 train disaster was Sina.com, the platform that supported the Weibo service. Weibo means "microblog" in Chinese. Weibo was China's answer to Twitter, which China's censors had begun blocking in China during the Tibetan protest of 2008. Like Twitter, the service restricted users to tapping out 140 characters per message. Unlike English characters, however, a single Chinese character can have multiple meanings—even puns—and hundreds of years of history and context bound up in its expression.

For instance, the former President of China, Jiang Zemin did not appear on the parade platform with other leaders during Beijing's celebration of the Communist Party's 90th birthday in late 2011. Weibo users in the millions conjectured whether he was gravely ill or if he had actually died. The media muzzle on the condition of the former leader simply created more buzz in Chinese cyberspace. Censors filtered out of Internet communications any mention of Jiang Zemin and deleted blog posts conjecturing on the welfare of the *apparatchik*. Not to be deterred, Weibo users simply used the ancient Chinese character for river—*jiang*—to represent his surname, though the character they used was different from that of the surname. Censors quickly caught on to the ploy and filtered out ALL of the characters in the Chinese language that could mean "river," whether or not they sounded like the former leader's name.[6]

With millions of users on the Sina.com platform—and on the vibrant QQ microtext service, supported by the Chinese company Tencent—the sheer volume of texts and permutations of characters used for discussion would have been humanly impossible for censors to respond to in real-time. The only other solution would have been to shut down the services completely. Sina.com's service supported 140 million users at the time of the train accident, while Tencent's supported 200 million. Between the two services, users had generated an amazing

26 million messages on the railway tragedy alone.[7] The CCP would have potentially alienated nearly one-fifth of all Chinese citizens had it chosen to simply blackout a homegrown service offering. Such a rash action on the part of China's leadership would have sent a signal to the international business community that the government at a single stroke could destroy companies and offerings it deemed inconvenient to its way of thinking. The action would have been like a cold arctic wind sweeping down from Siberia and ushering in a new ice age in one of the hottest business frontiers in the world—the Internet. Entrepreneurs and investors would naturally recoil from the prospect of collectively sinking billions of dollars into ventures in Chinese cyberspace. It wouldn't have been the first time, though, the central government would have considered the expediency of absolute control as preferable to a vibrant innovation ecology.

In 2009 the central government had tried to force every computer made in China or shipped into the country to have installed on their hard disks an officially sanctioned copy of censorship software. They called the software Green Dam Youth Escort. The application would block users from pornography and materials on the Internet censors deemed politically incorrect. The software would have put electronic surveillance on every desktop in the country. Millions of users logged onto the Internet to shout down the initiative. Chinese hackers even threatened to crash their own governments' servers should the authorities actually enforce the software installations on computers. The day before the initiative was to begin, on the last day of June 2009, the central government leadership back-pedaled on the initiative. The government turnabout on implementing Green Dam, however, did not deter censors from more targeted exclusion of international websites and online services it believed politically offensive—or that threatened the profitability of homegrown e-commerce companies.

Filtering for Profit

In 2008 China's central government blocked the international Internet platforms Facebook, YouTube, and Twitter, among others. Beijing didn't want protestors in Tibet or in Xinjiang to emulate dissidents in the Middle East who had threatened standing regimes. The beginning of 2010 saw Google withdraw from the field of battle with China's central authority when Google discovered the government sanctioned penetration of its customers' Gmail accounts. The attacks targeted foreign journalists and individuals who government authorities deemed dissidents. Google also publicly upbraided China's leaders for censoring links from search results to online sources the central government deemed illegal. As early as 2008, Chinese Internet minders had been interrupting services on Google so often that it made it difficult for users inside the country to develop the sort of relationship with products that companies seek. Google Docs was one such target. Service denial messages made (and still make, as of 2012) use of the word processing, spreadsheet, and presentation tools a frustrating exercise. The photo album program Picasa was also blocked. Perhaps the government felt the photo sharing program was a convenient vehicle for posting and sharing images that ran counter to how the CCP wanted citizens to view them. Google unilaterally shut down its server base on the mainland and withdrew to Hong Kong. China, in principal, respects the territory's right to free, unhindered speech and the rule of law.

The Google look-alike Baidu.com benefited directly from government interference with Google. Google's subsequent withdrawal from the mainland marketplace also provided Baidu with advertising fees Google most likely would have taken. In 2008 Baidu had only 30 percent of the search engine market in China as compared to Google's 50 percent. By the end of 2010 Baidu had 80 percent of the Chinese search engine market. Baidu hovered at about 3 percent of global market share at the end of the decade, while completely dominating the Chinese marketplace at about 75 percent of the online searches performed in the country.[8] Google still held the second position in China, with about 15 percent of the searches performed running through its Hong Kong *.hk address. BING—a Microsoft offering—with a worldwide share of the online search market of about 4 percent, overtook Yahoo! in March 2011 to become the second most used online search service in the world; BING's China slice of the pie was less than 1 percent of the domestic market at the time.[9] Google accounted for just over 19 percent of Chinese online searches in the first quarter of 2011.[10]

At nearly the same time as the dispute the government was having with users and PC vendors, the government was attempting to flex its muscles with Google.cn, the Chinese subsidiary of Google. At the height of the hullaballoo about the Green Dam software, Chinese Internet censors ordered Google.cn to stop posting links to pornographic websites. Google.cn's closest competitor in the Chinese marketplace—Baidu.com, which held upwards of 70 percent of the Internet search market to Google.cn's 26 percent—received no such warning.[11] Authorities did not censure Baidu.com about the issue, nor were its porn links in any way deleted by either the company or by Baidu.com. The move smacked of protectionism of the Chinese Internet market. According to some industry insiders, though, the relationship between Chinese Internet companies and their Party masters was double-edged.

One Chinese source told me under condition of anonymity, "The *technochiks* vex us pretty badly, too." *Technochiks* are the CCP officials who put in place censorship policies, filters, and staff to ensure information they deem politically incorrect does not leak through to the people. He continued, "I'm absolutely convinced that we're more a source of aggravation to said masters than we are a prop for them to pay as protection money to stay in business. As long as funds stream to the officials responsible for censorship and a range of business approvals, Chinese Internet companies can continue to operate. There's lots and lots of constant envelope-pushing going on here." Envelope-pushing is an allusion to the graft that many domestic companies have to pay government officials to operate. He continued, "I have loads of admiration for Google saying fuck you to the censors; but again, we don't have the leisure." One of the most vibrant industries in China, reliant on an e-commerce marketplace shielded from international competition, is the Internet cafe business.

Just the Internet, Please; Hold the Coffee

At one Internet cafe I visited in Suzhou, a city near Shanghai, I scanned nearby monitors to see what others were up to. Many had the popular QQ Instant Messaging window up and were typing and reading messages with friends. QQ users seem to take pride in the degree to which they can customize the long, narrow window that displays their list of friends—invited and uninvited. A user's most important decision, though, is choosing from among the scores of cartoon personas QQ provides through which users can chat with others in QQ-space: handsome warriors, winsome princesses, huggable pandas, and more.

In the West when we log onto the Internet we typically check our Facebook updates or email first. When a Chinese user sits down at home or in an Internet cafe the first thing she does is to log onto her Instant Messaging (IM) system, where friends are likely chatting away through a variety of text, audio, and video channels. The most popular IM system in the United States is AIM, which at the end of 2011 had 53 million users. In China, the most popular IM application is QQ, which, as of September 2011, boasted a whopping 700 million active user accounts. Chinese users will register themselves under several identities. Henry Jenkins from MIT performed a survey that observed that almost five times as many Chinese as Americans will manage a parallel life in cyberspace.

In the West users usually check up on the latest news and sports updates after they've read their email or Facebook updates. Chinese netizens, however, will go directly to their favorite web portal after checking QQ to see if any of their friends are online to chat with. Chinese use of the Internet looks something like this, according to a 2008 report by the China Internet Network Information Center (CNNIC): downloading (usually pirated) music (86.6%); Internet Messaging (81.4%); watching online movies (76.9%); reading online news (73.6%); using search engines (72.4%); playing online games (59.3%); and then email (56.5%). Most Internet cafe users are less than 30 years old; three-quarters of which have a high school education or less. It is not unusual for most users to be playing online games on one side of the screen, watching a movie (usually pirated) stream on another portion of the screen, while chatting with their friends through QQ about some trivial aspect of their lives—all at the same time. The Chinese, it seems, are true multi-taskers when it came to navigating cyberspace. In 2005 QQ was able to leverage its instant messaging (IM) interface into the most popular web portal in China, QQ.com.

To open the home page of a Chinese portal is to understand a bit of the frenzied life of the average Chinese. Pages are dense with photos of movie and singing stars; the latest gossip scrolls up bordered windows; advertisements square and round, rectangular and oblong scream for precious real estate; sponsorship bubbles float around the page, chasing after the user's cursor like a hungry fish chasing a mosquito skimming the water. "There's something for everybody [on QQ.com]," one 20-something-year-old user enthused at the Internet cafe I visited, "young and old; and we can all share with each other!"

Into the Fray

Western companies like Yahoo! that tried entering the Chinese market with their Copy-2-China business models did not find the success they sought. Chinese users consider Western-style sites boring. Western sites err on the side of simplicity in their appearance and messages; Chinese sites satisfyingly overwhelm the Chinese user with a smorgasbord of functions that rivals any Chinese dinner banquet. Baidu.com runs counter to the cluttered look offered by most websites for Chinese consumption. Baidu's interface is Google-simplistic: a white screen with the bare minimum of Chinese characters to point out what to do to search for keywords and other, hidden features.

In 2006 Yahoo! China failed to topple Baidu. Yahoo! was soon after bought by the Alibaba Group, owners of the business-to-business (B2B) directory of product-suppliers Alibaba.com. The Alibaba Group leads online retailers in the number of transactions made in China. The core product offering of the group is Alibaba.com, the world's largest online portal connecting potential buyers directly with suppliers from around the world. Users only have to type the name of the product they would like to have manufactured into a search box on Alibaba .com. They also identify the country—usually, China—and perhaps even the province in which they would like the search to take effect. The application displays a list of products that match the keywords. It's up to the user to scroll through the list of photos and descriptions to find potential suppliers. The onus is on the potential buyer to screen suppliers for quality and dependability. Alibaba was the third most visited e-commerce website in the world in 2011 after number one Amazon.com and then eBay, according to Comscore. The company makes its money through membership offerings to suppliers. Alibaba revenues in 2010 were US$845 million.

The overwhelming majority of online shoppers in China use a system called Alipay to settle accounts through the Internet, although buyers still settle nearly a third of transactions on the Internet through cash, paying the delivery service at the door. Alibaba established Alipay in 2004 to support purchases made through its other company, Taobao, which was a direct competitor of eBay. Alipay electronically places payments in an escrow account the buyer releases when she accepts the goods ordered. More than 8.5 million transactions each day made their way through Alipay by the end of 2010, for an annual transaction volume of US$140 billion. PayPal, within the same period, had a transaction volume of US$92 billion.

In 2011, Jack Ma, the Chairman of Alibaba Group, transferred Alipay assets to a company in China he personally owned, despite Yahoo! being a major shareholder in Alibaba. Ma claimed that Chinese government regulations forbidding foreign ownership of online payments had forced him to perform the share transfer.[12] The transaction was a huge embarrassment for Yahoo!, which was already losing global market share and had little independent presence in China. The incident clearly illustrated the extent to which business in general in China—and the high-stakes Internet marketplace in particular—were still frontiers where the rules were made up along the way.

In 2010 the Alibaba Group oversaw nearly 400 billion yuan (US$62.5 billion) in online transactions. Jack Ma predicted the company would manage 1 trillion yuan (US$156 billion) through its websites in 2012.[13] It was the Alibaba Group's late entrant Taobao that beat eBay in a highly publicized competition for market share. Taobao is a website with a cacophony of product offerings for sale.

In 2003 eBay bought the Chinese e-commerce site EachNet for US$180 million with much bravado. eBay exported its revenue generation model to China, which involved charging fees for transactions, listings, and other services. eBay and its Chinese partner, EachNet, controlled 90 percent of China's online shopping in 2004. Taobao, however, understanding the price sensitivities of Chinese shoppers, offered its services for free, making its money through online advertisements. Taobao trounced eBay. In 2006 eBay beat a retreat from its online base in Mainland China and retrenched in Hong Kong. It folded its EachNet investment into a joint venture with Tom Group Ltd., to maintain a presence in Greater China.[14]

In 2010 Taobao controlled more than 80 percent of e-commerce in China. Taobao's stature also extended into the labor market. In 2009 Taobao reported that its site had helped create half a million new jobs, mostly through young people opening new online stores. Taobao's ungainly growth spurt, however, forced the company to morph into something more manageable and nimble in the face of rising rivals.

In 2011 the company split into three entities: eTao, Taobao Mall, and Taobao Marketplace. eTao is a search engine focused on finding merchandize. The search service would help direct customers to Taobao Mall and Taobao Marketplace. Analysts saw eTao as a direct threat to Baidu, both of which look to advertising revenues to make a profit. The Mall was more a showcase of brands for about 70,000 companies, Chinese and foreign. Taobao Marketplace was more for small vendors. Taobao Marketplace was free for sellers, though it used the same advertising revenue model of its parent.[15] However, the Taobao business model had some weaknesses that upstarts began to exploit as early as 2009.

Taobao early on in its development began garnering a reputation for supporting the sale of counterfeit goods. That worked fine for a segment of the population that could not afford the real thing but wanted the look and feel—the cachet—of the genuine article, whether it was a purse, a mobile phone, or a dress. Nevertheless, the United States Trade Representatives (USTR) office lodged a complaint that Taobao supported the sales of thousands of fake products with designer labels, costing American companies billions of dollars in lost sales. In 2011 a Taobao Marketplace spokesperson said that in 2010 Taobao had deleted nearly six million listings from its site that infringed on trademarks. It had taken the cooperation of six thousand brand owners from around the world to identify the offending offerings. In the first half of 2011 Taobao Marketplace took down an additional 47 million listings that violated trademarks.[16] Taobao, though, had another, more sensitive vulnerability that irked thousands of buyers in China every day.

On average, it took two to five days for items ordered on Taobao to make it directly from the seller to buyers, which, as any consumer who's "got to have it now" knows, is a long time to wait for fulfillment. Sometimes, the boxes in which the items were shipped were crushed. One item my wife ordered took the agreed-upon but unsatisfactory four days to arrive. She told me the item was coming from Shanghai to our home in Suzhou, 150 kilometers west of Shanghai. A swarthy middle-aged man who had clearly only known manual labor in his life delivered the box. He smelled of cigarette tar and sweat. He was friendly and solicitous, and opened the box in the hallway in front of the entrance to the apartment. The trick to know in China, when ordering goods by mail, is to check the merchandise before accepting delivery. The review can be as superficial as opening the box to make sure what you ordered is what they put in the box. My wife and I, though, chose to be a bit more thorough by actually plugging in the appliance to make sure it worked as advertised. In Taobao's system, once the buyer accepts the package, the deal is considered done.

Another major challenge with e-commerce in China is the method of payment. Most Chinese do not have credit cards. Most, however, have bank cards. As late as 2009 sellers on Taobao took cash on delivery of goods to the buyer. As Taobao gained in prominence, it put in place its Alipay system. Most Taobao users open a bank account just for Taobao transactions. They do not want to expose their day-to-day bank account information to the outside world. When customers tell a bank teller the account is for Taobao, she will know what they mean. Though the account is generic, she will supply customers with a digital token that they plug into the USB port of their computer. When online shoppers make a Taobao transaction and wish to pay, they plug the tokens into their computers to complete what should be a secure transaction.

No longer, then, did users have to pay cash to swarthy men smelling of tobacco and looking suspect themselves. The ease with which users could then purchase and pay led to the creation of Internet users Chinese call Taobao Heads. Taobao Heads spend hours at a time each day perusing items to purchase. One husband told me of his Chinese wife, "We've got so much stuff now we're not using what she bought on Taobao. It's so cheap to buy! A lot of the things are unused, so we're giving things away to make room for the new purchases." The fervent commercial activity on the Chinese Internet made it plain to the central government that it could only push so hard when it came to filtering, cracking down, or outright blocking Internet channels of communication and commerce. Tech-savvy quarters of the CCP realized in 2011 they would have to join the game or have their power marginalized completely.

If You Can't Beat 'Em

Since 2008 the CCP has successfully blacked out all civilian digital communications in Tibet and Xinjiang. The extreme security measures have hardly impacted the country's overall economic growth rate. The territories, however, are poor, remote agrarian regions with little commercial activity to begin with and a population that has little access to the Internet anyway. The impact on the Chinese economy and international trade would be much more dramatic, however, if authorities placed a digital blackout on Shanghai. Hundreds of multinationals and thousands of Chinese companies in Shanghai alone rely on the Internet for secure transfer of information and financial transactions. In addition, hundreds of thousands—if not millions—of workers would be thrown out of jobs. Business owners would see their income streams dry up overnight. China's leadership would see several generations of work rolled back at least 20 years. The degree to which China would affect its standing and credibility in the world for maintaining a safe and stable environment in which to conduct business would be dramatic, on the order of the Tiananmen Square incident in 1989. After that incident, it took international businesses nearly three years to consider re-entering the China market after the world was shaken by the brutality with which authorities broke up the protest. China's leadership has known since then it can ill-afford a repeat of the response to mass discontent on the same scale as Tiananmen Square.

So the CCP decided in 2011 to extend its presence on the Internet beyond censorship into the commercial realm. The CCP sanctioned China Central Television (CCTV), the Party's TV persona, to start up its own online search engine. However, the Party would need to bring Baidu down a few notches to increase CCTV's online profile.

Reporters for CCTV televised an expose about Baidu that accused the state-sanctioned and protected Google-knock off of being monopolist in one instance,[17] libeling a respected professor in another report,[18] and ignoring dissatisfied Baidu users.[19] Think tanks even got in on the discussion, with Jing Linbo and Wang Xuefeng of the Chinese Academy of Social Sciences writing in the *Study Times*, a publication of the Communist Party School, "The combination of capital and the Internet is a mighty controlling power. The Internet is a special industry—once it is controlled by foreign capital, the impact could be severe."[20] They were referring to Baidu's listing on the NASDAQ. "If we judge by the indicator that a foreign control of over 20% stake is relatively controlled, and over 50% is majority-owned," they continued, "then most Chinese Internet companies that are listed offshore are controlled by international capital," the authors wrote. "International capital thus controls our Internet industry."[21] They rounded out the editorial by claiming the combination of capital and the Internet would have an impact on politics and the government. They added that China should strengthen supervision not only over an Internet company's capital structure but also its business operations, including its dealings with related parties.[22] Though the CCP was not willing to kill free enterprise and innovation on the Internet, it was willing to throttle it to maintain control of the country.

China Scrums

However popular it might be in the West to believe that the Chinese government will increasingly clamp down on Internet usage as completely as any Soviet-style police state, the reality of the balance between power and commerce in China is more convoluted. Nearly every day that I walk the streets of this fast-paced country I marvel (and sometimes, squirm; and at other times, become annoyed) at how nearly every interaction in China is a negotiation: whether it's crossing a busy street, vying for space while riding a bicycle in a bike lane, or buying vegetables from a street vendor. The more fractious an issue, the more each negotiation becomes a scrum. A scrum in the few-holds-barred game of rugby involves members of opposing teams going shoulder-to-shoulder against each other to kick a ball back to a player on their side. From the outside, scrums look like utter, violent chaos. And yet, deep within the mound of heaving bodies and grinding collar bones is a negotiation of sorts, to get the ball to the players who will push for a score for their team.

On the Chinese Internet, though, there is more than one team at play at any given time. And because of the vastness of the arena of the Internet and the restrictions to free expression in the physical world, there are many scrums going on simultaneously between blocks of users: e-commerce users, privateers, censors, and vigilantes.

Online scrums in China as a means to negotiate platforms, domains, rights, limitations, and penalties in cyberspace is creating a web space separate from the World Wide Web as the West has come to know and cultivate it. The Fractured Web, as Andrew Hupert calls the dislocation of a portion of the World Wide Web, is the new reality. Hupert was a professor of international negotiation at New York University's campus in Shanghai when we spoke. He told me over a cup of coffee in a trendy Shanghai cafe one muggy afternoon, just after the riots in Xinjiang in the summer of 2009, "No one cares that the central government has blocked Twitter or Facebook or YouTube. Chinese don't seem upset in the least about it. After all," he continued, "they already have their Chinese equivalents of the social networking sites, and the Chinese companies are overjoyed that the international competition is off their necks." In other words, Chinese politics and business are sometimes on the same side of the scrum; their interests aligned. That autumn Hupert had written on his blog *China Solved*—in reference to blocked Internet services like YouTube, Twitter, Facebook, and Google—"Usually industrial and national security policies are at odds with one another. This time they dovetail beautifully. This must have been a no-brainer for Beijing. Suppress potentially disruptive voices and protect key industries at the same time—in one fell swoop. Everyone from the Party leadership to the business community loves the idea." However, Internet businesses' alliance with the central government had shortcomings.

In the medium-to-long-term, Mainland users and China's up-and-coming hi-tech service economy will suffer. Chinese managers and businesses will find it difficult to understand how to enter and negotiate in the international marketplace; and Chinese technologists will find themselves in an application-ghetto the rest of the world considers insular and not applicable to international issues and norms. Hupert calls the insular market space the *Chinese Friendship Net*, a name taken from the government operated Friendship Stores of 20 years before. Only foreigners and high-level apparatchiks could shop in Friendship Stores; the rest of the populace had to stand in long queues and accept their rations from government shops. "For the moment, the *Chinese Friendship Net* is delivering all the same services and products as the international Internet—in some cases even more. But as the two Internets develop and diverge, we will return to a situation where commerce in China becomes separate but unequal. Those caught on the wrong side of the digital border will not have access to new media or technology—while a digital Chinese elite will have VIP access to the global net."

But the technochiks' efforts to fence off the Internet from the rest of the world will not go unchallenged. Hundreds of millions of Chinese netizens will push back on actions that curtail and control *all* of their activities on the Internet, as in the case of the Green Dam software initiative. The most dramatic scrums in the China Wide Web are and will continue to involve those that reach the threshold where politics and commerce meet, where the technochiks have drawn the boundaries of their domain for power. Anyone who crosses the border into the wider world risks being filtered out of cyberspace existence. The tension between unfettered access and censorship is rising quickly in China's Internet universe. The sheer number of new users logging on for the first time and becoming enamored with the plethora of service offerings and opportunities for expression will continue to rise into the 2020s. With less than a third of the Chinese population in 2011 regularly living with the Internet, China still has a long way to go before it reaches the same density of users as America. America's penetration was about 75 percent in 2009.

In addition, the 700 million citizens who still lived in the countryside at the close of the first decade of the new century had little recourse against corrupt government officials, unscrupulous real estate developers, and polluting factories. Greater access to Internet channels of communication will make local goings-on more transparent to the world, at nearly the speed of light. Indeed, one of the ways the

Party has been able to manage discontent in China's interior is through restricting the information that flows into the hinterlands.

Twenty years after the Tiananmen Square incident, citizens are more interested in balancing out the opportunities of self-expression and economic opportunity in their day-to-day lives than in democracy, *per se*. For Chinese, democracy—embodied by the Western notion of "voting the bums out of office" if they do a poor job, as well as a separation of powers—is worthwhile as long as it proves an effective means of allowing them to carry on economically the way they'd like to, with the least amount of "unfairness" reasonable in life.

As Rebecca McKinnon wrote:

" . . . One must also keep in mind that the people blogging online are the most inclined to view their glass as half full as opposed to half empty when it comes to personal freedoms: they are the educated urban elites who have benefited more than any other segment of the Chinese population from the past 20 years of economic reforms. There would need to be a much more profound and acute offline crisis for this group of people to find it worth risking the online and offline freedoms they have gained in exchange for the very uncertain gamble that they might be about to gain even more. This is especially the case when no viable national thought leader is able to emerge online under the current system of controls— and no viable alternative to the Chinese communist party has emerged offline either."[23]

The vast scale of the Internet, current commercial rewards, and the staggering riches that lay in store, though, has complicated the government's equation for control and restriction of information about the society and about the rest of the world. Especially important to Chinese officials is the way the rest of the world perceives China, as the less well-traveled of the Old Guard still harbors a tremendous insecurity about navigating in truly international streams. The Internet becomes like a wild thicket to Chinese propagandists, in which Chinese Internet subversives are able to hide and "nest" like sparrows.

Compounding the sheer number of current and potential Chinese Internet users with which government censors have to contend is the prospect of disruptive technologies that may seem to lighten the burden of socializing users, but may also complicate government agendas for control and "spin" of information. In the West millions of teenagers rely on Facebook and Twitter to chat about whether that cute girl in class really likes a guy or not; or what the hottest pop act is; or whether or not an old girlfriend is still hot or not. Meanwhile, in China, Facebook and Twitter are, as of this writing, blocked—considered tools of the subversive in light of the violent protests of Uighurs in Xinjiang or the ongoing investigations of corruption in the CCP. Instead, the CCP has sanctioned homegrown versions of the same applications with the hope that censorship controls will reign in any political impulses Internet consumers may have. The CCP also sees the Internet as a profitable new frontier through which its agencies may be able to further enrich themselves.

The clashes between the Chinese polity and its would-be masters will only increase in cyberspace. The sheer numbers of users rushing to access the Internet, combined with the disruptive technologies that continually destabilize the Internet ecosystem, are proving difficult for central planners to control. When Chinese authorities consider a country-wide event threatening their hegemony, they may compromise their image and their control of the Internet and shut down ALL access to it. Just as residents of Xinjiang found in 2008, consumers throughout China may not be able to get online through computers; nor may they be able to make phone calls on land lines or send or receive text messages between each other through their mobile phones. China then will enter a glacial age of digital and commercial innovation that will erode any strides the country was making to become an innovation nation. It will also cripple its efforts to become the world's premiere services outsourcing provider, a sector the central government has identified as strategically important to the country's economic interests and irrevocably dependent on digital communications technologies.

Chapter 3

The Silicon Paddies
of China

My host for the day at the Suzhou Industrial Park (SIP) International Science Park was a petite, articulate Chinese government official, Daisy Gao. Ms. Gao directed the promotional affairs of the Science Park, which is SIP's magnet campus for attracting information technology (IT), business process outsourcing (BPO), and R&D companies to the city of Suzhou. Suzhou is a short, 25-minute ride by bullet train due west from Shanghai. Chinese call Suzhou the Venice of China because it is laced with canals that run through the city and connect it to the Pacific Ocean and Lake Tai, China's third largest freshwater lake. Daisy represented the latest generation of Chinese government officials. She was in her late twenties, a newlywed when we met, spoke perfect English, and was professional and relaxed with Westerners. I first encountered the bespectacled promotion officer four years before, when I represented an American manufacturer looking for potential investment sites in China. Now, like SIP itself, she had shifted her focus to the services sector, especially the information and knowledge management industries. "We know manufacturing is very important to China's development," she told me, "but it is not enough to employ all the people. We have to develop the services industries, too."

The global growth consultancy Frost & Sullivan estimated in 2007 that the worldwide market for outsourced services was worth US$930 billion in 2006. The group forecasted that sector IT outsourcing (ITO), business process outsourcing (BPO), and outsourced R&D together would grow at a compound annual growth rate of 15 percent to reach a market size of nearly US$1.5 trillion by the end of 2009. By 2020, the global market for services outsourced to third parties could reach US$6 trillion.

IT outsourcing involves an outside organization of software and hardware engineers and project managers who support company computer systems, typically those for back-office functions such as accounting, payroll, and human resource systems management. Other IT outsourcing companies write programs called "embedded systems" that are found in everything from computer games to automobiles and manufacturing equipment. Businesses outsource repetitive tasks done by, for example, call center operators, payroll processing, medical recording, payments processing, and the like. In the instance of accounts payable processing, the Chinese service provider receives a scanned image of an invoice that must be paid by its American client. Relevant information such as the invoice date, due date, purchase order number, delivery date, product codes, and the like are manually entered into a computer system in China. The Chinese company then uploads the data to the client's financial accounting software. Now, the client has the order in its computer system and can track shipment progress and payment to the vendor accurately. The sectors that outsource the most back-office and IT support operations are banking, financial services, and insurance followed by high technology and then the healthcare industry, which primarily outsources its R&D expenditures.[1]

The Chinese government officials and entrepreneurs see that the shared services pie is increasing in size and want a slice of it. Entrepreneurs are in it for the riches and glory. The Chinese government, however, wants the many jobs that the services outsourcing sector can potentially provide. Jobs are important to the Chinese government because unemployed citizens are seen as a source of destabilization of the society. For those in power in China, social stability with economic progress is the key to prolonging their mandate to rule the country.

China—especially in east coast cities such as Shanghai and Suzhou—is focusing on service industries—or *tertiary industries*—which accounted for 67.4 percent of international direct investment in China in 2006, according to the United Nations Conference on Trade and Development. Official Chinese sources cited that in the first three quarters of 2005, the service sectors in 16 major cities in the Yangtze River Delta amounted to 39.2 percent of their combined GDP. Total output of China's tertiary industries accounted for just 32.3 percent of its entire economy, rising at an annualized rate of about 8 percent. The average rate in the industrialized world is as high as 64 percent according to official Chinese sources, so China has a long way to go to tertiary sector maturation.

The Chinese government has several motivations for promoting the tertiary industries in China: job creation, wealth creation, and to benefit the environment. Beijing knows that the light manufacturing sector—sneakers, toys, cigarette lighters, and other commodity-driven, labor-intensive manufacturing—will only employ a certain proportion of the working-age population. Issues, such as land use, resource intensity, technical training, and experience, constrain the degree to which China can industrialize. In particular, over the last two years, land for building manufacturing facilities has become highly restricted, and economic development zones in China can no longer expand the size of the land available for investment. The cost of materials has increased, too, as Chinese factories have sucked in greater amounts of metals, plastics, wood, and other resources to meet production quotas inside and outside China. The havoc unregulated light manufacturing has wrought on the environment will take decades to reverse. Air, water, and soil in some regions of China are poisoned to the extent that pollution has even entered the food chain.

The Chinese government sees outsourced service industry jobs provided by the travel and leisure sectors, financial services and banking, logistics, even arts and entertainment, as a social release valve to soak up the labor pool. Currently, Chinese universities are annually churning out hundreds of thousands of graduates who are un- and underemployed. Further, with per capita GDP in the nominally poorer interior of China rising, more students go beyond the compulsory nine years education to complete twelve years. The Chinese government will have the additional responsibility of creating jobs for the millions who do not go on to the university level but who are better educated than previous generations. The tertiary industry provides an outlet for this labor pool, one that light manufacturing cannot.

The Hi-tech Face of China

Suzhou Industrial Park (SIP) is the largest, most successful joint venture negotiated between the national government of China and Singapore. Originally, when Singapore was the majority shareholder, the area was called the Singapore Industrial Park. The Chinese side of the investment—administered by the local Suzhou government—held 60 percent of the shares in the venture for more than a decade, while the Singapore government and various private groups maintained the remaining 40 percent. But to call SIP an industrial park is misleading. SIP is more of a new city, an incorporation of four townships inside a 350 square kilometer plot of river delta that abuts downtown Suzhou with a highway separating old Suzhou from the new industrial park. Suzhou's government is intent on seeing all new industrial and high-tech developments established in SIP. The contrast can be seen in old Suzhou's cityscape of white-washed traditional structures now punctuated by the high-rises going up in SIP.

SIP—and its cousin on the west side of Suzhou, the Suzhou New District (SND)—started out courting foreign direct investment for manufacturing enterprises in the 1990s. Foreign investment in SIP is nearly 50 percent Western companies, followed by Taiwanese, Japanese, South Korean, and domestic Chinese firms that established offshore entities and then reinvested in China as foreign companies. (Foreign manufacturers had, until 2008, been able to garner tax advantages that domestic companies could not.) SIP has been very successful in attracting Western companies—especially in the hi-tech and knowledge industries. Its success is attributable to the Singaporean model of government administration. SIP administration has a greater number of English speakers than other foreign investment zones in China. SIP administration also has a sense of propriety and structure that Singapore inherited from the British. Emulating Singapore's business environment has helped to attract and retain Western investors, who find establishing operations in other parts of China problematic.

Since 2006, SIP and SND have excluded manufacturing that pollutes or produces low-value products. The zones have favored hi-tech, R&D, IT, and BPO companies to gentrify Suzhou and increase tax revenues.

To encourage more R&D and information management companies, SIP created the International Science Park. The Science Park was quite different from the rest of SIP. The Science Park was a sprawling complex of post-modern architecture. The total size of the campus was 690,000 square meters. The Science Park was built in four phases. The fourth phase was completed mid-February 2007. The first phase was primarily an incubator building for young IT companies that developed software and provided animation outsourcing services. The building itself seemed transported from the 22nd century. It was shaped like an elongated donut facing a small lake and divided by a strip mall of offices. Phase 2 focused on corporate R&D companies. Phase 3 was a high-rise building with R&D and IT outsourcing companies; Phase 4 consisted of two high-rise buildings, one that offered furnished apartments and the other an R&D complex. Phase 4 looked rather like a great, upright magnetron, with two curvilinear buildings erected in such a way as to spin around each other in opposition. Young Chinese, with sparks seemingly flying from their can-do faces, crowded outdoor corridors and walkways of the campus while inside the corporations themselves, one had to strain to hear even a whisper. The Phase 4 structure also featured a large, glaring flat panel display that showed advertisements for the park.

"Employment for people in their twenties and thirties is one of the issues China has to solve," said Daisy Gao. "We call it the 20/30 problem." After my tour of the Science Park, we sat down to talk at a restaurant on the SIP campus overlooking Golden Rooster Lake. We dined on vegetable and meat dim sum dishes. Daisy explained that the 20/30 problem was critical to the success of the economic and social reforms China was making in the run-up to 2020. The development of Chinese society could be compromised by the kind of unrest other nations faced when large numbers of young people were underemployed.

Indeed, the Central Government had long been well aware of the country's shortfall in jobs for its people. The Minister for Labor and Social Security, Tian Chengping, cited in 2006,

> "While employment is a difficult issue for all countries, it is more acute in China due to its huge labor force. The huge population and the weak economic foundation will put China under heavy employment pressure in a considerably long period of time. In the next few years, the urban labor supply will keep at 24 million plus annually. However, there will be only 11 million jobs available from economic growth and retirement. Thirteen million people will have no jobs. The difficulty is even sharper for central and western China, old industrial bases and resource exhausted cities. In rural areas, the labor force stands at 497 million, of which about 200 million have transferred into non-farming activities and 180 million remain in agriculture. There is still around 100 million labor surplus. Therefore, it is a rather arduous task to promote employment transfer and develop vocational training for the rural workforce."[2]

The key to jump-starting the technology-intensive services industry—the central government believed—was to entice overseas Chinese home to the motherland with their international training and experience.

If You Build It, They Will Outsource

Juliet Zhu, a government official from the promotion department of Suzhou's other economic development zone, SND, told me that the central government has made IT and BPO "encouraged industries" and has given Chinese cities the go-ahead to attract foreign investors with various incentives. To that end the Chinese government designated ten Chinese centers in 2006 as hubs for the development of IT, BPO, and R&D sectors. These centers were meant to provide the wedge that would open up China to knowledge-intensive industries valued at US$100 billion by 2020.

In late 2006, the national government identified certain cities as *kejibu*—literally, technology divisions—Beijing, Shenzhen, Shanghai, Nanjing, Hangzhou, Chengdu, Dalian, Xi'an, Wuhan, and Suzhou. According to government sources, the plan involved persuading 100 multinational corporations to transfer some of their outsourcing businesses to China, as well as to create 1,000 large-scale international service-outsourcing enterprises by 2010. The central government was going to channel hundreds of millions of dollars over several years into the cities to provide tax benefits to trained IT professionals and subsidies, and provide support for their families in the *kejibu* cities. Each would receive nearly US$8 million annually, which the city would then share with its economic development zones to spend on infrastructure and as incentives to woo investors and staff.

Juliet told me local technology centers provided residence permits, or *hukou*, to professionals and their families. A *hukou* from the city offered many benefits to families coming from rural townships. They could enjoy the city's education system, medical facilities, and social welfare benefits. City benefits were more generous than those in poorer regions in China. Prior to the easing of the *hukou* system, residents of particular cities were not allowed to live in other parts of China. It had been Mao's way of controlling the inevitable influx of farmers from the countryside into the more prosperous cities along China's east coast. Beijing's central planning, however, did not deal well with rationing resources to locations in which populations were in flux.

Technology centers made themselves attractive for talented professionals in the hi-tech fields by providing apartments at a rate of ¥600 (a little more than US$100) per month. In some instances, managers and specialists received steep discounts to buy a home. Foreign nationals, too, in high-value fields could also get long-term or permanent Chinese residency. If the foreign national had to travel out of the country frequently on business, he or she could acquire a multi-entry visa with a five-year term.

China's technology centers enticed Chinese nationals who held master's degrees to return and work in China. If they qualified to work in the hi-tech sector, they could be approved for subsidies that ranged from ¥50,000 to ¥100,000 (about US$7,500 to US$15,000) to buy a home in *kejibu* cities. For hi-tech companies that set up operations in technology centers, there were one-time subsidies of ¥200,000 to ¥500,000 (about US$30,000 to US$60,000). In addition, the companies could get the first year or two of operation rent-free, and enjoy a preferential tax rate for the first few profit-making years. R&D centers could also have their instruments and equipment imported into China duty-free.

Another *kejibu* that had its sights squarely set on becoming a base for high-end service offerings was Nanjing, a three-hour drive west of Shanghai. Nanjing is the capital of Jiangsu province. Nanjing's Jiangning district was the site of post-modern facilities used to house hi-tech incubators. In 2003 the district's economic development zone had only a smart looking administrative headquarters embraced by a tree-stitched hill, frantic construction projects, and a great modern metal sculpture that would come to mark the center of the first phase of the industrial park. There were few factories back then. During a tour around the Park the then-Director was always making sweeping gestures about where this residential area would be rooted and that set of manufacturing compounds would be built. It was difficult for me to visualize. The zone's plan involved developing industries such as automobile manufacturing, electronic information systems, and electrical controls for automobiles. Jiangning also had its sights set on being an R&D and software development hub. The opening of the iHub in 2008 was a milestone in the realization of the district's services outsourcing goals.

The iHub was nearly 20,000 square meters, with five multi-story buildings that supported office space, an exhibition center, and a car park. It was most recognizable from the highway by the huge, partly-submerged sphere that anchored the complex of buildings. Inside the sphere was an open, flexibly decorated exhibition hall and adjoining reception area. Staggered along the open corridors of the second and third floors and facing into the atrium were great open frames painted in primary colors that echoed the Microsoft Windows logo: yellow, blue, orange, white. More empty frames rooted to the floor greeted entrants into the five-floor administrative building fixed to the sphere. It was in the exhibition hall that the Singaporean development company responsible for the project had constructed a long, high stage from which the great and the good of government and business in

Singapore and Jiangsu Province pronounced the iHub officially open for business.

Ms. Pan Yin Yin, a small, nervous native of Jiangning, showed me around the compound. Clad in black military style fatigues, jack-booted security teams patrolled the area for miscreants, thankfully ignoring our stroll around the buildings. Typically in China security is presented as young men in oversized gray-green uniforms with peaked caps who lean back in the chairs of guard houses gateside. I suppose the Singaporean developer wanted to give the impression that not only was the complex going to see a movement up the industry value chain for investments in the area, but a new-found seriousness in security, as well.

The iHub was within easy access to supermarkets, hospitals, hotels, and even golf courses, Ms. Pan told me. She pointed at the open entrance to a lobby: iHub housed a business center for young start-ups, as well as a post office, restaurants, cafes, a travel agency, and banks. The facility was meant to be as self-contained as possible, just short of actually having residences within the compound, as did the International Science Park in Suzhou. Within a couple of years the campus would house scores of IT/BPO businesses, software development companies, and R&D centers. At the outset, though, few of the companies inhabiting the facility would be homegrown. China still had to rely on the Indian services outsourcers to illustrate how to meet the international standards multinationals required.

Crouching Dragon, Leaping Elephant

China began its daring attempt to go up against the Indian giants in the global market for IT and BPO as early as 2005. China saw tens of billions of dollars to be made and millions of jobs to be created in these sectors. The larger Indian companies, such as Infosys, Tata, and Mahindra Satyam employed thousands of Chinese staff by 2010. Chinese homegrown outsourcers had an uphill battle ahead to catch the Indian transplants.

Outsourcing was a US$70 billion-a-year business for Indian companies in 2011. Meanwhile, the Chinese sector was valued at about US$20 billion.[3] CLSA, the investment firm, projected China's reach at

$30 billion in 2014.[4] The Chinese, however, were looking to break the Indian hold on IT-based outsourcing services by 2020. China's government, however, had a long march ahead of it to attain that goal.

The Year 2000 (Y2K, as the IT industry called it back then) software re-engineering effort was a gift to the Indians. The West had millions of lines of programming code that needed to be reviewed and re-figured to take into account the changeover from the year 1999 to the year 2000. The change in the century would see computers record a "00" for the new year's dates instead of "2000." Calculations, of course, would no longer be accurate. Executives, governments, and the Western public (encouraged by the media) expected the worst: bills would be wrong, payments wildly out of whack with reality, airplanes would crash, and the world as we knew it would end. Arguably, India saved the West; or rather, its armies of software engineers updated the software that ran the financial record-keeping computer applications of the West.

India also learned about Western computer systems, Western systems development methodologies, and Western back-office business processes. Western executives figured after 2000 that if the Indians had managed Y2K well, they could cut their teeth on other computer applications in their businesses. And so the Indian ITO industry as we know it today was born.

China, though, is different. China had no Y2K to finance or educate its armies of fresh-eyed programmers in the hard-as-nails realities of Western business practices and operational processes. The Y2K crisis provided the Indians with opportunities for exposure and training in the business processes of Western companies, multinational corporations (MNCs), and non-MNCs alike. China does not have the troops of English-speaking, customer-focused, go-getters that India does to launch an industry to the stars. Instead, China is going to have to bootstrap itself to become a world-beater in both the ITO and BPO realms.

Certainly, the Chinese government has its heart in the right place and its intentions firmly set on services outsourcing preeminence. Newly fielded economic development zones throughout China were flush with cash by 2010, already investing in platoons of engineers and hi-tech infrastructures. Chinese were gaining success in forms processing and data entry, repetitive and detailed tasks. The most accessible areas for Chinese BPO operations at the end of the first decade were insurance claims processing, personnel records data entry, patient records entry, and invoice processing. Though gradually changing, the Chinese education system has for thousands of years emphasized rote learning and the regurgitation of facts and figures. As a result, Chinese tend to be more detailed and heads-down in their work than their Indian counterparts, albeit less innovative.

The Indian education system with its emphasis on English language skills also encouraged growth of the ITO business, and facilitated entry into the BPO space. Credit card processing, insurance claims processing, call centers, and more were natural extensions of the knowledge base and experience the Indians were gaining through their business analyses and IT implementations.

The Chinese capacity with English as a working language is far behind the Indians. India had the advantage—from an industrialization point of view—of 350 years of British colonialism. The English language had become an integral part of Indian society. English is also the primary or secondary language of the wealthiest countries in the world, countries with economies that are primarily service-based. These service-based countries have, for the past decade, been trimming the costs of the services they provide by outsourcing functions to India. The English language—and the desire to adapt and refine their English to suit customer requirements—has been a key factor in the success of Indian companies. An American in Ohio or a Brit in Birmingham can pick up the phone and discuss a customer issue with someone in Bangalore. That is near impossible to do with someone in Xi'an or even Shanghai. China currently has very little talent in the outsourcing space with such capabilities.

So, the Chinese have little credibility with Westerners when it comes to understanding and articulating the kinds of back-office applications that matter to knowledge-driven Western companies. Most Chinese IT companies cater to domestic Chinese customers; the vast majority of ITO companies support Japanese and Korean companies with programming projects for consumer electronic devices. Asian customers provide highly detailed specifications to Chinese programmers to leave little room for error. There is little opportunity for Chinese business analysts to gain access to corporate business processes outside of China. The Chinese need the access to develop the expertise and credibility Western companies look for when outsourcing their back-office functions to any vendor.

In the latter part of the next decade, before 2020, China will go through a mergers and acquisitions (M&A) phase that India has never really had to go through. India's development of its BPO industry is a direct outgrowth of its ITO industry. The Y2K phenomenon forced Indian outsourcers early on to develop economies of scale. At the turn of the century Indian service providers needed to support thousands of programmers, their hardware, and communications infrastructures. The Indians were then able to take the economies of scale along with the access they had gained to back-office functions to directly move into BPO. China has had no such kick-start, no such opportunity or financial base from which to develop the economies of scale to support massive BPO operations. BPO is all about mobility and scalability: moving the back-office operations of a company to another country.

Like so many industries in China, the BPO industry is fragmented, with more than 90 percent of BPO operations supporting only several hundred staff. Indian BPO providers routinely offer tens of thousands of staff to support Western MNCs. The overwhelming majority of out-sourcing companies in China, in contrast, lack capital and the numbers of skilled and experienced staff to run large projects of the sophistication Western companies require. The Chinese services outsourcing market will have to go through an M&A phase to build companies with the economies of scale BPO projects require. M&A in the sector will help domestic companies build the credibility they need to convince multinationals of their capabilities. China's services outsourcing sector, however, has to first shake off the legacy of its manufacturing cousin: rampant copying of customer designs.

One of the greatest challenges facing the nascent Chinese ITO industry is the concern Western companies have over Intellectual Property Rights (IPR) treatment at Chinese companies. Chinese companies across industries—especially in manufacturing—have generated a great deal of bad publicity and ill-will with Western companies. Many Western businesses see it as part of the corporate strategies of Chinese companies to steal designs, counterfeit products, and trade in black goods. The ITO industry has been tarred by the manufacturing sector's terrible record in this area, in a way Indian companies have never been affected. Western companies—even with their own domestic ITO partners—have historically been cautious about passing sensitive or proprietary information on to third-party vendors for processing. However, now Chinese companies have to prove to potential ITO customers they are able to prevent the leakage of customer information for illicit ends.

Chinese BPO providers have and will still predominantly support South Korean and Japanese companies. History and cultural affinity tie the Chinese, the South Koreans, and the Japanese together. The Indians are finding it difficult to enter these East Asian markets, mostly because of a lack of cultural affinity. The Indians through 350 years of British occupation were able to learn a great deal about Western proclivities; the Indians have had little opportunity to do so with the East Asian countries.

Chinese BPO providers continue to support South Korean and Japanese companies. However, Indian outsourcing companies, such as Tata and Mahindra Satyam, which have tens of thousands of employees worldwide, are well-aware of the potential for BPO in the East Asian markets and are aggressively establishing Chinese operations. The Indian operations based in China using Chinese staff will accelerate expansion of Indian market share in East Asia. Chinese outsourcers, however, are well aware of the threat at their doorstep, as visits to Indian and Chinese BPO shops showed me.

A Tale of Two Outsourcers

Mahindra Satyam, one of the so-called "big four" Indian outsourcers, was based just outside Shanghai in the Zhangjiang Science and Technology Park. The other company I visited, Shanghai SAFE, was a Chinese outsourcer based in downtown Shanghai. The executives of both companies were cordial hosts and took several hours each explaining their operations and plans for development of the outsourcing market in Asia. They also showed me around various departments, introducing me to managers and programmers. Through the tours I quickly realized the IT industry in China is the new sweatshop—for white collar workers.

Services outsourcing spaces are also cubicle cities, with lots and lots of movable-walls separating "bright young things" with heads down at their computers. If you visit such places around lunchtime in China, you will also see heads down *on* computers as workers take naps. ITO shops are organized by teams placed in different rooms. Each team works on one project for one customer. During both visits, I had to pass through entrances to various departments that were locked with keycards to limit access to the teams behind the doors.

Michael Su met me at the entrance of Mahindra Satyam's headquarters. Su was Marketing Manager for Mahindra Satyam's China operations. An affable Singaporean, dressed in a white button-down shirt and tie and black slacks, he quickly guided me the few steps to the firm's main conference room. Minutes later Su returned with his boss, Sushil Asar, head of the Business Intelligence and Data Warehousing division for Greater China. Asar personally delivered presentations about their global practice and the China-based development plans. These talks were followed by a presentation given by a Mainland Chinese engineering manager on Mahindra Satyam's projects in offshore development centers (ODC).

Mahindra Satyam impressed me greatly as a truly international company. I did not get the feeling during my half-day orientation that it was an Indian company *per se*. Something I appreciated about Mahindra Satyam's approach to meeting customer requirements was that the country desk drew relevant experience from its Asian operations. Asar gave me the example of an automotive customer in Japan: Mahindra Satyam used industry specialists from India and Japan to develop the business requirements and Japanese-proficient project managers and programmers in the Chinese city of Dalian to implement the project.

Mahindra Satyam was well aware of the rising labor costs and high turnover rates of staff in the Shanghai area. So, it had invested hugely in a campus in the Nanjing High and New Technology Development Area. The site was 70,000 square meters and would ultimately support a labor force of 2,500 professionals. It would be the largest Mahindra Satyam campus of its size outside of India. Private Chinese services outsourcing companies, though, travelled a different path in expanding their operations.

My hostess for the day at SAFE was Ms. Cai Jieru. Dressed in jeans and a white, short-sleeved blouse, this twenty-something met me in the marble lobby of SAFE's headquarters in downtown Shanghai. SAFE was clearly a successful company with about 1,200 staff in China at the time. However, stepping into their conference rooms and offices gave me the same feeling I always had when I visited the offices of Chinese local government agencies: the labyrinthine corridors, dim lighting that makes you squint to see, dingy walls, and the same clunky dark-wood conference tables. Waiting for me in the dank meeting room was Ms. Liu Jia Liang, Director for Development of the U.S. Market, and the Deputy General Manager for the SAFE Group, Mr. Huang Shaobo. Ms. Liu delivered the hour-long presentation about the company. Over 90 percent of its customers were Japanese. Their major shareholder was NEC, the Japanese corporation. I think having a major investor like that was a blessing and a curse: It was great from a cash flow point of view in the regional markets but it was a drag on developing a truly global presence, especially in the West. SAFE wanted to break into the American market. The company was unsure of just how to go about it, though, strategically and tactically. Though they had programming staff in Shanghai, they also "outsourced" many of their own projects to less expensive locations in China where staff turnover was less of an issue than in Shanghai.

SAFE felt like a college study hall, with long rows of tables at which young Chinese men and women played on their computers. It was lunch time at SAFE, and so the atmosphere of course was a little relaxed; but it had also been near lunchtime at Mahindra Satyam, as well. Upon entering their respective, secure domiciles, I got a distinctly different feel for the cultures of both organizations. The Mahindra Satyam corporatized environment had an IBM-feel to it.

Despite being a "foreign" investor in China, Mahindra Satyam had the clear advantage of the two in exploiting the Chinese market for its labor, its geographical position vis-à-vis the northeast Asia market, and even for the business of other multinationals already invested in China. Though SAFE was a Chinese company, it could be argued that it, too, was foreign-invested by a Japanese corporation. The intent of Mahindra Satyam's investor and SAFE's investor, though, determined the true trajectory of the companies: Mahindra Satyam came to China with operations already established throughout Southeast Asia and the West in order to use China as a platform to further address the international market.

NEC invested in SAFE as a job shop to specifically serve the Japanese market. The NEC investment would make it difficult for SAFE to break out of its East Asia orbit and establish beachheads in North America and Europe. The Japanese were high-maintenance, as it were, both technologically and culturally, and so would require resources and obligations that a budding company with a different kind of investor would be able to use in developing markets outside its immediate neighborhood. That's not to say SAFE would not be able to develop business in other countries; it would just be a lot more difficult than if they did not have such sizable Japanese projects and investment.

SAFE was representative of many domestically grown ITO shops that did not start as global players—as Mahindra Satyam had. The markets in northeast Asia were close geographically, culturally, and historically. So, it was easier for Chinese start-ups to work with regional clients rather than obtain customers from the States. The proximity of Japan and South Korea, as well as the potential size of China's domestic market, stunted expansion to the West. Conditions for domestic companies also reinforced the perception that Chinese companies would not be global players, with the exception of those that had acquired Western assets. However, even those companies would still have a difficult time convincing Westerners of their credibility in managing the assets to international standards.

Within the domestic Chinese market, as well, companies such as Mahindra Satyam would have more credibility working with the thousands of Western companies that had set up shop in China than would homegrown Chinese companies. Mahindra Satyam, and companies like it, would likely already be hosting services through its India centers for Western multinationals investing in China. Mahindra Satyam was more disposed than SAFE to speak the Western company's language (business-process and corporate-cultural), even in China. Counter-intuitively, though, BPO operations in China's interior could possibly leap-frog their East coast cousins in their share of the Western market and in their sophistication.

On the Hunt for BPO in Deepest China

Chengdu is a large, sprawling city of more than five million inhabitants who live under a Los Angeles-style canopy of haze and pollution. As the capitol of Sichuan province, the city has a reputation for its spicy food and friendly residents. It is also the largest Chinese city nearest Tibet. By 2010 the city had also gained a reputation throughout China and with many Western multinationals for becoming a services outsourcing hub that met international standards. In the spring of 2011 I made a visit to the Chengdu Tianfu Software Park Co, Ltd., where I was met by Cara Long, who worked in the business development department for the Park. Cara was a reserved, sober young lady with short, bobbed hair. After a formal presentation about the park, which she delivered in fluent English, she took me on a tour of the complex.

The area had more the feel of a university campus than an industrial park. Despite the frigid drizzle, maintenance staff ambled about the lawns pruning angular shrubbery and emptying trash bins. Few company employees, barricaded behind darkened windows, were outside during business hours. I was surprised how cold, it became in the six-seater golf cart that we drove around the campus. Perhaps because it was so cold, the driver drove the cart so fast that I could hardly take in the architecture of the place, which had the most modern design of any I'd seen elsewhere. Still, I was able to catch some of the names and identify some of the logos of multinationals that had landed operations in the Park: IBM, Accenture, Maersk, Amazon, Siemens, and more. Cara explained to me how such a remote city as Chengdu had come to attract so many brand-name multinationals to invest in the area.

The key to Chengdu's success actually lay in the eastern seaboard cities with BPO enterprise zones becoming victims of their own success. Cities like Shanghai, Suzhou and Dalian—near the Koreas—were rapidly becoming expensive as salaries increased to reflect the dearth of experienced talent in the area. Local economies, as well, were also becoming more expensive as foreign and domestic investors bid up real estate property prices. Services outsourcers were amongst the first to build operations in Chengdu, to reduce the costs of their operations. Chengdu, in the mid-2000s, had a surplus of university graduates from schools built during the 1950s. Mao Zedong moved much of the military-industrial complex of the country to the remote region to more easily hide the sector from nuclear attack by the Soviets. The military had established universities and R&D centers in Chengdu and other locations in the Sichuan and Hunan provinces to bolster the country's military capabilities. So, Chengdu already had a tech base upon which to build when high-cost services outsourcers on the coast needed to outsource some of their own projects.

The technology requirements of the domestic outsourcing companies became the blueprint for the kind of infrastructure multinationals would also need to support remote operations. Most of the multinationals—about 40 percent of which were Western—used Chengdu as a platform upon which to maintain backups of the data used in transactions in their home countries.

The government-run corporation that managed the Park also had its own software development outsourcing resources with which it supported its customers in the Park. Cara, who had relaxed considerably during the tour, showed me the offices of two groups: one was an application development department; the other was an embedded systems team, called Android Lab. The first group had about 40 programmers, nearly shoulder to shoulder, at desks separated by low partitions and upon each of which sat a flat-screen monitor and keyboard. Ninety-percent of the software engineers were young men, with a handful huddled in collaboration at the desks of co-workers. Park management had placed the Android group in a large hall with marble floors and little adornment. The Android engineering team was only about 20 people large. Facility designers had organized the desks to allow the team to expand at any time into the remaining space to easily quadruple the size of the group when necessary. Rapid expansion of engineering resources seemed feasible under the Park's management regime.

Unique among the dozens of economic development zones I'd visited in China, the Tianfu Park Corporation offered training packages to companies in the Park. Training courses prepared staff for work in various programming languages and in business English, as well as other disciplines. The Park Corporation had also set aside space for business incubators and offered subsidies to startup businesses, much as was the case in Suzhou. The Park had about 100 companies in its incubator, each with three-to-five staff, mostly fresh graduates. It would be years, if not decades, though, before Tianfu and other services outsourcing campuses would make a substantial impact on employing the millions of university graduates pumped out of the country's schools—China's 20/30 employment challenge.

A significant challenge ahead for the country in promoting the services outsourcing industry was finding and matching eligible staff for positions in services outsourcing. Finding staff with good levels of English was a major challenge for China-based outsourcers. Another challenge confronting companies was excavating potential staff with a hospitality mentality. Though workers may not necessarily face customers in the same way as hoteliers and restaurant staff, they do require an education in how to be considerate of the needs of others. China's go-go society does not support such an education in the home. Most parents want their children to distinguish themselves as high-income earners. The faster the better. Most university curricula are geared toward engineering and the sciences. Parents, children and the society at large see little value in studying the ins-and-outs of psychology, human interaction, and problem-solving.

School systems are more intent on harmonizing individual initiative into group behavior. Teachers and professors teach students to look to those in authority to proactively address potentially contentious issues. The society encourages citizens to take a passive-aggressive approach to conflict resolution. In some instances, passive-aggressive quickly morphs into explosive behavior. Neither approach is appropriate in solving a customer problem, whether across a sales counter, telephone line, or international dateline. It is increasingly incumbent on services outsourcing companies in China to train staff in weeks-long boot camps to instill many of the soft-skills Western and Indian service providers take for granted. The education system and lack of parental guidance are creating a dearth of talent in a sector the government is betting on to provide millions of jobs.

By 2010 the lack of skilled, experienced staff in the high-tech services industries was creating a huge drag on China's development of its ITO and PBO industries. Escalating salaries for staff, compounded by companies poaching employees from other companies, was threatening to stall growth of the sector. Already, with the global financial crisis of

2008–2009 decimating millions of IT-related jobs in the West, salaries for such workers on the global market began normalizing. Salaries for Western IT and other services staff dropped near Chinese levels, eroding the cost advantage between workers in the two regions. The nearly free cost of working on the Internet platform accelerated the phenomenon after 2010. Chinese services may grow too expensive in the international marketplace before they can eclipse Indian competitors.

Beijing did not put all its employment-related eggs into the services outsourcing basket, however. The leadership has been intent on hanging on to its heavy metal manufacturing industries. Central planners are betting heavy metal sectors would provide millions of jobs in the coming decade, meet industrial demand in its own domestic market, and also provide the capital-intensive products that will conquer markets in other countries, as well.

Chapter 4

Heavy Metal

C hinese authorities arrested Liu Zhijun on February 11, 2011 for "severe violation of discipline"—the Chinese Communist Party's (CCP) code words for "corruption."[1] The 56-year-old Liu was found to have embezzled and accepted 187 million yuan (US$28.5 million) in bribes from the showcase Beijing-to-Shanghai portion of the high-speed railway project. Also, under Liu Zhijun's tenure, the Ministry had racked up debts of RMB 1,980 billion ($307 billion).[2] In contrast, the United States Congress in 2009 passed an economic stimulus package of nearly US$800 billion to stave off recession for the *entire* United States economy. Zhao Jian, a researcher at Beijing Jiaotong University, said that "the debt load had grown too large for the government to afford."[3] CCP minders replaced Liu Zhijun with Sheng Guangzu, 62, head of the general administration of customs. Hubris, corruption, and ineptitude would connive to create one of the worst train accidents in China's history.

When high-speed bullet trains on China's premiere Hangzhou-Wenzhou line collided at nearly 400-kilometers per hour five months after the arrest of Liu Zhijun,[4] the nation's grand plan to sell its own made-in-China bullet trains to other countries became as much a casualty as the dozens who lost their lives in the incident. The tragedy exposed the flaws of the country's initiative of "indigenous innovation" to adopt the sophisticated technologies of other countries to adapt for use in domestic and export markets. The collision also spotlighted the deep international distrust countries harbored over China's industrial model because of the nation's weak enforcement of intellectual property protection. The indigenous innovation directive was actually retarding China's efforts to acquire the state-of-the-art technology it needed to gain credibility in international markets for high-speed railways, automobiles, and ships, among others.[5] Global markets also found that Chinese industry's emphasis on market share over profits created deflationary pressures at home and abroad for supposedly high-value products. A rare set of conditions in China's own society trumped economic principals and set the trajectory for its problematic heavy metal export model.

China's greatest economic asset since its leadership approved of the country opening up to the world in 1980 was its large, relatively young population—the largest in the world. Though overwhelmingly from the countryside, the youth of China offered international manufacturers a ready, relatively docile, and hungry workforce and a willing army of potential consumers. Mobilized to use the latest equipment to produce low-cost products, China was able to kick-start its economy into modernity. Inflationary pressures, energy requirements, and environmental hazards made labor-intensive businesses increasingly difficult to maintain in the country. Beijing began shifting the nation's policies in the mid-2000s to emphasize the development of more capital-intensive industries. The sectors required increasingly sophisticated technologies to become viable international players. The key to the strategy was, again, China's large population of workers, who also represented the largest pool of consumers in the world.

China's leadership had known for years that multinationals would bring their billions of dollars of investment and intellectual property to build and exploit the domestic market place. The scope of the potential market of nearly one-and-a-half billion consumers would cause international business leaders to make almost any deal to sell into China.

Nearly all of the technologies that China has used since it threw open its economy's doors to the world in 1980 have been imported; the technologies it already had in hand were remnants of 1950s Soviet era central planning—great, hulking, inelegant equipment mostly oriented toward heavy industry applications. China needed the more efficient designs the West and Japan had to offer to heft the nation out of market purgatory. Without rapid adoption of the foreign technologies China would not have been able to "catch up" with the world technologically after having ignored the Industrial Revolution 400 years before. Drawn by the promise of riches "beyond compare," foreign makers assisted in that technology transfer so they could profit during the nation's economic growth spurt. Foreign investors already knew that the Chinese industry plan was to tweak the technology just enough to suit domestic demands, then to become a competitor with the very companies that had helped the Chinese companies become successful.

China started with low-end, low value products to begin its economic ascendancy: toys, textiles, shoes, and the like. Then on to more capital-intensive products like cargo ships, which required a great deal of financing to construct, but relatively little in the way of high technology. Kick-starting the automobile industry was also a capital-intensive exercise that required far greater technological sophistication, quality, and safety standards than shipping. High-speed trains represented the pinnacle of any modern society's capability to mobilize capital and some of the most sophisticated technologies available in the world. Though relatively low-tech, however, ship building would prove the most important to the strategic interests of the country.

Ships Ahoy!

The Daoda Heavy Industries shipbuilding port is easy to spot—once you're on the correct road. It's the shipyard with the wind turbine. Daoda is located on the Yangtze River, essentially at the mouth of the great waterway as it disgorges water born from glaciers in the Himalayas. It is about a twenty minute drive outside a small town called

Qidong, in the Nantong municipality, an hour's drive to the northwest of Shanghai. I found Qidong unusual in the number of motorcycles on the road and the high proportion of riders who wore safety helmets. Protection of any sort for riders in China was unusual. The few trees there were appeared sparse, wind-whipped. The area had a barren feel to it, despite the high density of bushes. It was mid-November 2010, and the wind was strong and cold.

Though ostensibly on a visit to Daoda to learn about how it was traversing the learning curve that bridged ship building and offshore wind turbine foundation manufacture, I still found myself drawn to the vessels in dry and wet dock under construction, snapping photos of ships under construction when the novelty of the lone wind turbine wore off. Surprisingly, the factory compound was emptier than I would have expected. The drive from the gate to the administrative office took several minutes. Large hangars dressed in corrugated steel painted white dotted the dockyard. Groups of workers in blue hard hats and pale green trousers and matching jackets with company logos stitched on their breasts moved in small herds. It was late morning.

One of the dry docks, along the concrete shoreline, encased the carcass of a ship under construction. It was splayed open, the double-walled hull cut cross-section. The main hull was a great black rectangle, the walls of its internal chambers painted the same color red as the hulking rectangular cranes perched on rails and framing the unfinished vessel. Silver-pipe scaffolding held the air in place within the chambers, like the small bones of a river fish.

Daoda was a typical Chinese business success story, the sort that the CCP is happy to air to show its citizens, and the world. Just ten years before a Chinese bridge builder named Li Aidong bought some land along the Yangtze River that he sold for a great profit. He started the shipyard in 2007, during the greatest boom in shipping—and shipbuilding—history, since seafaring records were started in 1774. The shipbuilder quickly picked up foreign customers, among them the German company Intersee Schiffahrts-Gesellschaft GmbH & Co (ISG). ISG's order—christened the *Pacific Tramp*—was nearly complete when I visited that cold winter's day. The pier along which the boat was moored was a beehive of activity. Construction workers ambled between the craft and a vessel on the opposite side of the pier, while forklifts careened down the boardwalk hefting all manner of fittings. Nine months later the craft was plying the South China Sea laden with cargo on its way to Ho Chi Min port in Vietnam.

Daoda was a small shipyard by the standards of the State-owned Enterprises (SOEs) that were deploying the central government's plan for China to become the largest shipbuilder in the world. China's prime manufacturers—the China State Shipbuilding Corporation (CSSC) and China Shipbuilding Industry Corporation (CSIC)—dwarfed Daoda, a privately-owned entity. The ship building SOEs employ hundreds of thousands of workers who build seafaring craft for commercial and military use, and are tasked with construction of vessels up to 300 thousand DWT (dead-weight tons). DWT is a measure of the total amount of cargo, fuel, fresh water, ballast water, provisions, passengers, and crew. Daoda, at the time I visited the shipyard, was permitted by the government to only construct ships up to 35,000 DWT—one-tenth the size of the craft the SOEs produced. The two SOEs between them controlled nearly 70 percent of China's shipbuilding capacity. The government, according to a Daoda manager, wanted to keep it that way. Government regulations restricted Daoda from expanding its footprint along the shore of the great river for shipbuilding purposes. The company hoped that in the near future it would be able to expand into building ships of 200,000 DWT. Companies like Daoda, however, would always remain bit players in the Chinese central government's plan to own at least half of all the ships that supplied the country with oil.

China was the second largest net oil importer in the world in 2009, supplanting Japan during the global economic crisis of 2008–2009. In 2009 China imported 204 million tons of oil. In 2011 China was the second-largest consumer of oil, with more than half of its crude oil imported. China will likely be importing about 65 percent of its crude oil by 2020.[6] China's extreme dependence on imported oil is a recent development, forced by its society's aggressive modernization drive.

The Chinese Communist Party (CCP) made it a main plank of its legitimacy in the 1940s to eject all foreigners and foreign influences in the country, including technology advances. However, insularity worked squarely against the country's economic development. By the time Mao Zedong had died in 1976 the country was essentially bankrupt, without any convertible currency of its own with which to trade with other countries. Premiere Deng Xiao Ping's policy in 1980 of opening the country up economically meant industry would require more oil to power its machinery. By the mid-1990s China was opening relations with oil-pumping countries that were neither aligned with China in terms of politics or religion (the CCP presents China as avowedly atheist). Oil and money—not ideology—had become the shared worldview. The sources of China's imported oil quickly became diverse, nearly all of it arriving by sea.

By 2010, China was sourcing nearly half its oil from the Middle East, with more than a fifth of that amount from Saudi Arabia alone. Iran provided China a little less than Saudi Arabia at 15 percent of the total oil pumped out of the region going to China. Oman, Kuwait, the United Arab Emirates, and Yemen also provided China with the precious cargo.[7] In 2011 China received about 30 percent of its oil from Africa. China had also developed cozy relations with a prickly Venezuela, based on shared oil interests. China had become beholden to the rest of the world for one of the most important sources of energy in its portfolio. The vulnerability rubbed sorely against the grain of the Chinese Communist Party (CCP), which had prided itself on the country's self-sufficiency.

China's leadership had realized by 2004, though, that it was making itself increasingly vulnerable to the vagaries of international politics and globalization by having all its oil brought to it on ships owned by other countries. The leadership published a series of proclamations making shipbuilding a pillar industry in China. The CPC designates an industry as a pillar when it becomes strategic to the economic and even defense interests of the country. China bought ships made in other countries and copied their designs to build their own cargo ships. China's leadership set its sights for 2015 to have 50 percent of its oil shipped on boats the country would forge itself.[8] It also aimed to become the largest ship builder in the world at the same time. Within a year of the leadership's new policy, China's fleet carried 20 percent of the country's crude oil exports; in 2000 it had only carried 6 percent of its own imported oil.[9] The global economic downturn of 2008, however, threatened to bring construction of China's shipbuilding industry to a halt. The deep recession staunched the flow of international trade across sea lanes from a torrent to a trickle.

As part of the nearly US$600 billion China pledged to pump into its economy to keep its industries afloat during the crisis, the leadership strong-armed its SOEs into placing orders with Chinese shipbuilders to keep the industry afloat. As the shipping industry righted itself in 2010 the world found China had become the top shipbuilder. The nation had displaced the South Koreans and the Japanese as premiere contractors for constructing sailing vessels that are as long as the Eiffel Tower is high. Greek and German shippers lined up at Chinese shipyards to have their crafts built at a fraction of the time and cost as other shipbuilding countries. China's lack of consideration for the fundamental economic principal of supply and demand, however, eventually cost shipping lines dearly.

The marketplace discovered by the end of 2011 that China had constructed far more ships than the market could use. Shipping rates again collapsed. Li Shenglin, China's transport minister, said, "They [Chinese shipbuilders] have led the shipping industry to a situation that is more depressed now than in 2008. This state of affairs could persist for quite a long time."[10] Central planning also drove China's automobile industry to the same dead end.

Fast Car

The Chery Automotive manufacturing plant was as modern as any I'd seen in China: a great cavernous space, brand spanking new, sparkling almost, with new equipment little touched by human hands. A stainless steel track snaked along the floor and then jutted upwards to the ceiling with half-finished chassis dangling from it. More than a hundred workers—all men, all outfitted in pale green slacks, matching light-weight jackets zipped almost to their chin—stood ready at their stations. The line was sparse, admittedly, but still impressive. The head of the operation—a middle-aged Chinese engineer with a PhD appended to the surname printed on his business card—was clearly proud of the facility. It was autumn 2004, and the plant was one of the newest and most sophisticated of its kind in China.

It was also one of the few that was not tied-up with a foreign auto maker, like Shanghai Automotive Industry Corporation (SAIC) had been with Volkswagen and General Motors; or Changan—out in Chongqing, in the interior of China—was with Ford.

In 2004 I was but one of half a dozen representatives from an American tier-1 automotive supplier invited to Chery's headquarters in Wuhu, Anhui province. Wuhu is about an hour's drive southwest of Nanjing, the provincial capital of Jiangsu province, and more than a 3-hour drive west of Shanghai. Wuhu at the time was a backwater town, without high-rises. Visits to the city over the years have always struck me as unique, as the city never really seemed to be well taken care of. Development in the city seemed to follow a different path than cities closer to the seacoast. The downtown area was the only one I'd ever seen in China in which buildings—a mere five stories at their highest—were actually shuttered in the manner of inner-city Detroit or Philadelphia. Sheets of plywood covered windows and newspapers taped to glass doors blocked investigations into the hollowed out structures. A visit nearly four years later, in 2008, would find a huge excavation near the eerie downtown for the construction of a dinosaur park. One part of the park was reserved for a giant spaceship in which children, their parents, and grandparents could walk through and enjoy alien sounds, lights, and rides.

Eventually I would learn from government officials at the promotion bureau of the economic development zone that supported Chery that the city government was an investor in the car maker. The provincial government of Anhui, as well as the central government itself, also had shares in the company. Chery was a national champion. Though smaller than SAIC and Changan, it was nonetheless an important component in China's efforts to encourage development of automotive manufacturing as a pillar industry for the country. Eventually, the Chinese leadership envisioned, Chery and other indigenous Chinese manufacturers would become export giants in the world, just as the Japanese and South Korean car makers had.

Chery had received a sweet deal from the local government: the plot of land on which it had staked its claim had been all but free, while it also had no tax burden as an investment in the national interest. And just as most taxis in Germany are Mercedes brand, all the taxis and most of the other cars on the road in Wuhu were Chery manufactured. In 2004 Chery had become one of the best known brands in

China; though, probably for the kinds of reasons that would one day make Chery blush: sub-compact, paper-thin bodies, and poor quality. In the mid-2000s, though, it was affordable to many Chinese families. Chery vehicles were the starter car for buyers who wanted to take a step up from the bicycle or electric bike as the primary mode of transportation to work and to the market.

Chery had invited the tier-1 automotive components manufacturer with which I was working to Wuhu to entice the foreign producer into a working relationship with the car maker. Tier-1 suppliers provide their products directly to manufacturers like Ford, GM, and Chrysler for final assembly. My client had decades-long relationships with each of the Big 3 auto makers. Chinese manufacturers in the mid-2000s were looking for the same sort of tie-ups with suppliers in the automotive industry. The Chinese were finding the learning curve for producing quality products difficult to ascend on their own. Auto makers and their government masters also wanted foreign suppliers to teach local suppliers the manufacturing processes the foreign producers had been using to reduce costs, waste, and time to delivery. In addition, they wanted Western vendors to transfer technology to their Chinese partners. For that purpose Chery and the Wuhu government had chosen a domestic company with which it had already been working, albeit with mixed results.

We had met the potential partners for the first time at the Nanjing airport, two brothers from Zhejiang province who had been supplying parts to Chery for the past year. The brothers were tall, swarthy chain smokers, the kind of country-folk who had struck it rich in a way that had become so common throughout China. Both were dressed in black slacks and black polo-style shirts with cheap black leather shoes. Their company had been open just a couple years. Chery was their shot at the big time, they understood—the account was theirs to lose. If the local government and Chery said they needed to work with foreigners to ensure their success, then they would grin and bear it.

The visit to the Chery plant later that day would confirm that the product the brothers were supplying to Chery did need help. One of the executives I accompanied on the trip was a South Korean who had returned to his home country from America. The stout, blunt-speaking executive opened a passenger door of a QQ car that had just rolled off the assembly line. He ran his hand along the rubber seam of the door, prodded the window, shook the door. He slammed the door shut. "No good," he grunted. A year later Chery would be accused of taking bold shortcuts to upgrade technologies for its brand.

In 2005 a South Korean division of General Motors sued Chery for the wholesale copying of its Daewoo division's Matiz. General Motors was able to prove without much effort that every part of the vehicle—from the frame through the engine as well as the chassis design—was exactly the same as the automobile the SAIC and GM were building under the GM brand for the Chinese market. A vice-minister of commerce and a vice-director of the State Intellectual Property (IP) Office publicly supported Chery, claiming GM did not properly patent its technology for the Matiz. Eventually, the companies came to a settlement on the dispute. The IP infraction did not thwart Chery's plans to expand its market overseas. After all, the prize was a slice of the US$553 billion car export market.[11]

In 2007 American entrepreneur Malcolm Bricklin announced with great fanfare he had signed an agreement with Chery to distribute its QQ sub-compact in America. American consumers, however, gave the thumbs down to the light-weight vehicle. Bricklin quickly retreated from the United States marketplace. Chinese car companies, though, did not give up on partnerships with western groups as a way of entering hallowed foreign markets.[12]

China's top five car makers during the first nine months of 2009 sold the European Union market a grand total of 745 vehicles, according to the European Automobile Manufacturers' Association. Brilliance Auto, Chang'an, Great Wall Motors, Landwind, and Lifan Group hit great walls in the western marketplace involving safety standards and carbon dioxide emissions requirements.[13] The companies simply could not meet the expectations of European regulators and consumers with products that were "good enough" for China's emerging market. German impact tests on cars sold by Brilliance and Landwind ended in catastrophe for the companies in which their cars—rammed against German-made walls—folded like empty beer cans. German media declared the Chinese brands "bad quality," tarring all Chinese auto exporters into the EU.

Though China had outstripped the United States as the world's largest car market by the end of 2010, China's automobile export numbers remained negligible. Chinese car makers had exported about a half-million automobiles in the same period, against the nearly 10 million vehicles they had sold domestically.[14] With an export value of about US$7 billion, about 60 percent of China's automotive exports were to developing countries. Popular markets for Chinese auto exports included Brazil, Venezuela, Indonesia, Burma, Thailand, and the Middle East. China's car makers also came under pressure in the same year for the same reasons as the country's ship builders had at the end of the decade: manufacturers had made too many of their products for the market to support at profitable levels.

In 2011, the domestic market share for cars made by local players shrank from nearly 45 percent to 40 percent year-on-year.[15] Perception problems involving the poor quality of Chinese-made automobiles prevented buyers at home from investing in the cars. At the same time, government subsidies to consumers to encourage them to buy Chinese models came to an end. In larger cities like Beijing and Shanghai, a government mandate made car ownership prohibitively expensive to a new middle class. Meanwhile, higher-than-average annual inflation rates decreased the purchasing power of middle income families. Domestic car makers responded by continuing to produce their automobiles in droves and by escalating their efforts to pry open the export markets. The railway tragedy involving two high-speed bullet trains in southern China during the summer of 2011 confirmed to consumers at home and abroad what they had wanted to believe all along about Chinese products: unsafe at any cost.

A Ticket to Ride

Just three weeks before the tragic mid-summer train crash in 2011, China and Japan were having a well-publicized shouting match about the bullet train technology China had transferred from foreign joint venture partners. The railway ministry's spokesman Wang Yongping pontificated, "The Beijing-Shanghai high-speed railway and Japan's Shinkansen cannot be mentioned in the same breath, as many of the technological indicators used by China's high-speed railways are far better than those used in Japan's Shinkansen."[16] Shinkansen is the name the Japanese have for their own high-speed rail network, inaugurated in 1964. The Japanese had had only one accident on their railway—someone had gotten their arm trapped in a closing door in 1985—and they had been vociferously warning the Chinese that the Chinese were running the trains too fast.

"The difference between China and Japan is that in Japan, if one passenger is injured or killed, the cost is prohibitively high," Yoshiyuki Kasai told the *Financial Times*. Mr. Kasai was chairman of the Central Japan Railway. "It's very serious. But China is a country where 10,000 passengers could die every year and no one would make a fuss," he added.[17] The Japanese were understandably distressed Chinese officials were pushing the trains to the safety limit the Japanese had placed on the technology. The Japanese operate their bullet trains some 20 percent under the same limit and did not want the Chinese pointing a finger at Japanese manufacturing prowess or holding the country liable for Chinese *hubris*.

The Japanese would not have been particularly concerned about the specific number of Chinese casualties in train wrecks but for the inconvenient fact that the Chinese had copied or incorporated Japanese technology into their own shiny new trains. In the case of the Hangzhou-Wenzhou rail line—the scene of the bullet train tragedy—Beijing-based Hollysys Automation Technologies Ltd. had adapted the signal systems equipment Japanese maker Hitachi had made to order for a different rail line in China. Hollysys had expanded the Hitachi equipment to work across much of China, without Hitachi's knowledge or permission. Hitachi, however, as a matter of company policy, had placed some of the inner workings of the signal system in a "black box." Black boxes hide the most intimate details of a technology design to make it difficult for buyers to understand and to copy. A senior Hitachi executive said, "It's still generally a mystery how a company like Hollysys could integrate our equipment into a broader safety-signaling system without intimate knowledge of our know-how."[18] Commercial interests, as well, strained relations between the rail ministries of the two countries.

According to the Japanese, the Chinese had been, for years, exporting high-speed railway technology off the backs of foreign companies forced into joint-venture arrangements and technology-transfer agreements with Chinese State-owned Enterprises. Yuriko Koike, Japan's former Minister of Defense and National Security Adviser and chairman of the executive council of the Liberal Democratic Party wrote, "Immediately before the Beijing-Shanghai railway was built, the Chinese Ministry for Railways initiated international patent claims concerning the technology used in the CRH380A. It is believed that China has now filed for 21 patents in accordance with the Patent Cooperation Treaty (PCT), with the aim of obtaining patents in Japan, the United States, Brazil, Europe, and Russia."[19] She went on to say, "Since 2003, China has filed for 1,902 patents related to high-speed railways, with 1,421 approved and 481 still being examined. But the 21 recent applications are the first based upon Japanese Shinkansen technology."[20] The Chinese State-owned Enterprise CSR Qingdao Sifang Co. had co-opted its motive technology from the Japanese manufacturer Kawasaki Heavy Industries Ltd. and was going overseas with the technology to under-bid Kawasaki for railway projects. Kawasaki, however, was not the only jilted bride.

Chinese railway SOEs also formed joint ventures with Germany's Siemens, France's Alstom, and Canada's Bombardier, only to become a competitor on the world market against them. Ma Yunshuang, a deputy general manager at CSR Qingdao Sifang, claimed "Our technologies may originate from foreign countries, but it doesn't mean that what we have now all belongs to them."[21] The technologies China had co-opted from other countries had been instrumental in developing a railway network that was the world's largest in 2011. By 2020 the railway would stretch some 16,000 kilometers (about 10,000 miles), at an estimated total cost of more than $300 billion.[22] In 2011 the Chinese rail system carried about a quarter of global freight and passenger traffic on 6 percent of the world's lines.[23]

Some of the largest companies in China related to the railway industry directly benefited from technology transfers from foreign partners: China Railway Construction Co., Ltd.; China Railway Construction (Number 384 on the Fortune 500 list, 2006); MTR Corporation (Number 832 on the Forbes Global 2000 list); and Daqin Railway (Number 1209 on the Forbes Global 2000 list, 2006).

One of the highest profile attempts cited of Chinese re-introducing heavy metal technology into the international market as their own is the case of the bid for the high-speed rail system linking San Francisco and Los Angeles. In 2010 China signed a cooperation agreement with the state of California and General Electric (GE) to build the bullet train route. Japan, Germany, South Korea, Spain, France, and Italy are all interested in getting a piece of the California gold, as well. The Chinese pledged to finance a part of the US$43 billion project, which appealed to California, which has for decades been creaking under the weight of debt.[24] The potential tie-up between the Chinese and the Californians was one of the main reasons then Governor Arnold Schwarzenegger visited China in 2010—to add some stardust to the final stamp of approval. The appeal of a Chinese-led rail project in California came down to simple math: it cost about $15 million to put in place a mile of rail-related infrastructure in China; whereas in the United States, costs may run between $40 million to $80 million.[25] But California was not China's first international train stop.

Chinese railway company authorities could have also showcased projects they were already working on in Turkey, Venezuela, and Saudi Arabia. The Saudi Arabia project was launched and completed more as a political gesture to one of the largest suppliers of oil to China than as an infrastructure project that would improve the lives of citizens or the economy. The state-owned China Railway Construction Company Ltd. completed the 20-kilometer long project in 16 months, in November 2010, to ferry nearly 75,000 pilgrims from Mecca to Medina during the annual Hajj. Millions of Muslims travel between the two cities to reinforce their devotion to their faith. The construction company, which was listed in Shanghai and Hong Kong, lost US$600 million on the US$1.2 billion deal. The *Economic Observer*—a Chinese financial magazine with a streak of independence—professed the Saudi project to have been the worst financial loss by any Chinese company going abroad.[26] Hong Kong investors knocked 14 percent off China Railway's valuation in a single day after the company announced the budget overrun.

Losses, however, were of little concern to SOEs in China. They were too big to fail: The companies commanded industries the leadership deemed strategic—key to the country's survival and dominance in the world. SOEs performed more of a geopolitical role in international markets than one of profitability.

As a result, Southeast Asian countries were less inclined to press the Chinese on questions of quality, transparency, and accountability, as their governments tended to be more beholden to the economic largesse China provided their exporters and tax collectors.

In 2010 China signed agreements with Laos and Thailand to construct high-speed railways in the southeast Asian countries. The US$7 billion Laotian line would continue to run northward from its capital Vientiane over the Chinese border into Kunming, in China's southern province of Yunnan.[27] In August 2011, Beijing announced that Malaysia would buy 228 trains, the first export deal for Chinese-made bullet trains.[28] The CPC's long-term vision saw high-speed rails connecting Shanghai with Singapore and New Delhi. Passengers would travel between China and India through Burma.[29] China's intentions to expand railway infrastructure throughout the developing countries of Asia reflected the more practical side of its plans to move up the value curve of manufacturing production—and the greatest threat of incursion into markets the West had considered secure.

Selling into Developing Countries

China's aim to scale the product value ladder by adopting and adapting foreign technologies for domestic use and then to export manufactures was not limited to ships, automobiles, and trains. By the end of 2010 Chinese companies were also busy manufacturing trucks, steam turbines, buses, motorcycles, cruise ships, tractors, cranes, and machines that lift and load goods. Though the central government tenet of indigenous innovation coupled with a lack of adequate governance placed constraints on how far up the ladder of technological sophistication the country could go, huge markets awaited the sort of capital intensive, low-cost heavy metal that was developing China's interior.

While the global economic downturn of 2008 nearly brought China's ship-building activities to a halt, it turned out to present an opportunity of a lifetime to heavy vehicle and construction manufacturers in China's interior. The relatively poor landlocked provinces suffered from a dearth of infrastructure that would create a base for industry in otherwise remote parts of the country. Roads, railways, and airports would also help tie the roughed regions to richer east coast cities and to southeast Asia. National policy would enrich the heavy metal entrepreneurs who would provide the equipment the country required to normalize the economies of the east coast and the rest of China. Most of the manufacturers would be found in the interior, near the lucrative work sites. In 2010 China's production of construction-related equipment represented as much as 20 percent of global production.[30] As the domestic market for the big machines neared saturation in 2011 and as the first wave of many of the largest infrastructure projects launched during the Great Recession neared an end, the machinists turned their sights to the markets of other developing nations.

The economies of the developing countries had been buoyed by China's and the West's growing needs for their natural resources. Russian, Middle Eastern, and African oil, as well as Brazilian wood and soy beans brought the regions much needed capital with which to develop their own infrastructures. India, as it continued to liberalize its economy, also became a major purchaser of Chinese construction-related equipment. Cranes, cement trucks, and earth-moving equipment the Chinese sold developing countries were less technologically complex than those of more established multinationals. However, Chinese-made equipment completed the jobs for which they were bought without the additional costs of service contracts and trained maintenance staff. South Korean, Japanese, and American heavy machinery manufacturers saw their leads dwindle dramatically in Brazilian and Russian markets from 2010 onward. Chinese heavy construction products met requirements less exacting than those of sophisticated producers at price points developing nations could afford. The approach permitted the Chinese to create markets for their equipment in the Muslim countries of the Middle East and in Africa.

China's efforts to conquer export markets for low-cost, technologically sophisticated products—like high-speed trains—may have been misplaced. The indigenous innovation initiative and CCP gerrymandering of domestic industries to meet political (and sometimes personal) expediencies hamstrung the country's ability to acquire the latest, cutting-edge technologies. Multinationals and national governments understandably resisted transferring such intellectual property. Foreign enterprises understood how Chinese policy would turn their technology contributions against them in the international marketplace. By the time of the tragic train accident of mid-2011, China was hitting a self-imposed ceiling to technological prowess that low price points alone would not be able to breach. Indeed, the low-cost proposition was cementing an image of the country that worked against its efforts to gain credibility in high-end equipment markets. Without positive brand recognition, Chinese companies—no matter how technologically sophisticated the product—would only be able to superficially penetrate western markets. Brand China needed a remake.

Chapter 5

Brand China

The year 2008 saw scandals erupt from China at a rate that seemed to outpace the country's supersonic economic growth rate. It was also the year China was to host the summer Olympics, which would brand the country as a thoroughly modern nation rising to superpower status. Unfortunately for the nation's image, this was also the year consumers discovered the paint on toys that American toy maker Mattel was sourcing from China was laced with toxic lead. Soon after the toy debacle, American buyers discovered Chinese producers had tainted pet food and toothpaste exported from China with the plastics-derivative melamine. The concentration of melamine was so heavy in the pet food that thousands of family pets throughout the United States died. The scandals laid a devastating blow to the image China had been working to project to the world in the run-up to the Beijing Olympics.

Country images are important to the bottom lines of nations and the extent to which they are able to successfully export products

and entire industries across borders. America after World War II successfully exported its fast-food and fast-drink culture around the world
with McDonald's and Coca-Cola leading the foray. Germany exports
its image as a producer of well-designed, well-engineered, high-quality
engineering products. The Danes export a spare, elegant design aes-
thetic in their personal-use items. China exports *Fake*.

Can China reverse the image its exporters and its government are
conveying to the world? What change in its national and corporate
psyches would it take to catalyze change? The magnitude of the altera-
tions would involve innovations of behaviors and cultural norms that
have been entrenched in the society for hundreds—if not thousands—
of years. If the government has not successfully rebranded the country after all these centuries, can Chinese companies seeking to establish
credible brands in international markets be successful? Unfortunately,
even the orchestration of the Olympics itself ran counter to the image
the country was trying to project to the world.

Certainly, thousands of goose-stepping soldiers during the opening ceremonies of the 2008 Olympics did little to dispel the lock-step,
militarist image most of the Western world had of China. However,
the international revelation that the little girl Lin Miaoke, who sang a
welcoming song to the world, was actually lip-syncing while another,
not-as-cute girl—according to Chinese political choreographers—
actually did the singing backstage was a major set-back to Chinese propagandists. The occasion merely confirmed to the West that Brand China
was—like so many other Chinese presentations—a sham. China's populace eventually condemned its own government when it discovered
authorities were complicit in a cover-up of enormous proportions.

For months, if not years, major dairy producers had been lacing
their dairy products with the very same melamine that had meant the
deaths of so many beloved pets in the United States. Since the end of
the previous year China's leaders had known Chinese children were
in danger from the poisoned milk powder their parents unknowingly
fed their infants. The leadership believed the 2008 Olympics, and the
carefully crafted image the event was meant to portray, was far more
important than the potential deaths of Chinese infants.

Eventually, the central government was unable to hide the fact that
more than a dozen infants had died from drinking melamine-laced

milk powder. Thousands more were stricken ill. When the scandal brooked international media channels, China's image in the world's eyes was once again tarnished. Most Western observers agreed that any progress central authorities had made in advancing China as "a country that had arrived" on the world stage, as a mature if misunderstood stakeholder, had evaporated with news of the scandal. Local governments and the national inspection bureau charged with ensuring the quality of consumer products—The Administration of Quality Supervision, Inspection and Quarantine (AQSIQ)—had been in collusion with dairy producers in the promotion, distribution, and export of the tainted dairy products. Foreign buyers of Chinese milk products from Switzerland to America to Japan stopped all imports and use of dairy products made in China. Cookies, chocolates, and yogurts meant for international markets tested positive for melamine. Authorities intended the executions of the director of the AQSIQ and the CEO of a leading dairy producer to signal the end of the scandal.

Central planners nationalized the dairy industry and reassured domestic consumers and international buyers of product quality. Draconian government inspections of the dairy supply chain declared the poisoning issue resolved. Late in 2009 and then again in 2010 the plastic reappeared in the dairy supply chain in half a dozen provinces. Western quality assurance engineers and plant managers in China explained to me the recurrence of melamine in the dairy products was part of the system, not an aberration. If the customer had a problem with materials or components the producer used, they said, then the factory would re-introduce the rejects later on. Producers would inject the rejected materials slowly back into the supply chain. They expected no one would notice, or believed that the relatively small number of defects would be acceptable to buyers. Domestic and foreign buyers found the government's claims of the integrity of any of China's products incredible.

A National Image Made in China

When I spoke with Andrew Hupert, an adjunct professor at the Shanghai campus of New York University, he noted that Brand China is characterized by negatives: difficult to deal with, fussy, duplicitous, and passive-aggressive. The promoters of Brand China have been its export-driven privateers. They make and sell low-end, low-quality, low-priced products for international markets using cheap labor, cheap materials, and government subsidies. They also create world-beating pollution issues for their own country and for others. Westerners bought the products in great, unsustainable quantities specifically because they knew what they were getting. It was—and will be for the foreseeable future—very difficult for Germans, for instance, to go to a showroom factory floor in, say, Frankfurt, and buy a Chery brand car made in Wuhu, Anhui province. For most Germans—and Westerners—China has not cleaned its systemic house well enough to warrant risking the lives of consumers. However, should the same shoppers need jumpers for their toddlers made in Shenzhen, in South China, they would have no mental resistance to dropping a few euro for the low-end purchase. Country brand images are monstrously difficult to shed.

For instance, at the start of the so-called "War on Terror" the administration of George W. Bush set out to demonstrate to the Muslim world just how warm, cuddly and cool the United States really was. The cognitive dissonance, however, between images on Aljazeera news of the American-led coalitions in Afghanistan and Iraq blasting villages to smithereens, and counting mistakenly obliterated weddings in the countryside as collateral damage, actually set America's charm offensive a blow from which, years on, it has still not recovered. The haste, waste, and off-handedness with which the Americans handled rebuilding a shattered Iraq forced the majority of the population to tire of the occupying forces long before they evacuated in 2011. China, as well, miscalculated its coolness factor with foreign audiences.

China's attempt at rebranding its country backfired in early 2011 when the country spent millions of dollars on producing and airing a series of 60-second videos for a month in Times Square in Manhattan. The images flashed by so quickly it was difficult for any viewer—Chinese or foreign—to distinguish the rich and successful Chinese people living it up and talking about how great their lives were and how China wanted to be everyone's friend. Some of the images were of Americans of Chinese descent. No one in Times Square, however, recognized the cast of characters screaming out at them from a virtual world. Chinese citizens, once they learned about the expensive promotion, roundly assassinated the production and the producers, and asked the pointed question, "Who are those people on the screen"? If China's own citizens found such a propaganda push unconvincing, how would such an effort be effective in other countries? What matters to most people's judgments are a country's core values.

Hupert told me about five Brand China core values Chinese central government leaders seem unaware they are expressing: China is opaque and mysterious ("Being mysterious is cool at first, but after a while it just gets creepy and passive-aggressive," he told me); state-sponsored corruption, which permeates the society and reads in China business handbooks as The Chinese Way; an angry country ("China's feelings have been hurt (again)," Hupert said, "and it will damage trade ties (again)."); the game is fixed ("Trade barriers and indigenous innovation regulations seem to have elevated thinking that 'it's easy to fool a foreigner' from a folk-saying to official policy."); product safety and quality problems ("Americans still associate China Inc. with poor quality, dangerous products and low-cost, lower-value Walmart goods," Hupert noted).

Chinese companies laboring under the Brand China image that want to break into the big, credible leagues of an IBM, BMW, Sony, or LG need to innovate in a variety of ways to dispel perceptions abroad about doing business with China. Corporate branding, product, operations, management, and strategic innovations must work in concert to convince buyers that Chinese corporations can meet international standards. Some argue a company's brand image is the most important of its assets. Brand image can be so precious that sometimes a monetary value cannot be placed on it. For most Chinese companies dealing abroad, though, their brand image is their greatest liability.

When Being a Chinese Company Isn't Cool

Brand innovation involves shifting the "personality" of a product, product line, or even company so it aligns with the expectations of potential buyers and maintains an identity customers trust and rely upon. The consistencies of message, of the quality of the offering, as well as delivery, all become part of defining the extent to which customers trust a brand.

Unfortunately, when Americans hear of a potential Chinese acqui-sition of an American company they automatically think the acquirer has Chinese government backing, or that there is some evil plot to subvert American values. In the case of China National Offshore Oil Corporation's (CNOOC) attempted acquisition in 2005 of Unocal, an American oil company, they would have felt justified. In the instance of Huawei, a communications equipment manufacturer that has attempted several acquisitions in the American market since the turn of the cen-tury, they may also have felt their supposition supported. Huawei has been unable to shed its convoluted holding structure, which involves the People's Liberation Army. And though Chinese Internet service provid-ers Sina.com and Baidu.com are not household names in the West, they are listed companies in the United States. The companies gained the greater portions of their vast market share in China at the behest of the Chinese Communist Party (CCP). The CCP in 2008 enacted restric-tive regulations that made it very difficult for foreign online operators to capture but a small part of Chinese commercial cyberspace. Central government curbs to control domestic markets and the *de facto* support of state-owned enterprises adversely impact the trajectory of Chinese companies that want to establish brands overseas. Andrew Hupert pointed out to me that China doesn't have an Apple or a Benetton to give voice to individual aspirations or personal ambitions.[1]

Companies like Haier—a white goods manufacturer, Lenovo, the computer maker, and Geely, which produces air conditioners—are well known by Chinese consumers. Whereas Geely was struggling to break into international markets in 2010, Haier remained the leading white goods manufacturer of the small refrigerators found in college dorm rooms the world over, among other product lines. Lenovo, though, has been the most successful at rebranding itself and recasting its image as an international player.

Lenovo originally began as Legend in the mid-1980s. The central government asked Liu Chuanzhi to distribute the then new-fangled personal computers throughout government agencies and SOEs. Liu did such a great job in distribution and training on the new technology, the government backed the establishment of Legend, sanctioning the design and construction of home-built machines. Lenovo continues to have strong ties with the Chinese Academy of Sciences. The government also provided a ready-made customer base for Liu to sell into, providing a platform from which the company could attain more than US$2 billion in revenues and more than US$40 million in annual profits in 2000. Legend rebranded as Lenovo in 2003 when it felt it was ready to break into international markets, by which time it was the ninth largest PC maker in the world.[2] Legend would have preferred to retain its name in foreign markets; however, the name "Legend" was already registered in the countries into which they wanted to sell their products.

Lenovo preferred to keep its Chinese name within the Chinese market. However, overseas, it chose a neutral, international-sounding name to distance itself from the image Brand China encouraged in the minds of potential buyers. The strategy paid off in 2004 when Lenovo successfully acquired the laptop division of IBM, which had been exploring ways of divesting itself of its PC hardware business at the time. The key in the rebranding strategy that catapulted Lenovo from ninth largest PC maker in the world in 2004 to number four in 2010 involved an agreement with IBM to use the IBM brand for five years, which included the use of the "Think" badge. "Think" was the label IBM used for its laptop series, popular with corporate customers. IBM also promised to support the success of the Think product line under new ownership through use of its own corporate sales force. The agreement dramatically reduced Lenovo's risk of losing the customer base with companies outside China that had bought laptop products from IBM. The concern was that customers would have fled because of quality and accountability problems related to the perception of Brand China.

Beyond Cheap

Chinese manufacturing has the dubious distinction of being of low-value and poor quality—i.e., cheap. Not even Chinese people trust many of their own brands. One of the habits I had to learn whenever I bought electrical appliances and other products in Chinese stores and malls was inspection. Service staff consistently pulled the item I wanted to purchase from its sealed box and plugged the appliance in and turned it on. They wanted to prove to me there on the spot that what I had bought was indeed operating as advertised. Nevertheless, the stigma infects nearly every product exported from Chinese suppliers. The preconception also adversely affects the efforts of the country to move up the value scale with increasing credibility.

Typically, product innovation involves making a better widget, or one with added features, or something that actually does the job it was bought to do. A British manager, named Peter, suggested to me that his staff did not have "application knowledge" when he first started up a factory in 2000. His factory made Do-It-Yourself (DIY) tools. He posed the question to me, "How can engineers extend a tool or create a new one if they've never used tools before?" He recalled an instance in the early days of his company when engineers had been assigned to modify an appliance for the local market. The staff returned several weeks later with a range of colored, detachable ears consumers could affix to the appliance. "My engineers would come to me with ideas I already knew were not workable," Peter said. "So, to encourage their creativity and also bring them down to earth, I would tell them, 'OK, there's the machining equipment—bring me back a prototype in a couple days. At the beginning, they would always come back and admit their idea was not workable. After time and experience handling and working with the tools, they eventually succeeded in producing some real changes for the product. Eventually, I made these innovators responsible for guiding someone more junior in their own department in the same way."

Product innovation, of course, differs from process innovation in that product innovation is punctuated by stages of product development with tangible results. Process improvement, however, should be a continuous activity, built into the character of the organization. Process improvement incubates product innovation. The Chinese HR director of a Western plant near Shanghai explained to me his company had a rewards system in place in which any and all employees are recognized for making genuinely innovative changes in their production processes. During the economic downturn of 2008–2009, the company began hiring engineers for an R&D department it decided to build. A year in, in January 2010, the company had already hired 13 engineers; they intended to double the size of the staff by summer of the same year. The department was responsible for localizing products its Western counterparts designed. Legend in the late 1990s also localized Western products. The incremental, "small-i" innovation increased its fortunes immeasurably.

Liu Chuanzhi, the founder of Legend, noticed that only well-educated Chinese users who had English-language training were able to use the personal computers the company was distributing. This was especially problematic as most of the customers were government agencies. Government workers were notoriously hide-bound bureaucrats who had missed out on a university education because of the Cultural Revolution (1966–1976). Struggles against educational institutions saw all of the universities and many schools closed and teachers shipped off for hard labor. Very few Chinese would have received English-language education by the time they were middle managers in the state-owned enterprises to which Liu sold the computer systems. Liu took the initiative to develop a Chinese language keyboard to facilitate the use of the computer for the millions of users who were not literate in the English language. Legend sales leaped with the innovation, which has since been replaced by the innovation of software and operating systems that depict the myriad characters of the Chinese language onscreen. Nevertheless, even with the most innovative kit, Chinese multinationals are finding that traditional management structures are liabilities when entering foreign markets.

Management Innovation

Management innovation involves creating frameworks for mobilizing the energies of human resources to provide products and services that prospective buyers want to purchase and customers continue to want to buy. Management succeeds when revenues per staff member are high, costs are low, and customers are happy. Management innovations are contextual; that is, they depend on the business conditions and the goals of the company. In the 1990s cutting middle managers from organizations to "flatten" company hierarchies was in fashion in America. Re-engineering organizations was closely coupled with "empowering" employees; that is, allowing those who worked directly with customers to be able to make decisions without having to call a supervisor. It could be argued that the MBA-degree is a management innovation. An entire industry grew up in academia, priming armies of corporate staff with rationalized skill sets to theoretically manage organizations with greater effectiveness.

Certainly, innovating arcane management structures will help Chinese companies gain the trust of foreign buyers. Re-energized organizations that have a higher degree of integrity and alignment between the inner-workings of the company and the customer target pool should realize greater gains. The greatest management innovation challenge for Chinese companies—especially those that wish to enter international markets as more than just an exporter—is to "de-Confucianize" their organizations. Chinese companies are far more hierarchical in their management structures than Western companies, especially American companies.

American companies pride themselves on being relatively "flat," with few layers of management separating leaders from front-line staff. Further, flat organizations rely on the experience front-line staff have with customers to re-adjust the organization to meet changing industry and economic circumstances. Confucian business structures, however, see a more pyramidal reporting structure, in which junior staff and back-office functions defer to an all-seeing, all-knowing leader who makes every decision. The organization structure mirrors Chinese society itself, at almost every level of life. Throughout society, the level of the hierarchy into which one is born or is able to insert oneself professionally may even be able to trump the law itself. In China, people see their positions in organizations as not only gaining them higher salaries and perquisites—or, if they are the business owners, greater profits—but as gaining them access to high-power individuals who will allow them to obviate the rules others are meant to follow.

Chinese professionals whose experience has solely been in Asian companies are not accustomed to voicing their ideas to management. "Most Chinese companies are extremely hierarchical," Peter, the DIY-company manager, told me. He has spent a great deal of time personally working with Chinese suppliers to improve the quality of their components and to meet international standards. "Most of the companies are run by a 'big boss.' Everyone hangs on his every word for a decision on matters. And no one dares make a mistake. So, everyone pretty much keeps their head down."

Both product and process innovation require "flatter" organizations. Optimally, in such businesses, management encourages the exchange of information and ideas. Leaders reward thinking that may even be outside an employee's immediate job description. Managers also tend to overlook mistakes or dead ends that do not disrupt regular company operations. Invention—especially disruptive innovations that create new product categories and even new industries—cannot be scripted. This kind of business model runs counter to the traditional Chinese standard.

Confucian management structures operate against information and knowledge transfer. The businesses become ingrown, with company politics focused on gaining access to higher echelons in the company to curry favor with leadership and to beat out real and imagined internal competition. Addressing customer needs is a distant priority as staff literally waits to be told by their immediate supervisor what they should be doing next. Western management models tend to thrive on a level of decentralization that, in the best of conditions, allows creativity and innovation to flourish. Junior staff is expected to discover or invent disruptive product or service offerings they present to senior staff. Silicon Valley is the most obvious example of the sort of flat, innovative business environments companies in America, and to a lesser extent in the European Union, try to emulate. Chinese companies and bosses, fixed by a sociopolitical system that rewards business and government "emperors," are far from realizing the Silicon Valley model of "contra-management." It becomes near impossible, then, for traditional Chinese managers to create operations that germinate invention.

The Operation Was a Success . . .

The objective of operations innovation is to achieve greater effectiveness and efficiency of the processes through which work is accomplished: how paychecks are processed in a hospital; how claims forms are processed in an insurance company; how products are made and checked for quality as they come off a manufacturing line. In the West, management has entrusted a great deal of decision-making to line staff, from production workers to customer service representatives, to make operations more efficient and the customer experience more rewarding. In China, cultural and educational conditioning makes operational innovation and related product innovation a challenge for managers to implement.

Michael, a British engineering manager at a foreign-invested clean-tech factory in China, lamented to me, "They [my staff] won't think outside the channel. I keep hearing, 'it's not in my job description!'" It's a common complaint in Western companies that are trying to get their local employees to think creatively about how to improve business and production processes, and even product design, in China.

The Chinese rocket scientist Qian Xuesan once asked, "Why does China produce so many clever people, but so few geniuses?" He died in 2009, at the age of 97, with the question still unanswered. Westerners and Chinese alike point the finger at the education system, which values rote-study and regurgitation of facts over exploration, discovery, and dialogue. One Chinese university student told me, "Professors don't have office hours [in which students can ask help with difficult subject matter]. If you ask the professor a question, he tells you in front of others you are stupid." For all that, many university students simply show up for examinations, having spent days and nights memorizing cardboard cut-out questions to pre-figured answers. Another barrier that discourages learning innovation from early on is family- and peer-pressure that molds the value of *face* in the society. Making mistakes, having a minor failure or any other action that loses one *face* is disgraceful.

As any politician in the West knows, oftentimes the longevity of his career hinges on the number of jobs he generates in his district. In China, a lack of new jobs in local and national economies can mean the undoing of the entire Chinese Communist Party (CCP). Since the late 1970s the CCP has relied on job creation to maintain its mandate to rule. The ideological posture of Communism with Chinese characteristics is essentially raw capitalism in the mold of the American robber barons of the early 20th century. However, China's preferred model for modernization actually emphasizes social stability over growth rates. Few other institutions in China illustrate that equation better than State-owned Enterprises (SOEs).

In the mid- to late-1990s central and local governments embarked on what was for them a frightening experiment: dismantling the thousands of SOEs that were dragging the entire economy into illiquidity. For decades SOEs had been the core of local communities: where people lived, schooled, retired and died. In 2004 in Shenyang, capital of the northern province of Liaoning, local government officials took me on a tour of a huge State-owned factory named the Silver Elephant. Local company and government representatives were looking for foreign buyers to buy parts of the company, or even form joint ventures with various superfluous divisions of the business. I was awestruck by the scale of the operation, which made a variety of products for the ship-building industry. Scores of great black vulcanized rubber bumpers, two meters high, stood in rank-and-file with no one to inspect them. I was also surprised by the sheer lack of activity and dynamism to which I had become accustomed in southern China, where SOEs were less a constituent of regional economies.

Privatization forced millions of workers into unemployment, their iron rice bowls melted down for the sake of privatization. The iron rice bowl was a metaphor for the enduring social security benefits SOEs would provide workers. Protests throughout the country became rife. The central government bet that with the ensuing chaos, privatization would stimulate management and operational innovations that would energize dispirited individuals and revive moribund organizations. Many local governments encouraged workers to take management respon-sibility, maintaining various levels of ownership in the local companies. Zhang Ruimin was one such employee-beneficiary. He understood the extent to which the entitlement mentality of workers at SOEs stymied business competitiveness. In the mid-1980s he set about reforming man-agement structures and operational procedures to transform the business into the international white goods maker Haier.

Since the trauma of the great SOE sell-off, the Chinese government has been loath to see companies *en masse* introducing further tumultu-ous change into their operations. The beginning of 2009 saw the dawn of new central government policy involving the re-nationalization of successful private industries. The drive, known as *guojin, mintui*, liter-ally means, "advancing the state and pushing the private sector back." Simply put, Beijing has been methodically absorbing successful private companies back into SOEs. SOEs deliver the CCP a greater degree of control over the economy. *Guojin, mintui* targeted aviation, oil refining, steel production, food and beverage, and the renewable energy sector, among others.

SOEs are also China's largest employers. In 2006, three of the five largest employers in the world were Chinese: State Grid, the electricity distributor (1,504,000 employees); China National Petroleum, the refiner (1,086,966 staff); and Sinopec, also an oil refiner (with a head-count of 681,000). Walmart was the largest employer at the time, with nearly 2 million employees; while the US Postal Service beat out Sinopec for the number four spot with almost 800,000 workers.[3]

SOEs do not have the same latitude as Walmart, however, in reduc-ing headcount when times get tough or when the company adopts a new growth strategy that requires a leaner operation. Walmart is known as a major employer in many rural areas in the United States. The retailer is given to shuttering its doors when local economies become too weak to provide profitability for the behemoth. SOEs, though, must await direction from central government authorities to make wholesale layoffs. During the global economic downturn of 2008–2009, Beijing directed SOEs to create openings to absorb the surfeit of university graduates who were unable to find jobs in the wounded private sector. The CCP's obsession with social stability trumped opera-tional efficiency. Beijing policy restricts China's top employers to incre-mental operational innovation. SOEs greatest responsibility when times get tough is to provide the least amount of disruption to the society.

Even if a SOE or a private company has a killer-widget it wants to sell into Western markets, it needs to have a plan that reflects an under-standing of international norms and product lifecycles. International markets tend to be less forgiving of product failures than the manic domestic markets in which businesses in China launch and recall prod-ucts with breathtaking speed.

What Was the Plan Again?

Strategic innovation means engaging current or new markets in a way that the company or industry had never done before to the end of greater profit. For instance, investing in operations in China was a huge strategic innovation for many American companies, most of which had made their fortunes within the borders of the continental United States. Most American companies that invested in China during the first decade of the new century had never had experience with any other market than the American: the domestic United States market had always seemed lucrative enough. When China had been accepted into the WTO in 2001 most American—and European—companies wanted to reduce their costs of manufacturing at home by setting up operations in China. By 2008, most American companies said in a poll with the American Chamber of Commerce in Shanghai that they were in China to sell into the Chinese marketplace. The marketplace in their home countries had changed dramatically, and the companies changed their direction to seek their fortunes on other shores.

What Western companies discovered in China as business strategy *per se* surprised them greatly. In some ways, the Chinese approach to business rather seemed more like anti-strategy: characterized by short-term thinking, immediate gratification, a lack of transparency in corporate governance, and a drive to conquer market share rather than to making profits. Donald Sull, author of *Made in China: What Western Managers Can Learn from Trailblazing Chinese Entrepreneurs*, actually codified the approach Chinese managers take in their own domestic market. He found that their approach was congruent with the way that business owners and managers in other developing countries like India and Mexico also developed and implemented business strategy. The acronym he gave the approach was SAPE: Sense-Anticipate-Prioritize-Execute.

The approach involves business managers in developing highly dynamic marketplaces, sensing the major trends affecting business, anticipating the next big trend, prioritizing their business tasks and resources to aggressively engage the trend, and then executing a conquest of market share in a take-no-prisoners fashion to drive the competition off the playing field. Sull discusses such winners in the Chinese market as Qinghou Zong, founder of the drinks company Wahaha, and UT Starcomm, maker of a mobile phone service for communities. However, much of what Sull codifies is simply reflexive behavior for Chinese executives. Business leaders in China perform little in the way of structured reflection on business approaches. Scopes for return on investment in China run in six-month cycles, twelve months for the longest-term thinkers.

One Fortune 500 company group of executives, with whom I participated in negotiations in the automotive sector, was appalled at what they saw as the lack of patience, foresight and sense of win-win on the part of the Chinese counter-party. The Chinese side kept insisting that the US$10 million the Americans planned to invest was far too much for the size operation under discussion. The joint-venture factory was to be placed in Chongqing, in the interior of China. "We can buy so much land with that money," the Chinese pushed, "and build a huge factory! Several factories!" For them, they saw such an amount of money to be used over a 5-year period as a waste of capital that could be put to use immediately, and thought the Americans rather naive about the possibilities of the Chinese market. The Americans simply saw three greedy Chinese business owners sitting across the hotel conference table from them. Perceptions on business strategy diverged so greatly negotiations never passed beyond a Memorandum of Understanding between the parties.

Chinese businesses that want to venture beyond their borders to diversify their interests in Western markets have to adopt Western-style strategies. Potential partners and managers and investors in the West want to see 5-year plans, balance sheets, and profit-and-loss statements. They want to review a single set of accounting books—instead of one set for the tax man, and one set for the business owners. Chinese companies that want to list on Western bourses like those found in New York, London, and even Singapore are finding that they must make their governance structures and inner workings far more transparent than they could have imagined. Chinese computer maker Lenovo simply left in place the American management structure and the laptop computer division team it acquired from IBM. The radical change in strategy most Chinese domestic firms are finding they have to take when they cross international borders are incredibly disruptive to their operations. Yet the changes are necessary if the companies want to effectively compete in foreign lands.

China's central government can do a lot to improve its country's image. It can also improve its companies' capacities for innovation. National policy may even facilitate the expansion of its multinational wannabes beyond merely gobbling up resource-rich deposits around the world by firmly enforcing corporate governance structures that meet international standards of transparency and objectivity. Still, for every Lenovo, it seems, there are scores of Chinese companies on international bourses that have reaped the scorn and distrust of investors the world over.

Red Flags

The most high-profile of the dozens of companies that came under sus-
picion in America for fraud was SinoForest. SinoForest was a Chinese
tree plantation company listed on the Toronto stock exchange. Instead
of filing for an initial public offering (IPO), the company took a less
onerous route to becoming a publicly held company through what is
called a "backdoor listing." Backdoor listings involve a company buying the stock market placement of a company that, effectively, has gone
out of business. Backdoor listings, also known as reverse-mergers—in
contrast to initial public offerings (IPOs)—have few regulatory requirements and little need for the level of transparency IPOs demand.

American short-seller Muddy Waters LLC researched the company's published financial statements and compared them to what
researchers on the ground in China tallied. The firm uncovered a
gross discrepancy about which Muddy Waters principal Carson Block
published a report. The share price of the Chinese company quickly
dived, but not before Block had sold the shares he had bought in the
company. Buying and then selling shares in companies within a short
timeframe is called "shorting" stocks. Block made millions of dollars anticipating that Chinese companies that had short-circuited the
due diligence involved in IPOs were simply betting on the gullibil-
ity of investors. Block also called out the Chinese company Rino
International, which had been falsifying sales contracts.[4] But as Patrick
Chovanec of Tsinghua University pointed out, denial and confession
were beside the point in such cases: "It's not that people concluded he's
[Block's] right about these companies. It's that they realized they don't
know *whether* he's right or not."[5]

Chinese central authorities, though, cared little about the governance structures of domestic companies. They paid even less attention to those making forays into international markets. The majority of
Chinese companies listed on domestic stock markets are state-owned,
and of those, typically only about 30-percent of the shares are on offer
to the public. The State controls the rest of the shares. The State also
controls the top positions in the companies, making profitability and
shareholder rights secondary to personal wealth creation and political

expediency. The Chinese Communist Party, however, does care if the trouble the companies get into involves government officials exposed for acts of corruption.

Mingyi Hung, T.J. Wong, and Fang Zhang observed in their study "The Value of Relationship-based and Market-based Contracting: Evidence from Corporate Scandals in China," that companies listed on Mainland bourses and involved in accounting scandals saw their shares drop nearly 10 percent, on average, over the six months on either side of the incident. The stock fell by almost a third, though, for companies involved in the bribery of government officials or the theft of state assets.[6] Central government authorities gave scant attention to the spate of scandals involving companies like SinoForest and Rino International, since no CCP members were involved. Beijing considered these companies and the dozens of others investigated by the United States Securities and Exchange Commission (SEC) as merely isolated instances of questionable fraud. The transgressions were not worth creating an international incident over.

Branding Beyond Nationality

As long as a self-interested, short-sighted tone of governance is embedded in Chinese society, the greatest innovation Chinese companies will have as they penetrate international markets and seek credibility along with sales, is to bury the fact they are Chinese. Lenovo and Haier are among the most successful to shed their national flags. Scandals in the country continue to stream through media channels, inflicting damage on China's image in irreparable ways. The national brand the central government seems to be supporting is not only impacting the image foreigners have of the country, but, increasingly, that of Chinese citizens, as well. Food safety, for instance, became a major concern to consumers in China with revelations of illegal steroids being injected into animals to grow lean meat quickly; re-cycled cooking oil skimmed from gutters and conditioned with chemicals for resale to restaurants; and poisonous insecticides sold to unwitting farmers in south China to increase the yields in their crops. Nightly, local television news spends upwards of 20 percent of its programming on stories related to fraud.

Given what seems to involve government complicity—if not simply malfeasance—at various levels to the transgressions, domestic companies find it difficult to differentiate their corporate images and product identities from those their own country projects to the world. They also have to defend themselves from the opprobrium heaped upon the competitors in their industries that have been caught defrauding customers. If companies choose to become national champions they face a series of hurdles that require innovations to the image they portray, the way they manage their business and manufacture their products and offer their services. To meet international competitors in the global arena, however, leaves Chinese companies at a disadvantage when compared with German, American, Swiss or a basket of other national identities from which companies with national ambitions are able to draw marketing prowess.

Chinese companies that wish to break into international markets actually work at a disadvantage because of the country's national brand identity: cheap goods sold without accountability that are most likely fake anyway. Companies may dramatically revise their work processes and revitalize their product images to suit buyers in other countries; however, the taint of being a Chinese company will continue to work against aspirants for at least another generation. Companies may be able to escape the crushing weight of their country's bad press by changing their names to something Western-sounding (like Lenovo), or acquiring Western product lines to brandish their owner's credibility. Geely, the Chinese car company, did exactly that with its purchase of Volvo, the Swedish car maker. The acquisition gave Geely access to the European market, much-needed technology, and allowed the Chinese car company to hide behind an established Western brand that portrayed quality and integrity. In time, as long as Geely does not try to eclipse the Volvo brand, Western consumers may express pleasant surprise that the Volvos they had been buying and driving since 2009 were actually Chinese made. Large corporate accounts have relaxed considerably about Lenovo's purchase of IBM's laptop computer division. Big companies have not seen any drop in the quality of product and service delivery that had persuaded them to buy IBM products at the outset.

Through a gradual but quiet accumulation of corporate reassurances, the national identity China's leadership has been clumsily attempting to project to the world may actually come to pass. The central government may itself one day be pleasantly surprised by passing commentary on the high level of quality and support of some of their own national corporate champions. The transition, however, will come despite their stewardship of international relations, not because of it. Private companies—the freer of government ties the better—will be the new ambassadors for a country that will one day find itself becoming increasingly mired in the middle age of modernity. The leadership will no longer be able to paper over the country's shortcomings with largesse to developing countries, and will have to whip its domestic industries in shape and truly liberalize its financial markets. It will have to deal head-on with a growing image abroad of a country interested in dealing with other countries solely for the natural resources partners have to offer.

In the long-run China's manufacturing prowess in the world will amount to little when compared to two new-century realities with which the country will have to come to grips. China's image as a bastion of *Fake* will gradually be supplanted by a reputation as the largest energy consumer in the world and the largest polluter on the planet. Solutions for the new-age challenges will require more than just corporate restructurings and bland reassurances.

Chapter 6

Declaration of Energy Independence

A black shroud enveloped the car. We had driven only a couple of kilometers down the country road when smoke blotted out the mid-winter sun. Suddenly we were driving blind. By the time my eyes had adjusted to the darkness, we had stopped. On the driver's side of the car stood the great cement tower of a coal burning power plant, some 30-stories high, vomiting thick charcoal smoke. The dirty vapor swirled through the air, carefree, and fluttered across the hood of the government sedan that we were driving. The mist wafted across the cracked, uneven road and caressed a riot of crooked brick walls and corrugated plastic roofs that lay scattered along shattered lanes. People lived and worked in the ramshackle warren. They went about their lives without interruption. We stepped out of the car. A man in a worn sports coat riding past on a rusted bicycle squinted at us.

The Yangzhou government administrator said encouragingly, "We can build a single-floor facility for your client here." Yangzhou is about an hour's drive north of Nanjing, on the Yangtze River. My host pointed at the exact spot where residents were in thrall to their own survival in the brick maze. They must have witnessed this roadside scene countless times before, with other government officials ushering other businessmen from around the world. They knew though, they were safe from immediate encroachment. Only they would be foolish enough or poor enough to continue life in the murky shadow of a coal burning power plant. People who lived in the cities had more options than they did in the countryside. One day, though, they too would be forced to relocate to an urban center in the name of modernity. For now, they tried merely to make themselves invisible in the swirl of black haze.

China's energy consumption needs will only grow as the country continues on its aggressive course to urbanize the population. Urbanites use 3.5 to 4 times more energy per capita than their country cousins.[1] China's central leadership set the goal in 2000 that by 2020 the country would quadruple its wealth, or Gross Domestic Product (GDP). The country's supersonic economic development during the first decade of the 21st century saw it install the total electricity capacity of the United Kingdom every year.[2] This equated to three or four 500-megawatt coal-burning power plants every week, a Massachusetts Institute of Technology Industrial Performance Center report cited.[3] According to the U.S. Energy Information Administration, the country's energy usage more than doubled between 2000 and 2010. In 2008 the Institute for Energy Research stated that America had the capacity to generate over one terawatt of electricity, or enough energy to power 100 billion homes. China surpassed the United States as the largest energy consumer in the world in 2009. The International Energy Agency estimated that China consumed 2,265 million tons of oil-equivalent energy that year.[4] China's growing appetite for cheap power is likely to rise to 53 percent by 2030.[5] By 2035 it is set to exceed U.S. consumption by 68 percent.[6]

Joseph Tainter, in his book *The Collapse of Complex Societies*, surmised that energy is the fundamental currency of a complex society. A society will need to consume more energy if it wants to move from stage-to-stage in its development—agricultural to industrial, industrial to information age; or, put another way, from the countryside to the city. It will remain a relatively simple society if, however, it does not have access to sufficient quantities of energy with which to develop itself or to maintain its current state. *Sustainable energy production in the face of continuing urbanization is one of the greatest technological challenges facing humankind in the 21st century.*

Energy consumption in the modern world is bound up in a welter of utilities, institutions, and habits indicative of urbanization. By the end of 2011 Chinese cities supported nearly 700 million residents—more than twice the population of the United States. The Chinese leadership plans to bring nearly 100 million more country folk to settle in its cities by 2020. Urbanization has also forced transportation requirements to go far beyond the horse and buggy to include air, sea, automobile, and rail. Industry, agriculture, and the increasing use of electrical appliances are requiring China's energy generation capability to grow larger every year.

The transition from an agrarian society to a post-industrial society means China will continue to build and renovate dozens of new cities. Urban development will bring with it new buildings, roads, and utility infrastructure construction projects. China has goals in the coming decade of connecting every town with more than 200,000 residents with roads to airports to which vehicles can get within two hours. All the construction implies continued and growing energy consumption by two of the most gluttonous industries in the world: steel and cement. In 2005 steel manufacturing alone accounted for more than 3 percent of China's GDP.[7] China accounted for nearly half of the global cement production in 2007, 35 percent of global steel production, and—nearly as energy intensive—nearly a third of global aluminum production.[8] The proportions will not be changing over the coming decade, as China builds electrical generation capacity to keep up with the society's transformation. Ensuring ample supplies of food and water get to an increasingly affluent population will also become problematic.

Food production is also a major energy sink. Planting, irrigation, and crop fertilization require more energy as citizens become richer and eat more. Further, an increasing amount of crops are going toward the farming of livestock, which requires greater amounts of energy to cultivate than grains.[9] Food distribution, which includes packaging and transport, are major contributors as well to any modern society's reliance on energy. The production of potable water requires huge amounts of processing by equipment completely reliant on electrical power. Finally, individual consumption is increasingly contributing to the load on energy requirements as we light our homes, play with our gadgets, cook, clean and dry our clothes, and generally manage our lives within the urban setting.

According to the International Energy Agency, China's energy consumption mix in 2007 involved industry taking nearly half of energy production; residential, commercial, and agricultural activities absorbing almost 45 percent of energy output; and transportation involving a little more than 10 percent of energy consumption. Meanwhile, the United States in the same year invested 20 percent of its energy capacity in industry; 35 percent to the residential, commercial, and agricultural sectors; and a whopping 45 percent of energy output to transportation. The European Union with its 27 countries had the most balanced energy consumption mix with just over 30 percent of energy output devoted to industry; about 40 percent for residential, commercial, and agriculture; and about 15 percent invested in transportation, according to the same report.[10] The sources of energy do not vary widely for modern and modernizing countries.

About three-quarters of the United States energy mix is from thermal sources—like coal, oil, and natural gas. Nuclear power makes up 10 percent of America's electrical capability, while hydropower follows up with 8 percent of the pie. Wind, solar, and other sources of alternative power make up the rest of America's source of power. China's mix is quite different from America's in that over 70 percent of China's generating capacity comes from coal, while America depends on coal for half its power needs. In 2008, China relied on hydropower for nearly 20 percent of its energy generating requirements. In the same year nuclear and wind-power each took about 1 percent of the power generating capability, with solar contributing negligible amounts of power to China's 800-gigawatts capability.[11] China's insatiable and growing appetite for electricity can only be met by resources that are relatively inexpensive to mine, plentiful, and readily converted to energy with a minimum amount of refinement. Only the fossil fuel sources coal, oil, and natural gas fit those criteria. Of the three, coal is king.

Coal in China's Stocking

China missed the start of the Industrial Revolution 300 years ago. Actually, China blatantly refused to join the wave of technological and social transformations sweeping the West. In 1793 the British envoy of England, Earl Macartney, demonstrated a small steam powered engine to the Emperor of China, Qianlong, amongst other technological marvels. The Qing dynasty Emperor was said to have commented, "Strange objects do not interest me." Less than 50 years later, in 1840, during the First Opium War, British gunboats driven by steam turbines ripped the Chinese navy to shreds in the harbor of Canton. The ships were fueled with coal, which the British had learned how to apply to ever more efficient furnaces that would generate energy in increasing amounts. The Watt, as a measure of power, is taken from the surname of James Watt, the inventor who contributed to making the steam engine commercially viable.

Today, the technology underlying James Watt's invention still drives pistons and drive shafts much the way it did 200 years before. And coal remains the primary source of energy that powers the cities of the two largest economies in the world: America and China. Coal makes up the overwhelming majority of the source of energy that drives the huge turbines in the power plants of the two countries. Coal is also used in the great steel forges that made cities like Pittsburgh and Allentown the industrial centers they were for more than a century. China's mobilization of coal, however, was long forestalled.

By the time Earl Macartney had arrived, during his first envoy to the Emperor Qianlong, the Chinese had deforested much of Guangdong province and Northern Vietnam.[12] At the time, and for thousands of years before, wood was the primary source of energy in China. In the late 1600s the British discovered a way to economically convert coal into the most efficient source of energy the world had ever seen and to harness the power in the steam engine. By 1830 Britain was consuming coal with an equivalent output of 15 million acres of forest—or about 20,000 square kilometers, about the size of the state of New Jersey.[13]

China's use of energy continued to be way below the average of other industrialized countries for the next 150 years after Earl Macartney's visit to the Qing court. The disintegration of the Qing Dynasty in 1911 accelerated the descent of the country into chaos. Civil war over the next 25 years effectively brought economic activity in the country to a standstill. After the Communist takeover of China in 1949 the nation saw energy usage gradually increase until the Great Leap Forward, in 1958—a great experiment in manufacturing based on millions of backyard furnaces. China's energy consumption expanded by more than 200 percent over the next two years, after which the greatest man-made famine in human history ground economic activity to a halt.[14]

Steel and concrete production, primarily powered by coal-burning furnaces, has been at the vanguard of China's energy usage since the 1950s. Within 20 years coal-fired plants were ubiquitous throughout China, powering the country's revitalized urban centers. One Chinese woman told me that when she was a school student in the 1970s she would come home each day with the collar and cuffs of her white shirt blackened by coal dust exhaled from factory smoke stacks.

By 2007 China produced half the world's concrete production and more than a third of its steel manufacturing—operations powered by coal.[15] China's coal import volume leaped to 125 million tons in 2009, up 211.9 percent year-on-year.[16] China made up 80 percent of the growth of world coal demand from 1990 to 2010. By 2010 China used half the world's coal.[17]

China became a net importer of coal in 2010 when China's monetary stimulus jolted the economy back to life after the nadir of global economic downturn in the spring of 2009. Demand was so great that the price of coal on international markets doubled between the years 2005 to 2010.[18] China in 2010 imported about 150 million tons of coal.[19] Much of domestically mined coal in China is high in impurities, making it inefficient to burn the mineral for electricity. So, China, to meet its exploding energy requirements, has been importing coal from America, Australia, and South America. It proved during the time to actually be cheaper to ship the coal to the energy-hungry operations on China's east coast than to transport shipments from the country's interior.[20] The ill-kept and poorly integrated cargo railway system made coal transport prohibitively expensive. The plethora of private mines—many of which were illegal—made rationalizing coal supplies problematic.

The coal mining industry in 2009 began a massive consolidation as the State found the free-wheeling approach of mining bosses—many of whom ran illegal operations—inconvenient to China's overall goal of increasing energy efficiency and reducing pollution; not to mention reducing the number of fatalities from mining accidents.

In 2002 the country registered a high of 7,000 deaths from coal mining operations. In 2009 the number had lowered to just over 2,600. The province with the worst safety record was Shanxi province, where subsidies, tax breaks, and particularly pliant local governments accepted pretty much any Chinese coal investor. The national government set about consolidating the mines in 2009. In 2010 the government took the tally down from more than 2,500 mines to nearly 1,000 through a process of merger and acquisition by State-owned Enterprises (SOEs).

In the long run, consolidation of the coal mines should be good for China. The country will be able to more easily and cost-effectively modernize mining operations. The government intended that modernization would save lives and increase the efficiency of production. Managing the coal mines under just a few nationalized umbrellas would make it easier to see that miners followed national directives and complied with national priorities.

China's future is tied solidly to coal, despite the leadership's recognition that coal is poisoning its air and contributing to climate change. China has no choice but to pursue its use of the stuff, whether domestically or imported. Xiao Yunhan, a member of the Chinese Academy of Sciences, sees China irreversibly dependent on coal for at least another two decades.[21] By 2030 China is expected to account for nearly 80 percent of the growth in the world's use of coal. Afterward, analysts expect the country's use of coal to flatten, if not actually begin to decrease.[22]

Barclays Capital analyst Micheal Zenker believed that as long as gas prices stayed lower than coal prices, gas-powered electricity generation could eat into the market for the steam coal that runs many of

China's power plants. The United States Energy Department projected that new natural gas generation capacity would outstrip new coal generation capacity by more than 30 percent into 2020. Less expensive gas-run power plants could begin replacing coal plants over the next decade. The conversion might even force a reduction in the number of coal plants built by as much as one-third.[23] Chinese and American researchers at the end of the first decade of the 21st century began working in earnest on ways to clean up coal's act by "gasifying" it. Their aim was to see that countries were able to use coal sustainably, with a minimum amount of damage to the environment. Nationalization of many of China's coal mines should also foster and facilitate implementation of innovative green technologies such as coal gasification. Visionaries even see coal gasification as helping China to some extent release its dependence on foreign oil imports.

Cleaning Up Coal's Act

The head of the Clean Air Task Force in China, Ming Sung, cited in 2010, "There are ways to generate electricity from coal with pretty much zero emissions." Sung helped design Shell Oil's first coal gasification plant in the United States in the 1980s. He explained the key to cleaning coal was to turn it into a gas first. "Make coal into a gas, either above ground—which is a traditional coal gasification technology. Or you can go underground. It's very efficient, and very low-cost. And that is the technology I feel will change the landscape," Sung added.[24] The United States was the leader in Coal to Liquid (CTL) research in the 1970s and 1980s until oil prices became so low as to make research efforts into alternative energy peripheral to the United States economic growth. At the turn of the century Made-in-America expertise migrated to China to carry forward research into and application of the technology.

China and the United States at national levels of government and in academic circles have realized the need to cooperate to reduce the dirty effects of coal. While not necessarily addressing the consumption and efficiency issues underlying the countries' addiction to coal, efforts began as early as 2004 to find economical ways to "gasify" coal. Gasification—also known as coal liquefaction—produces jet fuel, diesel, oil and gasoline, as well as carbon dioxide (CO_2). The CO_2 can be used in a range of products from injecting soda pop with bubbles to the production of ceramic tiles. Joint venture projects between China and the United States have been exploring CO_2 sequestration since 2005. Sequestration involves injecting the CO_2 into the ground— perhaps even into retired coal mines. For every ton of coal processed nearly a ton of CO_2 is produced, making sequestration a viable alternative to releasing the greenhouse gas into the atmosphere to contribute to climate change phenomena.

One such consortium between China and the United States involved West Virginia University (WVU). The institution worked with the Shenhua Direct Coal Liquefaction (DCL) facilities in Shanghai and Inner Mongolia.[25] The joint venture was underwritten by China's National Development and Reform Commission (NDRC) and the United States Department of Energy. WVU was also working with the Chinese on an environmental and economic analysis of the Shenhua DCL plant. The university was also investigating CO_2 sequestration processes related to the Shenhua DCL plant. Integrated DCL and ICL (indirect coal liquefaction) processes, liquefaction fuel testing, and other activities also held the institution's interest. The pilot projects demonstrated the feasibility of solid waste recycling, CO_2 sequestration, and zero water discharge.

Another effort involved The Pacific Northwest National Laboratory (PNNL), a Department of Energy facility, based in Washington state. PNNL worked with scientists from the Chinese Academy of Sciences to assess the viability of carbon dioxide sequestration underground in China.[26] A PNNL study found that China has enough underground capacity to sequester CO_2 for a century. Results also showed most of the potential repositories within 100 miles of major users of coal. Power generators, steel plants, cement factories, and other heavy industry typically accommodate large spaces that can receive excess CO_2. The finding implied that transport of CO_2 from domestically mined coal could go a long way to making sequestration viable economically, possibly without slowing the go-go pace at which China's economy is growing.

Though China is far from ready to kick its coal habit, the R&D insights American teams applied to Chinese quick-time implementation of engineering projects should help to somewhat reduce the threat burning coal presents to individuals and to the environment. CTL technologies, however, will do little to curb the society's growing appetite for coal, nor the consequences of a command-and-control economy striving to become a free market.

Economics Rules

The first time the economics of coal energy came to haunt the Chinese consumer was the winter of 2008, during a blizzard season the likes of which many parts of China had not seen in 50 years. Beijing suffered the coldest winter in 100 years. Entire provinces in central China were without electricity for several weeks. The reason, however, was not for lack of coal, but because of central government requirements that coal producers accept a rate for the sale of their coal to power plants as set by the National Development and Reform Commission (NDRC). During that frigid winter train cars laden with coal sat in depots without release from coal mine owners who chose to wait out the authorities, a negotiating tactic of the most aggressive sort. Eventually, the blizzards lifted, the weather moderated and demand eased, relaxing market pressures for higher priced coal.

The winter of 2010 in China's north proved as challenging from an economic point of view as the blizzards of 2008. China reached an energy tipping point in 2010, the same year it surpassed the United States as the largest consumer of electricity in the world. Though snows were not as heavy in north and central China in 2010 as they were in 2008, more people living in cities with greater wealth turned on their central heating systems to thwart the cold. Also, in the two years since 2008, China had built and manned more stores, more malls, more office buildings, and more factories than ever before, all drawing on coal-powered energy subsidized by the state. Coal producers exacerbated the energy shortages by refusing to sign contracts for 2011 under central government *diktat* that forbade their raising prices to meet mushrooming demand. By the end of 2010 coal contracts signed by producers accounted for only 29 percent of the total railway transportation capacity allocated for coal cargo.[27] Power companies hired intermediaries to find and bring to them the coal they needed to keep their furnaces glowing red. Intermediaries, though, typically inflated the cost of coal by as much as double the State's price level, forcing power plants to cut back on purchases. The State Grid—one of the two electricity networks in the country—reported Shaanxi, Shanxi, Hubei, and other provinces were having coal power shortages. Some regions in Shaanxi Province, a region rich in coal reserves, began implementing "brown outs." At one point, fourteen backbone power plants in the area had less than five days of coal power inventory left.

The central government expected coal producers to play their part in maintaining a harmonious society by keeping their prices from inflating in line with food and water costs. Coal producers, however, were not playing ball. The prices the National Development and Reform Commission (NDRC) insisted coal miners pay, 100 RMB to 200 RMB (US$15 to US$30), less than market rates per ton. Orders for the thermal coal that run power plants went unmet.

The standoff pointed directly at a major weakness in China's long-term strategy to continue powering its economic ascent over the next ten to fifteen years. The CCP was learning that the laws of economics—specifically, that of supply and demand—would bend to Party rule for only so long. Ironically, as long as central government planners did not allow the market forces to function inside China with regard to coal, other, counter-productive forces would circumvent government energy policy.

Coal burning's pollutants and the ill-effects on the health of the population, however, continued to pressure China to implement alternatives to coal-based power. China aggressively pushed ahead with investments in hydropower, wind power, and solar power. Battery technology to store energy for smart grids that distribute power throughout the country and power cars was also of primary importance. As long as China was the Workshop of the World the country would be hungry for energy.

In other words, a great deal of the energy China was using was because of the manufacturing of the sort of cheap goods Americans and Europeans clamor for. A serious refitting of China's energy signature required the three trading blocks to reconfigure—or re-balance, as economists like to say—their economies: the Americans away from consumption of goods and toward saving, high-end manufacturing, and R&D; the Europeans in liberalizing their labor markets and tax regimes to permit the growth of smaller, nimbler entrepreneurial enterprises; and the Chinese away from heavy industry—steel and concrete production and leather processing—toward services and higher quality production activities. Greater consumption for all the economies needed to be rolled back to ecologically sustainable levels.

Oily Risers

Urbanization is the primary driver behind China's increasing imports of oil and gas. By 2030 China will have become the largest consumer and importer of oil in the world, using nearly 18 million barrels of oil each day, almost double what it used in 2010. China will have to import three times more oil than it did in 2010 to sustain its thirst. Growing vehicle usage has been a major contributor to growing oil consumption in the country.

After decades of riding bicycles in every kind of weather to work, home, on family outings, and on nights out with friends, Chinese began junking their bikes in the mid-2000s. They began favoring Henry Ford's vision of the thoroughly modern family; that is, an automobile for every middle-class family. In America, the vision realized a penetration rate of 700 out of every 1,000 people owning a car in 2010. In 2010, China had a mere 30 car owners per 1,000 people. By 2035, 240 out of 1,000 people in China will own a car—only two-thirds of America's 2010 penetration rate.[28] In 2010 China had an estimated 40 million cars on its roadways. Most of those cars were bought after 2005. Fully 10 percent of the number of cars were in Beijing alone, a quarter of which—one million—had entered Beijing's famed ring roads after 2008.[29] By 2035 China will see 135 million cars on the roads.

Local governments are already seeing a downside to massive car ownership. Skies in many cities are perpetually polluted from car exhaust. Traffic has become gridlocked in a fashion that makes some drivers pine for the good old days of pedaling bicycles to work. During 2009, Beijing was adding 1,000 cars a day to its roadways. In the last two weeks of 2010 the Beijing municipal government announced that in 2011 only 250,000 cars would be permitted to be purchased in the city. Beijing residents responded to the pronouncement by swamping car dealerships in the few days left in the old year to grab their piece of the four-wheeled dream.

And though Beijing may have limited the purchase of the number of vehicles within its city limits for 2011, residents throughout the rest of the country were still on a mission to one day own a car for the family. The International Energy Agency estimated in early 2010 that China's rate of growth in oil consumption would run at about 2 percent per annum. The reality was that by the end of 2010 oil consumption had grown by more than 8 percent year-on-year, to more than 8.5 million barrels per day.

China's increasing thirst for oil and gas has pushed the central government into dramatically increasing its research and development budget for exploration of new sources. China discovered 38 oil basins in the South China Sea and the southern portion of the Yellow Sea from 2000 to 2010. Accelerated exploration programs yielded in 2010 a geological stratum of 'super-thick' oil and gas in the South China Sea.[30] Researchers also found natural gas hydrate in the northern region of the South China Sea, and at Qilian Mountain, at the intersection of northeastern Tibet and southwestern Gansu province. Policy makers announced at the end of 2010 the country would spend about US$75 million on oil and natural gas exploration over the next 20 years, a ten-fold increase over the previous decade. The excavation of domestic sources of natural gas is critical to China's efforts to achieve energy security. Natural gas deposits within the country's borders may offset annual increases in the importation of coal and oil, which expose the country to capricious changes in international markets. The relative cleanliness of natural gas exhaust may also help the nation realize clearer skies over many of its smoke-choked cities.

What a Gas

China's use of natural gas is a relatively thin slice of its energy pie, according to the International Energy Agency. In 2008 natural gas use represented only 4 percent of overall consumption. Still, the central government intended in 2010 to promote infrastructure development for natural gas to reduce its overall carbon footprint. Total consumption of natural gas in China in 2010 was 106 billion cubic meters—with growth of nearly 20 percent over 2009. Natural gas demand in China was growing in leaps and bounds entering the second decade of the 21st century. According to China's National Development and Reform Commission (NDRC), demand jumped 21 percent in the first quarter of 2011, from a year before, to 33.3 billion cubic meters.[31]

Manufacturing in primary and secondary industries used the overwhelming proportion of natural gas in China from 2008 through 2010. Primary industries include mining, ore processing, and steel and cement production; while product manufacturing dominates secondary industries. Commercial and residential consumption of natural gas vied for second place. *China Sign Post* reported that cooking dominated 70 percent of total use of natural gas in residences, followed by 18 percent for use by water heaters and 12 percent by space heating.[32]

China National Petroleum Corporation (CNPC) predicted that natural gas consumption would grow to 230 billion cubic meters by 2015. In 2010 Thomas King, president of BP (China) Holdings Ltd. in Shanghai, believed China's natural gas market would double from 2011 levels by 2015 to 260 billion cubic meters. Lin Boqiang, director of the China Center for Energy Economics Research at Xiamen University, projected the growth rate to average 20 percent per year through 2020. "The consumption growth rate will be more than 20 percent in the next 10 years because this is now the peak period for China's urbanization and industrialization," he told *China Daily*.[33]

Industry analysts expected China to consume 300 billion cubic meters of natural gas by 2020, accounting for 8 percent of China's total energy portfolio at that time. The Chinese leadership, though, wants to triple the use of natural gas to about 10 percent of its energy consumption by 2020 as it cuts reliance on more polluting coal. The segments of society believed to see the greatest growth in the use of natural gas from 2010 through 2020 are industry (400 percent), residential (500 percent), and power production (700 percent). The chemical sector stands out on its own as an industry sector that relies heavily on natural gas, with 250 percent growth expected from 2010 to 2020.

China's National Energy Agency (NEA) calculated that domestic natural gas consumption was 110 billion cubic meters in 2010, of which domestic production was able to address 94.5 billion cubic meters, a 12 percent increase from 2009.[34] By 2015 analysts expect domestic production of natural gas to reach 150 billion cubic meters,[35] still leaving a shortfall of 80 billion cubic meters of consumer demand that imports will have to meet. Fracking has come under serious consideration by China's energy industry as a means to accelerate access to domestic supplies of natural gas. Fracking involves forcing great volumes of water and chemicals into layers of rock and seams of coal to liberate natural gas. New extraction approaches, however, still may not be enough to counter growing consumption requirements for natural gas.

The NDRC reported that imports met about 20 percent of the nation's natural gas demand of 106 billion cubic meters in 2010, up nearly 8 percent from a year earlier.[36] However, Bloomberg reported that in the first quarter of 2011 China's imports of natural gas actually doubled over the same period a year earlier.[37] By 2020 imports could make up about 25 percent of the total intake of natural gas; while 2030 estimates see imports reduced to about 20 percent of the natural gas portfolio as domestic supplies increase and urbanization slows.[38]

Urbanization will continue to drive China's demand for natural gas into the 2020s. Though coal will play a dominant role as the country's primary energy source, natural gas fits nicely into an energy portfolio intended to reduce carbon emissions and increase energy efficiency.

Breaking the Addiction

It matters to the world how much energy China uses and the source of the energy. Issues such as pollution and natural resource depletion affect everyone on the planet. The rapid urbanization of 20 percent of the world's population has created a tipping point in the awareness of the degree to which fossil fuels are bad for the environment. China's accelerated use of coal and oil has also made many governments and non-governmental organizations wonder out loud about the degree to which supplies are limited for the world at large.

Domestically, China has all but run out of oil, and the central government in late 2010 began to become concerned miners were running down its deposits of coal. The deficit of both implies China will have to exploit the deposits of other countries with little regard for maintaining the balance of their ecosystems. Meanwhile, air pollution from coal burning power plants is circulating along China's seaboard northward, into Japan and Korea. The pollution circulates eastward into Canada and then southward into Seattle. Automobile exhaust from Chinese roadways is mixing with that of the stalled traffic of Los Angeles' own choked arteries, compounding health hazards for residents. By unwittingly taking on the energy liabilities of other countries, China also assumed the mantle as the greatest polluter on the planet.

China's export manufacturing sector absorbed supply chains that used to reside within the borders of other countries scattered throughout the world. The Americans, Germans, British, and countless other countries are also complicit in the concentration of energy consumption and pollution production in China. For example, automobiles that used to be made in Japan saw their components and assembly moved to southern China. Energy requirements bound up in managing the supply chain also moved to mainland China. Or consider the effect Walmart has had on Chinese manufacturing. Much of the stuff Walmart buys now in China was once Made in America in the mid-1990s. If Walmart were a country it would have the 25th largest economy in the world. Its purchasing power gave it the heft to push margins so low that American companies were unable to compete with Chinese exporters hungry for any business. The transfer of orders that would have otherwise gone to American factories took with it a sizable chunk of America's energy profile. Unfortunately, Chinese operations are only about one-quarter as efficient as American businesses in converting energy into wealth.[39] China's energy requirements, then, became more expansive than the country had prepared for in planning its energy infrastructure.

In 2005 China set about making itself more efficient in its use of energy to reduce its dependence on fossil fuels and the expense of building additional energy infrastructure. In its 11th 5-year plan it laid out a goal of saving 20 percent of the energy it used per unit of economic activity. In 2006 and 2007 the country's energy use in relation to its GDP growth was stubbornly high. Factories were working all out to meet rising demand from the West for consumer goods, while domestic construction projects continued to sprout throughout the country. It looked uncertain whether the nation would be able to meet its ambitious target. The global economic downturn of 2008–2009 proved a gift for China's energy statisticians. The downturn was the most dramatic contraction of economic activity in the world since the Great Depression of the 1920s.

The effect of the Great Recession in China was to shutter thousands of factories that could no longer manufacture and export stuff to the rest of the world. The downturn also forced thousands of other factories to drastically curtail production schedules to just two or three days a week. The change was traumatic for a sector that had seen a go-go manufacturing frenzy the year before in which most factories had three shifts working round-the-clock, seven days a week. GDP growth in 2008 slowed to its lowest rate in seven years, growing at only 9 percent. The net effect was to see China's energy use come into closer congruence with its GDP growth. The nation's electricity consumption in 2008 rose by only about 5 percent year-on-year, the lowest annual growth rate since 1998.[40] With wasteful, low-margin factories and heavy construction projects unable to continue operation during 2008, China actually saw energy efficiency as an achievable goal. The government claimed it slid into 2010 just .9 percent shy of its target.

China's and the West's addiction to fossil fuels is so deep and so historically abiding that humans would have to rip apart the very fabric of their societies to completely replace the energy sources. Trillions of dollars in infrastructure development, modes of transportation, power generation construction, even the way we eat and store and process food stuffs would have to change irrevocably. The worst case scenario of simply running down stocks of fossil fuels without sufficient replacements already developed would be a Mad Max world. Mad Max was the trilogy of films made in the 1980s in which the Australian actor Mel Gibson fights for survival in a world that most highly values the oil and gas that power their ancient cars and dilapidated shanty towns. Civil society has broken down and brute force rules a world that can no longer sustain the level of complexity to which it had become accustomed. The forebears of the dystopia seem not to have invested heavily at national levels in alternative energy sources like wind power, solar power, and nuclear energy, as China began doing in 2008.

Though coal and oil will clearly continue to reign over China's modernization efforts, the country has developed national policies of energy independence. China's plan is not only to become as self-sufficient as possible from the potential tyrannies of unstable fuel providers outside its borders, but from the caprice of international markets, as well. The nation's leaders also see a pressing need to seek independence from fossil fuels themselves, the low-hanging fruit that within a few short decades may all be picked.

Chapter 7

Consider the Alternatives

The lunch banquet in the cold, drafty restaurant dining room halted. Guests at the meal put down their utensils to listen intently to the portent. "The offshore wind industry will have terrible accidents because of quality issues and the speed of construction," Mr. Wang said. Mr. Wang was a young man, portly, good natured and a lively host. However, his voice had become grave with the prognostication. Even his colleague, a young Chinese named Leslie, seemed to pale at the prediction. Wang was a senior business manager in the offshore wind division of the private shipbuilder, Daoda Heavy Industry. The dockyard I visited at the end of 2010 had been under the Yangtze River three years before, all swift, muddy currents bounded by hard clay and tall weeds. Now, the hull of a 30,000 dead-weight ton (DWT) ship lay off to one side of the new dock. Workers were fitting the deck with equipment. Across from the ship, an 80-meter tall wind turbine stood like a sentry at the water's edge. The turbine maker had shipped the working model to the dockyard to test the stability of its concrete foundations. Daoda, like so many of China's wind turbine component makers, was learning through trial and error. Daoda's leap into building wind turbine foundations spoke volumes about the entire alternative power sector in China.

In 2005 the central government articulated a policy to develop alternative energy sources to supplement its use of fossil fuels. The leadership provided subsidies, tax breaks, and protection from international competitors in the domestic market to achieve its goals. The largesse within three years had made wind power and solar power companies formidable in the international markets. By 2020 Beijing would like to see the same market supremacy for their champions invested in electric vehicle technologies, nuclear power industries, and hydropower. The aggressive timetables for cultivating the sector, however, has meant product over-capacity, design flaws, problems with quality, high maintenance costs, and the ire of potential international partners. The tragedy of the Fukushima-Daiichi nuclear power plant in Japan in the spring of 2011 brought a momentary pause and review of the nation's plans for a green future.

However, by the beginning of 2012, memories of the tragedy blurred while markets and moneymen began stirring for new investment in the sector. It was clear, as well, the country would continue to run a chronic shortage of energy as long as urbanization was a primary component of the country's efforts to modernize. The negative impact on the environment and pollution-related illnesses also saw Beijing accelerate production and use of alternative energy technologies. China, it seemed, could not afford to wait for a future held ransom by fossil fuels. Its wind power industry was meant to negotiate new terms for powering its new society.

Wind at My Back

In 2010 China surpassed the United States in the total amount of wind power capacity installed for use. With 16 gigawatts erected in 2010 alone, China's total capacity leaped to more than 42 gigawatts. In 2010, the U.S. had installed about five gigawatts, increasing its portfolio of wind power to 40 gigawatts.[1]

In early 2011 the central government revised its original target of having installed 100 gigawatts of windpower capacity by 2020. The original goal had been 30 gigawatts, a target it had met in 2010. The new 2020 goal implied that China would need to build one-and-a-half wind turbines every day from 2015 until 2020 to meet government requirements. The most popular wind turbine model built during the first decade of the new century generated 2.5 megawatts of power, one that would be powerful enough to power 2,500 American homes. The towers of the typical triple-blade wind tower stretch upwards from 75 meters to 100 meters, with blades that range in length from 20 to 40 meters.

China's central government had been promoting the wind power industry aggressively since 2005. At the time, nearly 80 percent of the market went to foreign players like the Danish producer Vestas, Spanish maker Gamesa, and Indian manufacturer Suzlon. During the mid-2000s the central government identified three wind turbine manufacturing champions it would cultivate: Sinovel, Goldwind, and Dongfang Electric. Within three years of the central government initiative the Western wind turbine manufacturers found themselves with only 20 percent of the domestic market. Beijing achieved the goal of cordoning off the China wind power marketplace primarily by controlling auctions for wind farm producers and reserving prime wind zones for country champions. Central government also applied another constraint on foreign wind power turbine makers.

In 2005 the country's National Development and Reform Commission (NDRC) placed a domestic content restriction on wind turbine makers in China. The NDRC is one of the most powerful ministries in China, controlling the direction of China's modernization, the speed at which development should occur, and the degree to which the country should be open to foreign direct investment. In the case of domestic wind turbine manufacturing, the NDRC directed that wind turbines had to have 70 percent or more of their content from domestic suppliers. Foreign makers complained about the policy, claiming it was prejudicial against foreign companies and even in contravention of World Trade Organization (WTO) regulations. The WTO's mandate is to ensure a level playing field in international trade. The NDRC knew that foreign makers by and large relied on supply chains outside of China to maintain the level of quality and technological sophistication their wind turbines required. Central planners wanted more foreign component makers in the wind power industry to relocate to China. Beijing intended for more technology and know-how from Western suppliers to be transferred to China's manufacturers. The domestic content policy also gave domestic component suppliers time to mature their own wares while foreign companies established operations in China. Many foreign component makers balked at transferring their businesses to an environment in which they knew intellectual property was at risk.

Eventually, at the end of 2009, the NDRC relented in enforcing the policy. The face-saving reason for the U-turn was that China was a modern, international economy that was open to all producers, no matter the country of origin. Poul Kristensen, then President of the Danish Wind Energy Association in China, told me the real reason was that Chinese suppliers did not have the technology, training, or experience to make the components wind turbines really needed to work in a country with a geography as varied as China's: great deserts in the northwest; flat grasslands in Inner Mongolia; humid sub-tropics in the southeast; and the corrosive sea spray of the coastline. China had to make the business environment for foreign wind power parts suppliers more inviting than in the past.

The technology gap was so large in 2010 between Chinese and Western suppliers that Western suppliers were actually educating potential Chinese buyers on specifications. For instance, the CEO of a Danish wind turbine components maker told me that when his company asked Chinese buyers the dimensions of the blades for the wind turbines the Chinese were building, they would reply they didn't know. Chinese turbine makers insisted the Danish vendor was the expert, and so should inform the Chinese purchasers how large Chinese products should be.

China's ambitions in wind power for 2020 seemed way beyond practical reach for the country in 2010. Chinese manufacturers were unfamiliar with the manufacture of the sophisticated internal components for wind turbines, the secret chemistries of outer coatings for blades, and even the proper upkeep of the machines. Ultimately, much of the cost of installation and maintenance came down to the quality of the turbines themselves. Torben Jorgensen explained to me that

Chinese makers did not have a concept of Total Cost of Ownership. Total Cost of Ownership not only involves managing the cost to manufacture a product, but to maintain it over its lifetime. Jorgensen was Head of Technology at Fritz Schur Energy, a Danish producer of hydraulic pitch control systems for wind turbines. Steep subsidies, cronyism, and a mercenary approach to the manufacture and sale of turbines meant that makers produced turbines with an aim to manufacture and sell them off as quickly as possible without much—if any—liability for performance and longevity. China's manufacturing culture of "good enough" also implied that maintenance costs would skyrocket as turbines that were supposed to have lifetimes of 20 years would likely remain viable only seven or eight years. Chinese wind turbines were about half the cost of those built in the West. On average Western companies invested US$3.5 million in constructing the typical 2.5 megawatt wind turbine. At the subsidized rate China's electric grid operators charged consumers for power drawn from the wind, wind farm management companies would need at least 15 years to breakeven on their investments on wind turbines. Maintenance costs would likely make supporting wind turbine farms a loss-making proposition.

Current technology know-how, quality issues, and increasing maintenance costs saw wind turbines becoming more a liability to achieving renewable energy goals in 2020 than a national asset. In 2011 the NDRC declared a moratorium on building new wind power farms. The Commission called an audit on installed wind turbines—half of which were sitting idle, unconnected to the power grid, while the half that was connected suffered incessant maintenance problems. The leadership's issues with implementing a coordinated wind power plan gave the government pause in harnessing its solar power products export industry.

A Little Ray of Sunshine

Hebei Zhongming Energy & Technology Co., Ltd. was obligated by its local government masters to produce 60 MW of Photovoltaic (PV) solar cells by the end of 2010. The company registered the business on 40,000 square meters of land in April 2010. In May 2010, Hebei Zhongming was still building its solar panel factory when I met with company representatives. They had yet to hire the company staff. When I asked from where the company would hire the large work-force needed to man the operations, the sales representative answered, "from down here." "Down here" was the Yangtze River Delta, where hundreds of other companies since 2005 had been manufacturing PV cells for export. Hebei, on the other hand, was in the arid north, near Beijing. Hebei Zhongming was a subsidiary of Tangshan Mingshi Industry Co., Ltd., a State-owned enterprise that also managed a local logistics park, various real estate properties, and oil extraction conces-sions. The new entrant into the Chinese PV market was representa-tive of domestic PV projects by private and local government investors gambling on handsome payoffs. Investors in Hebei Zhongming, how-ever, were not the only shareholders greedy for quick profits.

Hans Suo, Director of Sales for SunLink PV in Zhangjiagang, Jiangsu province, told me in 2010, "Two hundred fifty more companies are entering the PV market this year." By the end of 2010, however, it was clear Suo's projection was wrong: *600* new entrants had actu-ally piled into the PV manufacturing marketplace. SunLink had been in business since 2004. The new facility I visited had the capacity to build 100 megawatts of photovoltaic (PV) panels each year, or enough to power 100,000 American homes annually. It would not complete construction and fit the remaining floors of the operation until it saw if the market could absorb the additional capacity, however. At full capac-ity, SunLink would be able to double its production in a year. Chinese companies continued to jump on the PV manufacturing bandwagon throughout 2010. A booming export market had driven down the price of production equipment and local governments continued to provide subsidies to start-ups in the industry.

As early as 2007, though, the National Development and Reform Commission (NDRC) warned of over-capacity in PV production. The global economic downturn of 2008–2009 saw the price of PV cells plummet as international buyers were unable to place orders due to supplier over-production and the cash and credit constraints of interna-tional buyers. The Spanish market in particular was hard hit as govern-ment subsidies evaporated. The country became mired in debt and high unemployment. The country's battered real estate sector had been a main buyer of Chinese-made PV technologies. National policy in Spain had supported feed-in tariffs to reduce the cost of tying solar panels into power distribution grids, as well as providing tax incentives for the purchase of solar power generation. The German market, too, was hard hit during the global economic downturn; it revived by the end of 2009, though. However, the German government reduced feed-in tariffs subsidizing solar power by as much as 16 percent. Germany had been China's largest market for solar power equipment for years. The German change of heart struck a severe blow to China's PV makers.

In October 2010 the NDRC raised the warning that Chinese suppliers were over-producing PV products. Over-capacity was driving prices down at an alarming rate, making it difficult for all but the largest players to profit from the marketplace.[2] Over-production of PV products had brought the price of solar panels down by nearly half between 2008 and 2010.[3] During the same period PV exports to America quadrupled. The rapid drop in the prices of solar panels for the export market prompted U.S.-based PV makers in 2011 to petition the United States government to place a 100 percent tariff on imported Chinese solar panels. The request cited that Chinese makers benefited from government-provided loans, cheap land, tax breaks, and an undervalued currency. By 2012 Chinese PV makers found they had few places in the world remaining in which to sell their wares. The domestic market for solar power products was nearly non-existent, however.

Professor Cui Rongqiang, a professor at Shanghai Jiao Tong University's Solar Energy Research Office, believed China's total domestic PV consumption capacity was 130 megawatts in 2010.[4] The figure implied that a single operation like SunLink at full production could satisfy all of China's PV requirements in just over a year. By the end of the year Chinese companies had a combined capacity to manufacture 4,000 megawatts of photovoltaic cells annually, according to Cui Rongqiang.[5] Nevertheless, solar power remained nearly twice as expensive as coal in China when it came to generating power.[6] Hence, power generation and coal production operations had little interest in taking on additional electricity generation capacity that would make their contracts uncompetitive. Commitments to take on additional capacity from wind power made integrating solar power into the grid even less appealing. In lieu of a national policy of feed-in tariffs to subsidize the sale of PV products to power suppliers, Chinese PV makers would continue to cannibalize themselves. Local PV producers waited throughout 2011 for a national policy as robust as China's own for wind power to open the domestic PV market. Without central planning support, China's domestic PV makers would find it difficult to make a profit in the cut-throat domestic market. Domestic PV suppliers, then, were held hostage by the export markets.

The central government, however, preferred to support very large showcase projects. For instance, wind power, though erratic, delivered the megawatt jolts a hungry modernizing society needed to grow and prosper. The large scale of wind farms also made it easy for officials to highlight the success of their policies. Traditional PV makers, however, based sales on batches of panels for projects that generated mere kilowatts of power. Efficiencies of most PV products that Chinese vendors made, as well, were well below that of oil and coal. State-of-the art polycrystalline cells operated near 25 percent efficiency at best. Solar farms would need huge swathes of precious land to become technologically and politically viable in China. So national and provincial governments proposed technology applications for PV products on a scale never before tried in other countries.

The Hongqiao light rail station became the world's largest standalone Building Integrated Photovoltaic (BIPV) project in May 2010, just in time for the start of the Shanghai World Exposition. It began transmission the same month. When passengers entered or exited a train at the station they were actually in a power plant. The structure could produce 6.3 million kilowatt-hours (kwh) of electricity per year, enough to power 12,000 Shanghai households. Its 20,000 solar panels covered a roof area of 61,000 square meters. The station is colossal, a huge rectangle at the opposite end of which is the Hongqiao International Airport, a major hub for domestic flights. Soon after, other cities and provinces throughout the country unveiled their own plans for BIPV.

China's Ministry of Finance, Ministry of Science and Technology, and the National Energy Administration—a department in the NDRC—launched the Golden Sun program in July 2009. It provided upfront subsidies for qualified large-scale PV projects from 2009 through 2011. One of the grandest projects under the Golden Sun program involved the company Astronergy.

Astronergy unveiled plans at the end of 2010 for the world's largest standing BIPV solar power structure. Astronergy was a Hangzhou-based crystalline and thin film solar module manufacturer. The project would involve roof mounted solar panels on Hangzhou east railway station. Hangzhou is a city as rich per capita as Shanghai, though much smaller, It is a two-hour drive to the west of Shanghai. The 10-megawatt project would cost 270 million RMB and was expected to generate 9.8 million kilowatt hours per annum. The Golden Sun program funded roughly 8 megawatts of the project. The National Solar Photovoltaic Building Demonstration Projects program sponsored the remaining 2 megawatts of the project. Other cities, though, insisted on crowding into the solar-powered spotlight.

Not to be outdone by either Shanghai or Hangzhou, the Beijing Economic and Technological Development Area (BDA) launched its own demonstration project at the end of 2010. The plan was to install 20 megawatts of rooftop solar power systems with an expected budget of 460 million RMB (about US$71 million).[7] China invited bids on its first solar thermal power plant project in 2010. Beijing also invited solar power projects based on exotic technologies.

The central government sought to launch a 50-megawatt project in Hangjinqi in north China's Inner Mongolia Autonomous Region. The bidding process would be overseen by China Machinery and Equipment International Tendering Co., Ltd. The $240 million project came under the umbrella of China's National Energy Administration, the new government arm that was set up in 2008 to oversee the China energy sector. The 50-megawatt project would be the first of its kind in Asia. According to local government statistics it could generate up to 120 million kilowatt-hours of electricity. Solar thermal heating uses mirrors to concentrate solar radiation to turn water into steam, which is then stored in a heat medium. The heat can then be extracted to produce power at night or even on overcast days. Concentrated Solar Power (CSP) was still in the experimental stages in China when officials made the announcement about the 50-megawatt project. The technology for CSP in China was only just getting out of the laboratory. Significant foreign technology would be needed to move the industry out of its infancy. Scientists chose the Hangjinqi in Mongolia as one of the few locations in China's orbit that had enough solar and water resources to support a project of that size. The site selection process underscored the weakness of the technology: China is running short of water due to drought, water transpiration, industrial use, and agricultural waste. Chinese visionaries intent on a solar future, however, were not daunted by such natural resource constraints.

Chinese scientists built a huge glass enclosure in the Gobi Desert that drew heat from the cooling sands to channel convection currents up a chimney to run a turbine atop the structure. Wind turbines near the chimney supplemented power generation from the plant during the winter, when the sun was not as strong as in the summer months. The turbine also ran at night as the cooling sands provided enough hot currents to continue powering the generator. The first phase of the plant began operation on December 10, 2010, with a capacity of 200 kilowatts. In 2011 the generator would provide 400,000 kilowatts of electricity per year, saving the equivalent of 100 tons of coal and 900 tons of water. Funded by a local company in Inner Mongolia with 1.38 billion yuan (US$208 million), the project has an additional two phases of construction to go before completion in 2012. The final project will cover 277 hectares and have a total capacity of 27.5 megawatts. Power from the plant will feed into the north-central grid that supplied Beijing.

China has 2.6 million square kilometers of desert resources, in the north of the country, as one of the lead scientists describes the Gobi. One imagines, with the sands of the desert encroaching on Beijing, the world may one day see solar chimneys downtown in the capital itself. Though the north might be arid, the south of the country provides great potential for a rich and contentious source of electricity—hydropower.

Damming Neighbors

Burma's military junta in October 2011 took the unprecedented step of cancelling a US$3.6 billion project to construct a hydroelectric dam in Myitsone, near the country's northern border with China. The dam would have drawn power from the legendary Irawaddy River. The dam was a joint project between the Burmese and Chinese governments. The Burmese government cited the project would destroy the homes and livelihoods of thousands of local residents. The cancellation enraged the Chinese leadership. The Myitsone dam, however, was not the first of China's hydropower projects to upset China's neighbors. Unfortunately for the South Asian neighborhood, China's plans to dam upstream sources of Asia's greatest rivers would not be easily foiled. China's energy needs are insatiable and growing.

In 2010, electricity generated through hydropower made up 20 percent of China's power portfolio, or nearly 200 gigawatts. The Three Gorges Dam project alone generated nearly 10 percent of all of China's hydroelectricity, enough to power more than 20 million American-style homes. The country's leadership made it public in 2011 that it planned to double its hydropower capacity by 2020.[8] Relentless urbanization, industrialization, and consumerism accelerated the country's search for, and construction of, power generating facilities, conventional and alternative. Hydropower is low-hanging fruit, from an engineering point of view: the rivers are open and accessible, and Chinese engineers have a great deal of construction experience in the sector. China's plan to dam waters that feed into Southeast Asia has not been lost on the region.

Southern states already blame Chinese hydroelectric dams along the Mekong river for reducing the torrent to a trickle downstream. The Mekong (*Méigōnghé*, in Chinese) starts in the great glaciers of the Tibetan plateau and reaches into China's Yunnan Province, Burma, Laos, Thailand, Cambodia, and Vietnam. More than 60 million people rely on the river for their livelihoods, which is the world's largest inland fishery, according to the Mekong River Commission.[9] Some analysts also blame the dam projects in part on the drought that parched southeast China in the spring of 2010 and 2011—waters that would otherwise flow freely were made into reservoirs to conserve water, not irrigate the land. During droughts in China water levels along the Mekong dropped several meters in Southeast Asia, to their lowest levels in recorded history. The drought killed off fish and plant stocks. The dry spell also crippled hydropower stations in Yunnan province and essentially took offline 90 percent of hydropower stations in next-door Guangxi Zhuang autonomous region. During the period intemperate conditions also debilitated Guangdong's electrical supply. Guangdong received a substantial portion of its power from the hydro–stations based in Guangxi. Despite setbacks in power generation in Yunan province, Beijing leveled its sights beyond the Mekong River.

The Salween River (*Nùjiāng*, in Chinese), one of the world's longest free-flowing rivers in the world, was still undammed as of 2011. The river runs through Burma and Thailand. China wanted to change the state of affairs, placing several hydropower projects along its reaches. Numerous political obstacles—cross-border and internal to Burma and Thailand—saw the hydro-projects repeatedly delayed. However, in the summer of 2010 the Chinese central government approved projects on the river that it had formerly mothballed because of concerns voiced by its neighbors. The move indicated that the Salween's days of remaining untouched were numbered. China, however, was not content with merely altering wetlands.

At the end of 2010 China began work on the highest hydropower project in the world. Engineering teams dammed the Yarlung Zangbo River in the Tibetan Himalayas to build the first in a series of hydropower dams to meet the energy needs of a developing Tibet. The river flows from the glaciers of the Himalayas into India as the sacred Bhramaputra river. Sinohydro Bureau No. 8 began damming the river on November 8.[10] The project was the first of its kind in Tibet. The 7.9 billion yuan ($1.2 billion) investment would provide a total installed capacity of 51 megawatts.

Understandably, Indian officials were disturbed by developments on the Yarlung Zangbo River. Chinese authorities barred Indian inspectors from the construction site, which is located in Gyaca county, 325 kilometers southeast of the Tibetan capital Lhasa.[11] The project was the first of four, which were located very near the border of a territory long-disputed by the two countries, Arunachal Pradesh. Most Chinese citizens are oblivious to the Indian project, in sharp contrast to the Indian population, which was watching the development with some anxiety. The Chinese projects touched a deep vein of Indian devotion to the Brahmaputra.

China's designs on some of the most vital rivers in the world have all but convinced downstream neighbors like India, Laos, Vietnam, Thailand, and Burma that China has eschewed its policy of "Peaceful Rise" in favor of one of "Energy—Whatever the Cost." A pause in the development of its nuclear power program, however, showed the leadership was capable of exercising some humility.

Nuclear Deterrents

The nuclear tragedy that unfolded in Japan at the Fukushima-Daiichi nuclear plant during mid-March 2011 forced China to announce a moratorium on approvals and construction projects for nuclear plants. The call was a major face-losing move for a leadership that trumpeted its nuclear power prowess at every turn. The decision represented a huge and considerable turn-about after plans just announced in its 12th 5-year plan for an aggressive push into nuclear power. Original plans for a handful of new power plants along the east coast mushroomed into the development of more than 50 new plants—nearly half in China's interior—by the year 2020, with a combined output of 40 gigawatts. However, China's own dramatic history of earthquakes and the increasing dearth of water resources made placing nuclear power plants in China's hinterlands foolhardy at best, tragic at its most catastrophic. At the root of China's accelerated nuclear timetable was its Faustian relationship with coal.

Coal shortages during the Spring Festival of 2008 brought the most heavily populated portions of China to a standstill. China experienced its fiercest snow storms in a hundred years in some places. Price caps of coal stunted deliveries of the fuel to power plants; snow and ice on train tracks froze delivery of what precious coal was available to power plants. Months later, the National Reform and Development Commission (NDRC) accelerated development of nuclear power plants dramatically.

China was going to trump Mother Nature and natural resource economics by building nuclear power plants in China's interior. The inland geography of the country, however, increased risks beyond the standard mantra accompanying any effort that seemed to outpace reason. The most problematic facilities planned for development in China's interior included the one in the Ningxia Autonomous region, in central China; and those planned for construction along the Yangtze River, in Chongqing, Sichuan, Hunan, and Hubei provinces.

In April 2009 a director of the National Nuclear Safety Administration, Li Ganjie, listed the top safety concerns about the nation's new nuclear power development policy as:

- a lack of well-trained, experienced professionals in the field;
- immaturity of China's own research and development capability and track record in nuclear power;
- a dearth of experience building and installing state-of-the-art nuclear power stations;
- a lack of management expertise;
- a lack of safety supervision experience and manpower;
- the still-birth of environmental regulation of nuclear facilities;
- a lack of experience and facilities for waste management;
- a lack of civil discourse to gain public support of nuclear power plants near the homes of citizens.

However, the very fundamentals of the feasibility of the nuclear sites were also being ignored in a country rife with earthquakes and tremors. For instance, just hours before the 9.0 quake off the coast of Japan that damaged the Fukushima nuclear plant, China's Yunan province suffered a quake that registered 6.0 on the Richter scale. The Yunan quake injured nearly 350 people. Eighteen thousand homes collapsed and another 30,000 had some damage. Just a few hundred kilometers away from ground zero, three years before, was the tragic Sichuan earthquake, which caused nearly 100,000 casualties.

One of the few lines of defense nuclear power housings have in the event of structural damage is the abundance of water. Water can buy time if radioactive emissions breach protective moderators and casings, and keep temperatures at a level that may otherwise rupture containment vessels, resulting in a spread of nuclear contamination. In the case of the Fukushima facility, operators had been bathing the nuclear cores with thousands of tons of sea water in an effort to work out options for safely shutting down the reactors. The irradiated sea water eventually moved far out to sea.

Plans to place reactors along the Yangtze River in China's interior assumed the river would always have sufficient levels of water to sustain the cooling of the reactor during normal operation. Designs also assumed the river would have the thousands of tons of water reactors would need in case of an emergency. The 2000s, however, had actually seen decreasing levels of water in the river. In 2009 I peered over the edge of the railing of a public square in Chongqing, in China's interior, at the juncture of the Yangtze and Jialing Rivers to find a mud flat. Flat bottom boats that typically ply the muddy waters lay beached like helpless whales. China's energy plans included the development of scores of hydropower projects along main river routes that were already highly stressed due to drought, urbanization, and agricultural practices wasteful of water and pollution. Of course, any intentions nuclear operators had in China to flush distressed nuclear cores with water from rivers would also meet with extreme local opposition downstream. The nuclear accident in Japan also threw a spotlight on the technology China planned to use in its stepped-up plan for nuclear plant construction.

In the aftermath of the 2011 tsunami off Japan's coast Chinese utility firms were quick to defend the technologies they were employing in their roll-out of the country's nuclear power program. The Fukushima plant, which was hardest hit during the tsunami, became operational in 1971 with technology that today is more than 40 years old. By the time the Japanese tsunami had destroyed the reactors at the Fukushima plant, China was already deeply invested in the third phase of its nuclear power technology, local proponents claimed. Most of the reactor designs for Chinese power generation were based on the Westinghouse AP1000, considered a proven and cost-effective means of producing power. Each reactor produced 1,250 megawatts, or enough to power more than one million homes at American consumption levels. The first new reactors were set to be completed by 2013; however, the moratorium put actual finish dates in doubt. China's plan with the AP1000 design—as with most foreign imports of technology—was to adopt and adapt the designs to suit domestic requirements, especially involving the use of uranium from local sources. Uranium, like other minerals, comes with a host of impurities that are specific to the regions in which they are mined. Beijing was not going to allow that constraint to interfere with its aggressive plan for expansion of its nuclear power network.

Westinghouse obliged the Chinese penchant for purchasing technology with the full intent of adapting it to its own commercial uses. The American company formed a joint venture with the State Nuclear

Power Technology Corporation and Shanghai Nuclear Engineering Research & Design Institute to design the CAP1400, a variation of the AP1000. China Huaneng Group planned to build the reactor in Shandong province. The CAP1400 would have the capacity to produce 1,400 megawatts of power when switched on in 2017. The Huaneng Group was not the only company intent on implementing new nuclear power technology in China.

The China Guangdong Nuclear Power Company started construction in 2009 and 2010 of two reactors using designs from the French firm Areva. The 1,660 megawatt reactors were based on an approach called European Pressurized Reactor (EPR) technology. EPR physical designs emphasize safety during worst-case scenarios based on meltdown of the radioactive core, making the design highly appealing. However, in 2009 nuclear regulatory bodies in France, Finland, and the United Kingdom stated concerns to Areva, pointing to the lack of independence between operational and emergency electronic control systems. Regulators indicated that if one control system went down it should not take down the other system.[12] The Areva design likely came up as a concern in safety review discussions during China's moratorium on nuclear plant development.

During the moratorium, however, individual companies and even local governments trumpeted their continued progress in establishing nuclear power footprints. For instance, Cui Shaozhang, deputy general manager at Huaneng Nuclear Power Development Co., announced the world's first high-temperature, gas-cooled reactor would be installed in Rongcheng, Shandong province. The Rongcheng plant would use helium in its cooling system. Theoretically, its reactor cores would be able to withstand temperatures exceeding 1,600 degrees Centigrade for several hundred hours without melting down.[13] Helium is an inert gas, not subject to exploding, like hydrogen. Nearly a month after the Japanese nuclear disaster, however, it was plain China's headlong plunge into a nuclear future was in for some detours.

The central government chose to approve only four of the ten projects it had planned before the Fukushima incident. The nuclear stakes, it seemed, were just too high for the country to gamble. The leadership's aim to modernize its society and to install an engine of high economic growth was laudable. However, even the CCP had to admit it could not command the earthquakes to still and the waters to part. Local residents in Pengze, Anhui province also realized the limitations of the central government's omniscience when they began protesting the construction of a nuclear power plant in their backyard. Anhui province is about a two-hour drive west of Shanghai. Townsfolk, former government officials, and scientists banded together in late 2011 to protest the location of the plant.

He Zuoxiu, a prominent retired physicist who helped develop China's nuclear program in the 1960s, told the *Financial Times*, "China has to stop its 'Great Leap Forward' approach to nuclear power." The Great Leap Forward was Mao Zedong's attempt to rapidly catch up with Western industry in the 1950s. The effort was a complete disaster. "China has to have nuclear energy—we need the power—but we need to slow down and take a more measured approach, and really learn the lessons of Fukushima."[14] Another ambitious and problematic national program involved what China and many other societies around the world consider an energy- and environmental-silver bullet: the electric vehicle.

Welcome to Electric Avenue

The driver threw the stick shift into high gear and sent the 31-seat electric bus careening full-tilt down the length of the factory parking lot of the new Zonda Bus factory. It was a Saturday morning, late summer 2010. The bus disgorged the group I was traveling with at the far end of the factory. Zonda Bus is one of China's largest bus companies, with export sales to the Middle East and Europe. The company was also on the leading edge of battery technology research. The company's focus was on making its buses go faster and further than most battery-driven vehicles in their class in China. The operation I had visited was located in Yancheng, Jiangsu province, about two-hour drive north of Shanghai. Several factory managers and local government officials led the group of delegates with whom I travelled through a series of rooms. A single working machine that had some vital part to play in the manufacture and assembly of huge battery packs for the buses dominated each room. The company spokesperson announced the batteries in their buses could charge and discharge more than 1,000 times, and operate for more than 500,000 kilometers. The battery-equipped buses could approach speeds of 110km/hr. The 50 buses the company had just provided Tianjin for the Davos meeting in September 2010 could run for 500 kilometers off a single charge—300 kilometers with the air conditioner running all day.

The Chinese government made it plain to the world in 2008 it was intent on introducing electric vehicle (EV) technology onto the country's roads. In October 2010 the Minister of Science and Technology, Wan Gang, announced that China would be producing one million electric vehicles for Chinese roads by the year 2020. The number was still a small portion of the projected 46 million to 71 million cars expected to be sold that year, but still the largest EV market in the world. According to the Energy-Saving and New Energy Vehicle Development Plan (2011–2020), by the year 2015 China would have 1.5 million new energy vehicles on the road. By the year of 2020, the number would be as high as 5 million. To realize this goal, the government planned to invest RMB 100 billion between 2011 and 2020 to get the industry going. During the summer of 2010 the central government also announced it would stimulate the consumer market for EV through a subsidy of 60,000 yuan (nearly US$10,000) for each EV buyer. Mass manufacture of electric vehicles in China that met international standards for quality, safety, and reliability would not be available until 2015 at the earliest. Local governments were also setting the pace for the consumer market by mandating fleets of public transportation run on electricity.

For instance, at the end of 2008 Beijing rolled out 1,000 new energy buses onto the city's roadways. In the spring of 2011, the city introduced 50 Foton Midi electric taxis to the streets of Yanqing, a suburb of Beijing. In 30 minutes the car could be charged to 80 percent capacity. The plan for the first charging station in Yanqing included 25 charging piles. Future phases of the plan included 36,000 regular charging piles, 100 fast charging piles, one battery replacing station, two battery recycling stations, and ten service stations installed by 2015. The local Beijing government also intended to give each charging station subsidies of no more than 30 percent of its initial investment. The Beijing city government's long-term plans involved putting 5,000 new energy vehicles into operation, including 500 electric taxis, by 2012. Local government support of the nascent manufacturing industry stimulated investors throughout the country.

A visit to the Jiangsu Aoxin New Energy Automobile Company, Ltd., also in Yancheng, revealed a near-empty hangar in which small teams of workers languidly assembled small, compact electric vehicles. The simple suspension chassis and skin-thin bodies of the seven models on display underscored just how much of a learning curve Chinese industry had to go to match the robustness and sophistication of combustion-engine vehicles. The lady bug–like AV2 and AV3 could seat two uncomfortably in a space that would see most Westerner's knees pressed firmly against the dashboard. The load of the "Dynamic Free Dream" sanitation truck would need to be dumped after a single swing around any Chinese high-rise apartment complex. Meanwhile, the AXG mini bus with its maximum speed of 40 km/hr and a range of only 100 kilometers, would be easily run off the road by a swarm of China's ubiquitous electric scooters. Clearly, the factory was only geared to supply made-to-order quantities of vehicles.

Nevertheless, Chinese companies by 2010 were racing ahead in the EV industry in the same way they were in other alternative energy fields. The stage at which the EV industry was in 2010 was very much like the Chinese automotive industry in 2002, when I had visited the newly opened Chery automobile factory in Wuhu, Anhui province. Chery is the maker of one of the most popular cars on Chinese roadways, the QQ. In 2010, though, Chery opened a US$500 million R&D center in Wuhu for research and development of its own EV technologies, mostly developing control systems. Other car makers in China as well were plunging ahead in pursuit of profits in the new age industry.

Concerns abound, however, that the EV market in China still suffers from quality issues. Western analysts believe that more sophisticated battery technology, control systems, and materials technology are a greater leap than Chinese manufacturers are able to make on their own. The slack time between the scrum of car makers entering the EV market and consolidation of the market is a prime opportunity for American, German, and Japanese technology companies, with greater experience in the field, to make their presence felt in China. As is the case with wind and solar power, the foreign companies may find China a more welcoming and lucrative environment in which to do business than their home countries offer. As Marco Gerrits, a former Daimler auto engineer and a consultant with Boston Consulting Group in Beijing told *Fortune Magazine*, the foreign companies could capture up to half of the EV industry in China.[15] If the Zongda bus trip was any indication, though, the window of opportunity for foreign car makers and other alternative energy technologists was closing fast.

A Battery of New Energy Technologies

China's central planning approach to implementing alternative energy sources has consistently led to over-capacity issues across the sector. The country has a simplistic formula of acquiring technology from abroad, adapting the technology for domestic use, and then exporting revised products. Aggressive production schedules have exacerbated over-capacity realities by introducing problems with quality and maintenance, especially in the wind power industry. Foreign competitors in the wind- and solar-power industries have filed complaints against the Chinese government for supporting unfair trade practices. If not for the Fukushima-Daiichi nuclear accident in Japan, Beijing would have continued constructing dozens of nuclear power plants at a rapid pace without proper quality and safety controls. Nevertheless, within a year of the Japanese disaster Chinese residents were protesting the construction of nuclear plants in their hometowns. They complained authorities had seeded projects without the consent of locals, and without concern for their safety. China's hydropower program has also strained relations with its neighbors. Hydroelectric dams are a keystone of the country's plans for energy security. Bordering states have accused the dams of drying rivers that have sustained local societies for millennia, and of contributing to climate change in the region. Electric vehicles have escaped the harsh criticism wind energy, solar power, nuclear plants, and hydroelectric dams have because the industry is still nascent and fraught with technological challenges.

In 2007 China's central planners were on a national drive to develop battery storage technology for domestic EV makers.

State-owned enterprises would also license the technology to companies around the world. Breakthrough energy storage technology would help increase the range electric vehicles could travel. Storage technology would also manage the variances in electricity production from conventional sources, and from the more erratic solar- and wind-power alternatives. During peak electricity production times, when customers were not inclined to consume much energy, storage facilities would place the excess power in inventory. During peak consumption periods, the power grid would be able to tap into the inventories to reduce the cost of electricity to customers.

In 2010 China began its efforts to develop a countrywide "smart" grid. Smart grids monitor electricity production and consumption at the household level to increase efficiency in distribution of electricity. The century-old technology currently involved in moving electricity from production at the power generator to consumption in residential and commercial property is very much like using a fire hose that is always gushing water. Whether a user needs a cupful, a bucketful, or no electricity at all, a fountain of energy is always available on traditional grids. The most efficient means of electricity generation is one in which consumers need power produced "just in time," to borrow a term from supply chain management. In lean manufacturing, communications technologies enable suppliers to know when to produce a certain amount of a product to meet customer requirements at the moment. Smart grid technology seeks to attain the same awareness, production, and distribution of energy. The hope is also that smart grids would help reduce air pollution through a more measured approach to electricity production that burns dirty coal.

The pollution fossil fuels produce, however, is not the only energy-related environmental hazard with which Beijing has to contend. The manufacture of alternative energy technologies is also creating dangers to health. Much of the pollution created by the manufacture of wind- and solar-power and electric vehicle technologies is toxic to the degree it is making entire communities in China unlivable, poisoning thousands and killing hundreds. Aggressive production quotas and unrealistic delivery schedules have exacerbated the national crisis. Cleantech as China produces it, it seems, is not as clean as its name advertises.

Chapter 8

Errors of Emission

I n September 2011 an angry mob of 500 villagers broke through the chain-link fence of the Jinko Solar Holding Company solar cell factory and ransacked the premises. A torrential rainfall had flooded mismanaged vats of toxic waste that had flowed into a stream in Haining, Zhejiang Province. Residents in the area reported the day after the deluge that they had seen thousands of dead fish floating in the surrounding waters. Government inaction had ignited community fury.

Though the local Environmental Protection Bureau (EPB) had punished the facility five months before the incident for improperly storing and managing the waste, the factory had continued to operate business-as-usual. The operation was supposed to have shut down and paid a fine of 470,000 yuan (US$73,600) until its waste management system was robust. By the time the autumn rains had swept through, the facility had still ignored all injunctions the EPB had set against it. The result was a rampage by angry local citizens that cost the company thousands of dollars in damage. The incident demoted the "green credentials" of the Jinko Solar Holding Company, which is listed on the New York Stock Exchange.

The irony of green- and clean-technology manufacturing in China is just how terribly polluting the processes are without the proper technology, safety controls, and management procedures in place. China's rush for market share and its quest to fill its voracious appetite for energy, however, have seen many of the safety and environmental stops pulled out of operations to meet production goals that are unhinged from economic fundamentals. Privateers and local governments perceive health and safety measures as terrible inconveniences to being profitable in the cleantech sector. Cleantech in China, though, isn't very clean during the manufacture of many of its products. The manufacturing side of the solar power industry, wind power technologies, and the batteries for electric vehicles present new hazards to human health and habitats. The residents of Haining were not the first victims of unfettered waste from the manufacture of photovoltaic (PV) products in China. Nor, likely, will they be the last.

The Dark Side of the Sun

Whereas in 2000 there was only one PV ingot manufacturer in the world, by 2009 there were more than 20. The Alibaba supply chain sourcing online search engine identified 29 polysilicon ingot producers in China in 2011. Richard Winegarner, president of Sage Concepts, a consulting firm in California, cited it usually takes at least two years to get a polysilicon producer operational. Many of the Chinese companies, he said, were attempting the same feat in half the time.[1] The approach implied a huge number of corners were being cut from a dangerous process that has sharp edges of controls and technologies in place for a reason: to reduce the toxic imprint on the environment and on the lives of human beings. After all, *the raison d'etre* of producing solar panels is to provide energy sources that complement and may even one day supplant fossil fuels as primary power sources. Energy from the sun, transformed into use for us humans, is meant to be plentiful and clean, reducing the carbon footprint to near zero. Opportunities to provide willing international buyers solar power components in the mid-2000s were too difficult to ignore. Investors and manufacturers in China with little experience or sophistication in the industry rioted the market.

Willing buyers, prompted by feed-in tariffs in Spain and Germany, drove the price of polysilicon from US$20 per kilogram to US$300 per kilogram from 2003 through 2008.[2] The new factories that were to come online in 2009 had an estimated capacity of 80,000 to 100,000 tons of polysilicon—more than doubling the 40,000 tons produced in the entire world in 2008. Makers and buyers of polysilicon products, however, ignored the true costs of manufacturing in China.

Production of the polysilicon ingots involves superheating quartz-ite gravel or crushed quartz to create silicon. Subsequent heating and "doping" with chemicals sheds as much as 80 percent of the initial metallurgical grade silicon. A highly toxic byproduct of the process is silicon tetrachloride. Subsequent phases of production require the use of poisonous solvents that only become more harmful after they inter-act with the silicon. One of the byproducts is fluoride, which, in great doses is harmful. High concentrations of fluoride found in river water were the catalyst for the townsfolk of Haining to go on a rampage of the Jinko Solar plant. Manufacturing of the final product, however, requires yet more chemistry.

Production of the actual cells that workers piece together to create solar panels involves slicing the PV ingots into thin wafers. The cutting equipment uses an abrasive slurry applied to a fine wire to "grease" the slicing process. The slurry is a mixture of glycol and powdered silicon carbide that operators pump into the wire-saw machine. The used slurry contains super-fine particles of silicon, called kerf. Sawing sloughs as much as 50 percent of the ingot into the slurry and the water used to rinse the wafers. If wafering operations choose to recycle instead of discharging the used slurry into the surrounding countryside, they often hire third-party contractors to carry off truckloads of the stuff to recapture reusable materials. However, little is known about the chemicals and the disposal processes Chinese contractors use to separate the slurry "wheat" from the more toxic chemical "chaff." Many contractors simply pile up bags of the processed, chemical-laden slurry on their properties.

American managers at CRS Reprocessing Services, based in Louisville Kentucky, were absolutely salivating about the potential of the Chinese market when I met them in Shanghai in 2010. Since

2003 CRS had been cleaning up after PV makers in America, Europe, and Japan, and was just breaking into China. The company builds the equipment and implements the processes needed to recycle chemical slurry for re-use. The company claims a 98 percent re-capture rate. Prospects for growth for the company in the China market were huge, as, according to CRS, Chinese PV makers had, until a recent change in government policy, been pouring the poisonous slurry into plastic bags they piled up in the back of their factory compounds. One CRS director told me of a potential Chinese customer of theirs who had so much of the slurry built up "you could actually see the dump from satellite photos, if you knew where to look." It's the waste that can't be easily detected by any other means than human suffering, however, that has caused the greatest media scandal.

Villagers called out the polysilicon maker Luoyang Zhonggui in 2008 after farmers were fainting in their fields from the white powder factory workers were dumping on their plots. Factory owners simply eliminated waste management and recycling equipment and processes to save on the high energy costs of heating the fusing chambers to 1,800 degrees Fahrenheit, and on the prices of chemicals made more expensive by the increased number of polysilicon makers jumping in on the ground floor of a rising industry. Profits marginalized the people in the village of Gaolong, Henan Province near the Yellow River. Analysts believed Luoyang Zhonggui, though, was merely representative of the vast majority of polysilicon foundries put into operation practically overnight in China.[4] The factory's understanding and implementation of technology pioneered 50 years before by the German company Siemens was incomplete, so the Chinese national research institute that established the Luoyang Zhonggui plant augmented German know-how with their own groping. Local and national government hopes were that the manufacturing processes developed for the Luoyang Zhonggui plant would serve as the anchor for a solar power supply chain in the area. Instead, the factory site served as ground zero for dangerous levels of land and water pollution. Factory staff was dumping liquid silicon tetrachloride waste in the fields farmers tended.

Soil samples showed high concentrations of chlorine and hydrochloric acid, which do not exist naturally. The chemicals are byproducts of the breakdown of silicon tetrachloride. Chemical decomposition released a mix of acids and poisonous hydrogen chloride gas. The gas made breathing difficult, sometimes causing dizziness.[5] The fine dust remaining from evaporation collected in the lungs and guts of residents. Crops wilted under blankets of a white dust and water kettles materialized small rocks as water boiled away in them. The degree of human suffering rivaled cases of lead poisoning in China, another by-product of the good intentions of cleantech. Production of the lead-based batteries that go into China's electric bikes, however, was causing an epidemic throughout the country that local governments found difficult to curb.

Get the Lead Out

My American guest, a middle-aged woman from the United States, looked on admiringly at the flow of electric bike (e-bike) traffic that flowed past us on the busy downtown Suzhou street. Suzhou, my adopted home in China, lays about 150 kilometers west of Shanghai, and has an average income level nearly equal that of Shanghai. Still, the city of Suzhou, with only about 1.5 million residents—small by Chinese standards—retains a parochial feel. Most of the streets in the city and outlying economic development zones still have bike lanes. Fume-belching cars glut the narrow streets within the ancient moat of the city and spill outward to suburban compounds. However, car purchase and maintenance still lay beyond the reach of average residents. My guest commented on how environmentally conscious the Chinese seemed to be by riding the e-bikes instead of motorcycles or cars. Of course, economics, policy, and human laziness had more to do with the transition from bicycle to e-bike. Chinese were growing richer and wanted to get to places faster and with less of their own physical energy to invest.

Since the 1950s China has been famous for the sheer number of bicycles that plied the streets of every paved road and rutted dirt path in the socialist country. The bicycle represented the most egalitarian of transport means—the workers, the farmers, the intellectuals, and the cadres all got to work or shopped by bicycle. Only apparatchiks of the highest levels had automobiles assigned to them. At its height, the Chinese market for bicycles boasted 500 million bicycles.

In 1999 I had the pleasure to cycle with thousands of Chinese along broad bike lanes in Beijing unimpeded by the onslaught of automobiles. It's easy to experience quietude as one cyclist among thousands of others. Camaraderie finds you as you enter conversation with a stranger alongside whom you've been pedaling for several miles. By 2011, however, nearly 150 million of those cyclists had turned in their Flying Pigeon brand bicycles for e-bikes, up from a mere 200,000 in 2001.[6] Private car ownership in China hit the 100 million mark at the same time. E-bikes, though, cost between US$250 and US$400 to buy, and one RMB a day to charge the battery.[7] The affordability of e-bikes assures sales will still grow nearly 20 percent per year through the following decade. The environmental and health costs of e-bike ownership, however, are far out-of-sight of Chinese consumers.

Double-digit growth in the production and consumption of e-bikes has contributed hugely to a lead poisoning problem in China. Ninety-eight percent of all electric bikes run on lead-acid technologies; the remaining market uses nickel-metal-hydride and lithium-ion batteries, which are relatively non-polluting.[8] Christopher Cherry, a professor at the University of Tennessee at Knoxville, cited that batteries made in China that contain 22 pounds of lead can create about 15 pounds of lead pollution.[9] He said e-bikes during their lifetimes can use up to five batteries. "Electric bikes result in far more emissions of lead than automobiles," Cherry added. "They always use more batteries per mile than almost any other vehicle."[10] Though the batteries are supposed to be recyclable, it is difficult to know what really happens to the lead in the old batteries as recycling happens in small, garage-like establishments on city streets.

In 2006, it was estimated that 34 percent of children in China had levels of lead in their blood that exceeded World Health Organization standards.[11] In the latter half of 2009 local citizen revolts forced local authorities throughout China to reveal six lead poisoning scandals. Excessive levels of lead in the blood stream can cause seizures, coma, and, eventually, death. Lead poisoning can also harm the nervous and reproductive systems. Villages saw most of their children stricken with lead poisoning from air and water emissions from nearby battery plants. A total of about 3,300 youngsters in Shaanxi, Hunan, Yunnan, Fujian, and Henan provinces who lived near lead smelters of battery factories were found to have dangerously high levels of lead in their blood.[12] In town after town children's blood samples registered three to five times the amount of lead considered hazardous to health. Lead poisoning is the leading cause of geographical clusters of cancer in China.

Wang Jingzhong, vice director of the China Battery Industry Association, told the *Wall Street Journal* that the e-bike battery industry had grown by 20 percent a year since 2005, with no end in sight. He cited some 2,000 factories and 1,000 battery-recycling plants in the country. Wang Jingzhong added, "It is a chaotic situation."[13] In 2011, China had about 2,300 e-bike and e-scooter makers buying the lead-acid products from battery makers. The fragmentation of the industry contributed to an epidemic of lead-poisoning incidents that, along with industry growth, saw little hope for immediate relief.

In December 2009 Guangzhou authorities in southern China closed down a battery factory after they acknowledged 25 children living near the plant had excessive lead levels in their blood.[14] A month later Jiangsu province saw more than 50 children and as many adults who lived by the Dafeng Shengxiang Power Supply Co. Ltd. battery factory in Hekou village suffer lead poisoning.[15] Weeks after the Hekou incident, south of Jiangsu province, in Hubei province, authorities announced 30 people—including 16 children—had been found to have excessive levels of lead in their blood. Local authorities in that instance actually ordered a halt in production at the Hubei Jitong Battery Company.[16] A hospital in January 2011 tested 280 children who lived in Gaohe Township in Huaining County. Two hundred had high levels of lead in their blood. The township is in Anhui province, about a three-hour drive west of Shanghai. Most of the children lived in a village called Xinshan, which sheltered two lead battery factories—the Borui Battery Co. Ltd. and the Guangfa Battery Plant.[17] In the first four months of 2011 police arrested nearly 75 people involved in producing lead-based products, and purportedly closed hundreds of smelters and battery factories.[18] Closing the doors of a factory in China, however, doesn't necessarily mean closed for business.

Migrant worker Xiang Hongfen and her husband found out that their employer Guangfa Battery Plant had poisoned their 12-year-old daughter and 7-year-old son. The local county government declared the Guangfa plant and a battery plant in neighboring Borui village closed. Xiang Hongfen and her husband, though, were both directed to continue working at Guangfa factory, which was actually still conduct-ing business.[19] Neither the company nor the local government would pay for the family's medical bills. The government used the excuse that the family's residence permits (*hukou*) were from another city, making them ineligible for health coverage locally. With no other work to be found in the poor district, the couple continued the life-threatening labor. The relationship between the local government and the battery factories often goes beyond ignoring suspension orders. Sometimes, there is a level of collusion that foils attempts at effective enforcement of regulations meant to protect local residents.

For instance, Guo Linyu worked at the Dafeng Shengxiang Power Supply Co. Ltd. as a battery maker. He told *The China Daily* in 2010, "The Company was informed in advance of any visit [from health and safety inspectors]. Each time an environment department official was about to check the factory, our boss would tell us to stop working and start cleaning the workshops."[20] The Haijiu battery factory also illustrated the cozy relationship between business and govern-ment. Environmental regulation enforcement at the Haijiu battery factory was patchy at best. However, the operation passed every inspec-tion for six years running during the first decade of the new century. Shen Yulin, the environmental protection director for the area, said he had only 65 inspectors to cover more than 2,000 factories across 400 square miles.[21] For six years workers repeatedly checked into the local hospital for illnesses related to lead poisoning. Authorities did not cen-sure Haijiu until a revolt by local residents in the spring of 2011 raised the issue beyond the ability of the town to cover up the epidemic.[22] Zhejiang residents who lived near the Suji e-bike battery factory would find that a familiar story.

The Suji e-bike battery factory was located in the country-side near the ancient resort city of Hangzhou. Since 2005 the busi-ness had been providing on the order of 1,000 jobs to the agricultural outpost. The tax revenues and additional largesse paid to local officials made them giddy with the area's new-found wealth. Ye Cai'e, who lived near the Suji battery plant, said that local officials threatened, "Whoever makes noise will not receive compensation or medical treat-ment."[23] Nevertheless, the owner's dark relationships with local officials were not enough to protect him from charges of malfeasance leveled by central government authorities. It took the lead poisoning of 53 children and 120 adults and a high-visibility protest in 2011 to force Beijing to intervene on behalf of the victims in the area.

The end of 2011 saw the foreign enterprise community in China rocked by a scandal related to lead poisoning. Shanghai authorities closed the operations of American battery maker Johnson Controls and 14 other lead smelters in the municipality. Johnson Controls had purchased the plant from a local Chinese businessman in 2005. Shanghai officials had closed the Pudong district plant after back-to-school medical examinations of 25 children detected high levels of lead in their blood. The government had chosen to slow local economic development slightly by closing the other plants, as they were finding it difficult to pinpoint the exact source of the contamination. Johnson Controls, a Tier-1 supplier to Global 500 automotive makers, responded to the investigation by saying their plant was run along more stringent standards than even Chinese regulations met.[24] In February 2012 Johnson Controls announced they would permanently close the plant. The answer to lead poisoning from e-bike battery production, recycling, and disposal, many say, lays in a move to Lithium-ion batteries. Lithium-ion is the basis of the technology promoted in other, larger electric vehicles like automobiles, vans, and buses. Lithium and its rare earth relatives, though, have their own dirty secrets.

Rare Earths, Common Pollution

Lithium-ion technology is more expensive to implement than the lead-based approach to battery making. Lithium-ion technologies can mean the end of most of the battery makers and the e-bike retailers in China's cut-throat marketplace. Higher environmental standards, however, gradually forced e-bike makers who wanted to break into Western markets to adopt lithium-ion technology. The rare earth element lithium, though—like its cousins at the bottom of the periodical table of elements—are buried in layers of radioactive geological and political detritus.

Lithium, neodymium, dysprosium, europium, lanthanum, terbium, cerium, and other rare earth minerals are key to the production of a host of cleantech, consumer electronic, and even military defense applications. Lithium, for instance, is the foundation of the chemical reactions at the heart of electric vehicles meant to replace traditional petrol-burning transport. Neodymium is used to build the high-strength magnets that help generate electricity in wind power turbines and high-power motors in electric vehicles. The motor in each wind power turbine needs about one ton of neodymium to generate one megawatt of power, enough to power 100,000 American-style homes.[25] Dysprosium is crucial in the manufacture of hard disks in computers, and also in the composition of magnets used to propel electric vehicles. Europium oxide is central to the production of compact fluorescent light bulbs, meant to replace energy-greedy incandescent bulbs. Cerium and palladium will become increasingly important components in the manufacture of low-cost catalytic converters to reduce the amount of carbon-emissions cars belch. The switch to cerium and palladium will matter more greatly than ever as China and India adopt American-style car cultures. Despite the name of the family of elements, rare earth minerals may be as abundant in the earth's crust as copper and lead, according to the British Geological Survey.[26]

China was able to corner the market in rare earth minerals as part of a national plan set in motion at the end of the 1990s. The country produced the ores at such a low cost that mines in the United States and Australia were unable to compete. The governments of the United States and Australia, in particular, actively chose to support closure of the mines in the early 2000s and cede market leadership to the Chinese. China has 37 percent of the world's estimated reserves, about 36 million tons. However, China came to control more than 97 percent of production. Post-Soviet bloc countries have nearly 20 million tons of rare earth resources, while the United States has almost 15 million tons. Australia, India, Brazil, and Malaysia also have large deposits of the ores.[27] Greater use of rare earth metals to reduce fossil fuel pollution, however, instead excavates a different sort of pollution—and a conundrum for environmental activists.

Rare earth miners pump sulfuric acid into the ground to wash the rare earths from the clay and dirt binding them. Operators rinse the rare earth deposits with yet more acid and chemicals to separate the rare earths from each other. The acid baths drain into the ground, seeping into ground water and into nearby streams and lakes. The poisons, however, are not just chemical in nature, but also radioactive. The effects of the pollution on the lives of local residents are devastating.

For instance, Baishazhen, a village in Guangdong province, near Hong Kong, became a favorite site for local mafia to strip mine in 2005.[28]At the time, all the world's gadget makers had supply chains snaking through the region. Also, China and other international champions in the wind power market began increasing production of wind turbines. Soon after Baishazhen became an entrepot for the trafficking of rare earth minerals, rivers that were once clean and clear ran muddy, foul, and toxic. Lakes retained cocktails of toxic solvents, killing off all animal and plant life in them and surrounding them. Baishazen had been Mr. Song's home his entire life.

The 81-year-old farmer witnessed the streams that ran past the walled compound in which he lived become fetid and clouded, undrinkable.[29] Guangdong provincial government officials claimed the chemical run-off had poisoned thousands of acres of otherwise productive farmland. Any plants Mr. Song and other residents cultivated near polluted streams quickly died. Even his well smelled of the acids the illegal miners used to excavate the rare earths. In mid-2011 the central government took steps to stop the illegal mining interests in south China. However, China's far northern frontiers were an entirely different story. State-directed development of open-air lakes of corrosive toxins to catch rare earth mining run-off was the rule, literally.

Inner Mongolia harbors one of the richest deposits of rare earth minerals in the world. Since the mid-1980s a vast city-sized industrial complex has grown up in the city of Baotou, perpetually shrouded by a fog of noxious vapor and dust. Squads of helmeted security guards patrol the area to keep the curious at bay and to squelch any potential dissent from residents who band together to protest their toxic home. Perhaps more poisonous than the production facilities themselves is the artificial reservoir of waste that tails off from the operations. By 2010 the lake had grown to become five miles wide and 100 feet deep, spreading three feet annually. Rare earth refinement operations pumped 7 million tons of deadened, poisoned earth into the poorly constructed lake every year. Poor quality construction saw the toxins leeching into the ground to contaminate the water tables upon which farmers depended to irrigate their crops. Residents also bathed and cooked their food with the poisoned water.[30]

The nearby village of Dalahai has suffered extraordinarily from the pollutants. Mr. Su Bairen told visitors about the artificial lake, "It turned into a mountain that towered over us. Anything we planted just withered, then our animals started to sicken and die." The residents themselves suffered from respiratory illnesses while their hair turned preternaturally white and their teeth fell out. Cancer rates increased dramatically and generations born after the construction of the lake were born with soft bones. Studies performed in the late 2000s on the area determined the reservoir emitted ten times the amount of radiation of the surrounding area. The length of time that this level of environmental degradation and human poisoning had been going on with local and central government sanction casted doubt on China's claim that it restricted the export of rare earth minerals for the sake of the environment and livability.

In the autumn of 2010, China protested against Japan's incarceration of a Chinese fishing trawler that had rammed Japanese coast guard vessels. Beijing placed an embargo on the export of its rare earths to Japan. Throughout most of 2011 the central government chose to keep the pressure on international markets by placing export quotas that were 30 percent less than what they had been the year before. The restrictions heavily impacted the bottom lines of American and European cleantech and electronic appliance manufacturers. Foreign governments lodged a complaint with the World Trade Organization that China was hording rare earths for its own industries. Beijing claimed that it had to rationalize the rare earths mining industry for the levels of pollution the informal mines were creating.

Much like the country's coal mining industry, the central government was finding that supporting illegal rare earth mining was reaching a point of diminishing returns. Illegal coal mines in China's north had claimed the lives of thousands of workers through mining accidents, and shortened the lives of tens of thousands more through the inhalation of carcinogenic dust. The central government directed the buyout or forced closure of hundreds of the mercenary coal mines to reduce the number of accidents that were embarrassing to the country. Beijing also began implementing measures to increase productivity in legal coal mines and reduce pollution and destruction of the local land

and surrounding communities. Foreign companies and governments remained unconvinced by Beijing's defense of its coal mine restrictions on the export of rare earth minerals.

Foreign producers of cleantech and consumer electronics already had known for years that China intended to dominate the sectors worldwide. Closer to home, the country published in its 5-year plan that it would accelerate its development of wind turbines by 2015. Country planners also envisioned a million electric vehicles on Chinese roads by the year 2020. In the name of energy efficiency, China was increasingly pushing its consumers to invest in compact fluorescent light bulbs, as well. The technologies, though, all required amounts of rare earth minerals in quantities ranging from a fraction of an ounce to tons for each unit produced. Production requirements added up to mountains of the substance for which no tax existed to rationalize its use. Material prices did not reflect true costs when safety and environmental considerations were factored in. Government policy in no way incentivized nor underwrote research into alternative materials that were less despoiling of the environment and less dangerous to human health.

China's move to restrict export of rare earths prompted the United States and Australia to have their domestic rare earth mines shipping ore before 2015. Analysts expected rare earth mines in North Vietnam to expand their operations, as well. Though the price of rare earths from China quadrupled in the five years prior to 2010, the new sources will likely decrease the spot price of the minerals on international markets. Increased mining and lower material costs will probably encourage production of yet more cleantech meant to protect the environment. Unfortunately, the means by which miners in China extracted rare earths achieved exactly the opposite result: rape of the land and the gradual poisoning of local residents. Much the same can be said of the production of solar power cells and the batteries in electric bicycles, as well. Cleantech production in China is in dire need of review and enforced revision.

When There Is No Longer a Backyard

The concept of clean and renewable energy is laudable: essentially, energy for free developed with technologies that on balance are good

for Mother Nature. The promise of cleantech is that perhaps societies may even leave the earth a bit better off than in the age of fossil
fuel use. The reality, however, is that the Industrial Revolution worldview coupled with a vicarious approach to consumption is also poisoning the planet. Certainly, China's leadership, in its rush to become
wealthy and regain stature in the world as a superpower, is culpable
in the extent to which it is disregarding the health and welfare of its
own people. The country is also harming its future as more children
are born with health defects that make them wards of the State, instead
of fully capable contributors to society. Willful greed, negligence, igno-
rance, and complacency on the part of local governments, law enforcement, environmental protection agencies, mafia, and tycoons alike have
turned millions of acres of the country into no-man's lands, uninhabit-
able for generations. Silicate solvents, toxic slurries, lead refining processes, and rare earth extraction methods are levying hidden costs to
society. Future generations, however, will have to pay the price for the
country's impatient modernization. China, however, is not the only
country culpable. Other countries have or are committing crimes
against Nature and communities in the name of "clean" energy.

Developed nations like the United States, Germany, and Denmark
have shifted production of cleantech products from their own countries to China. The developed countries have for years had environmental regulations on their books that either outright prohibit refinement
of the materials their cleantech required, or that make production prohibitively expensive to source and build domestically. Environmental and
human welfare considerations observed in other countries and attendant
costs are a prime reason the Chinese were able to undercut prices for
rare earths on the world market: flagrant disregard for safety and environmental concerns trumped the true economic cost of intensive mining. Eventually, though, societies and corporations must bear the expense,
arguably far more costly than if shareholders and government interests
had invested in a sustainable approach to excavation at the outset.

For instance, in 2011, Mitsubishi, the Japanese conglomerate,
became mired in a US$100 million investment to clean up the Bukit
Merah rare earths mine in Malaysia. Nearly a dozen people in the village developed leukemia after mining began, most of who died from
the cancer. Project managers expected the cleanup to require 11,000

truckloads of radioactive earth to be entombed atop a nearby hill. The effort also required storing 80,000 steel barrels of slurry. Large-scale cleanups of lead-laced sites, silicate tailings, and slurry dumps will prove a major expense to companies and local governments in China. Instead, the highest priority for shareholders seems to be to get rich as quickly as possible before the total cost of ignoring pollution issues becomes prohibitive. In some instances the price includes a quorum of residents dying of poisoning. The deaths and illnesses force the local residents to revolt *en masse* to embarrass government and business interests to remediate the violations. Sustainability of the processes that go into the production of cleantech—no matter the country of origin—is becoming an increasingly important issue for the world to confront.

The planet is running out of habitable space as the population looks to top the 9 billion mark by the year 2050. Narrower confines, unbreathable air, and toxic water will move from becoming important environmental challenges to critical social issues. Societies—no matter the level of economic development—will have to grapple with the monetary and human costs of clinging to the Industrial Revolution model of modernization. The crude excavation of natural resources to produce energy and the materials to maintain our standards of living are becoming increasingly problematic. Sustainability now is a buzzword—a fluffy, fuzzy concept that current economic theory ignores. The discipline of economics is still heavily based in the outmoded worldview of Adam Smith. Economics and modern concepts of wealth would certainly be different if humans took into account the actual—not subsidized—costs of living in a closed system. We live in an ecosystem called Earth.

Government subsidies and preferential treatment for natural resource extraction and processing give the illusion that alternative sources of energy are uneconomical. Within the constraints of current economic theory it would certainly seem the case. A truer accounting would include the costs to the environment of unsound mining and manufacturing processes. Calculations would also take into consideration the social costs of carrying communities that are no longer able to function because of poisoning. Then, the modern world will have a truer picture of what humanity will still be on the hook for in repaying its debt to the Earth. China's payment on the loan it has taken out from Nature will come due sooner than it thinks.

An over-crowded country like China never had many backyards from which local residents could refuse admittance to highly polluting mining, refining, and production processes. Eventually, under the current industrialization model, one form of heavy pollution or another in China will come from someone's backyard. The fact is as unavoidable as a cloud crossing a city line, a breeze blowing through a chain link fence, or a river coursing through the countryside. The increasing frequency and size of protests against environmental effronteries is an indicator that the Chinese are becoming aware of their codependence on their local ecosystems. The rash of lead poisonings of children in 2011 within the Shanghai municipality strikes at the heart of the affluent in the country. Pollution in China refuses the constraints of geography and class. Nature has begun to tell the nation's citizens they have something to lose if they continue to account for their production and consumption habits through off-balance sheet chicanery that hides the true upfront costs of modernization with industrial revolution characteristics.

That so much of the world's production has been transplanted to China is speeding the country's recognition of the true meaning and intent of environmental sustainability. The United States, with its very large backyards, relatively low population density, and transplantation of much of its dirty industry abroad will be slower than China to act on rebalancing the books Nature has been keeping. The country has the potential to bolt ahead of the United States in addressing issues involving pollution and natural resource exhaustion. Increasingly, China must take into account the total cost of applying Industrial Revolution thinking in developing its society. As new environmental and energy issues arise, so too must a new way of thinking about modern society's relationship with Nature.

Chapter 9

Dragon on a Diet

In the spring of 2011 Old Zhang limped out of his ramshackle homestead, a long fishing pole in hand, just as he had nearly every morning of the past twenty years of his retirement. He picked his way down to the Nanpan River. Born and raised in Luliang County, Yunnan province, he had always had the Nanpan as a constant companion: as a child running along the shores of the mighty offshoot of Himalayan glaciers, shouting rudely at fishermen; then, as a husband and father, plying a fishing boat in the Nanpan's swells. Over the last handful of years, though, along with some of his elderly neighbors, the Nanpan had passed away. Still, every day, Zhang went down to visit what remained of a reservoir of the once-mighty tributary. When he was younger the reservoir had held over more than 1.5 million cubic meters of water. Luliang had for decades been the province's most water-rich plain, providing irrigation resources throughout the state. The only reminder there had once been a reservoir in Luliang were the small cigar-sized fish, flash-dried in the cakes of mud hardened by sun and wind.

Zhang now was no longer sure where the bank ended and the riverbed began. The entire area was terra-cotta red, the land so dried and cracked that spaces had opened up in the ground that could fit a big man's hand, fingers splayed wide. Some crevasses ran as deep as a meter. The breadbasket of Yunnan Province had not seen rainfall for more than four months. Luliang had fallen on hard times. He knew from TV and from friends and neighbors that other parts of the country were in the same dire straight. Shandong province, in north China, was threatened with the greatest drought the region had seen in 200 years. Aggressive industrialization and urbanization in China was sapping the country dry.

After 2005 China's dearth of water resources was set to derail all of the gains the country had made in its economic development since the early 1980s. Privatization of agriculture, just after the death of Mao Zedong in the late 1970s, saw an explosion of the agricultural use of water. Farmers were the first to realize the wealth born of entrepreneurship when the Communist Party grudgingly gave its stamp of approval to those first sprouts of enterprise. The trickle of enterprises became a flood of trade with the cities, based on a natural resource the Communist Party had not pinned to economic realities: the cost of water lost to indiscriminant waste.

On average, China has just one-third the water resources of other countries. Water availability in the nation, however, is unevenly distributed. While south China has just over half the population of the country, it has nearly 85 percent of the nation's water resources. The south supports 40 percent of China's croplands. The north, by contrast, has only about 15 percent of the country's water, 55 percent of its population and 60 percent of its cropland.[1] For instance, the citizens of the sea port city of Tianjin, which faces the Korean peninsula, can only provide its population of 10 million with one-tenth the amount of water of the average citizen in the world.[2] The per capita share of water in Tianjin municipality in northern China is only one-10,000th of that in Tibet.[3]

To rectify what is at heart a systemic issue, the Chinese leadership is falling back on technology to address its shrinking water tables. *The extinction of water in the country presents the single greatest threat to the country's growth and stability.* Aggressive urbanization of 20 percent of the world's population and the development of mass consumerism, bolstered by globalization, are exacerbating the problem. To its credit, China's leadership was not debating whether there was a water problem and where the fault lay and who was to pay the bill. Instead, the clique of technocrats swiftly took to engineering approaches to ensure the nation's water security. Policy directives saw the greatest water works ever built diverting water from the water-rich south central part of the country to the city-provinces of Beijing and Tianjin in the arid north. Desalinization plants came online to supply much-needed water to municipalities. Local governments were also gradually raising water rates to reflect just how precious water had become in the country. Water use, however, is more nuanced than engineers and economists reckon.

Watergy

The leadership was not taking into account a simple, yet fundamental equation in addressing the nation's increasingly dire water challenges: the relationship between water, energy, and food. The constraints on the relationship became more restrictive with high-speed urbanization. It takes relatively little energy to take the water from its source and use it to irrigate fields in a country in which clean, drinkable water is plentiful. Growing food, feeding livestock, quenching thirsts, washing clothes, and taking showers take relatively little energy. As fresh water becomes more difficult to find and extract and then to distribute, costs mount as the society needs to generate more energy to meet its needs. Requirements for water grow as the population increases and/or the society becomes richer. For example, urbanites eat more meat than their cousins in the countryside, and take more showers and drink more soft drinks than country folk. Analysts call the relationship between water, energy, and food "watergy."

In 2004 China consumed eight times more water in generating 10,000 yuan (about US$1,500) of wealth than more advanced countries like the United States, and four times the global average. The country's industrialization drive saw China using four times more water for every 10,000 yuan of value-added industrial output. During the early 2000s, factory products were mostly low-end commodities—sneakers, toys and textiles—while infrastructure projects like building bridges, roads, and high rises took up the simple majority of economic output. While modern economies in the West recycled as much as 85 percent of the water used for industry, China recycled as little as 60 to 65 percent of its industrial water.[4] The most intense use of water for industrial purposes, however, laid in the production of energy.

Turning Water into Oil

The dearth of water for industrial use poses a huge problem for China's energy generation sector. With about 70 percent of China's electricity produced through the burning of coal, China will have to make crucial trade-offs in how it uses water in perpetually drought-stricken regions. In areas where coal mining is prevalent as well as in coal-burning plants, water is processed in abundance. In some instances, coal lays buried in deep-seated aquifers, from which the water needs to be pumped to enable the miners to do their job of clawing the coal out of the ground.[5] Further, coal mining itself requires that each ton of coal extracted from the ground be washed with four- to five-cubic meters of water. Each year, China consumes 40 million cubic meters of water alone to wash the coal it exhumes. The waste water the process leaves behind is laced with poisonous heavy metals, salt, and sulfates.[6]

The copious, unregulated use of water in coal mining in China is resulting in ground water drying up and water tables dropping across the country. Water shortages are prevalent in the towns that rely on wells and ground water in their daily businesses. Land erosion and desiccated farmland are becoming an increasing problem. About 75 percent of the nearly 100 state-owned coal mines faced water shortages in 2008, with 40 percent saying they faced serious water shortages. Most dramatically hit have been the coal-mining centers of Shanxi, Shaanxi, and the western part of Inner Mongolia.[7] Homes have slid into great sink holes that spontaneously appear. The shelves of earth that had been supporting the dwellings have been knocked away through the siphoning of water tables and hollowing of earth below.

In a well-meant but ecologically disastrous approach to alternative energy sources, Chinese coal companies in the mid-2000s developed coal-to-liquid (CTL) technologies. CTL is more popularly known as coal gasification. The technology turns coal into liquid either before or after mining. The liquid coal can then be refined into diesel fuel to run cars. Coal gasification can take three to five tons of coal to convert it to one ton of diesel for cars. The intention was to help China wean itself from oil imports.

China became a net importer of oil in 1993, after it was unable to produce more than 3 million barrels per day. The International Energy Agency projected in 2009 that China's net oil imports would top 13 million barrels of oil a day by 2030, more than China's total output in 2008.[8] The primary cause for the dramatic leap in oil consumption in China was the country's adoption of the automobile as a right of private consumption. China actively sought to develop its automobile industry and cultivate a strong urban consumer base from the early 2000s. For nearly ten years car sales grew by double-digits annually. Second to its explosive automobile market was a domestic petrochemical industry deeply invested in the refinement of oil for plastics and fertilizers, among other uses.

The growing requirements of modernization in China for oil—especially foreign oil imports—made energy security a centerpiece of government policy. The country's leaders have always been of the mind that their country would never fall prey to another country holding it ransom over energy supplies. Still, China's leadership found importing oil unavoidable once domestic supplies had clearly peaked in the late 1990s.

In 2008 the National Development and Reform Commission (NDRC) called a halt to all CTL projects in China except two. The NDRC wrote on its website that CTL was "a technology-, talent- and capital-intensive project at an experimental stage with high business risks." CTL technologies also required ten tons of water to produce just one ton of oil products.[9] The two projects the NDRC permitted were already underway by the Shenhua group, in Inner Mongolia and in the Ningxia Hui Autonomous Region. Ironically, the regions in China with the greatest reserves of coal—Inner Mongolia, Shanxi, and Sha'anxi—are historically amongst the most arid in the country.

Mining operations that had been running full-tilt in the region for decades wasted vast amounts of water. In China, technology may not be able to skirt around a profound constraint of Nature itself.

Manufacturing Water

The immediate thought that comes to mind in a region that is chronically and increasingly without water is to manufacture potable water. The ocean, of course, is the greatest source of water, however unfit for human consumption and land-based life it might be. Desalination is the process by which great air compressors suck sea water up huge pipes to essentially evaporate the salt from the water. China's first desalination plant went into operation in 2010, in Tianjin, a city-province on China's northeastern coast. Tianjin's water supply was in crisis. Urbanites and industry had overused and polluted and wasted most of its natural potable water resources. Desalination was seen as a key to the region's water and energy dilemma.

The Beijiang desalination plant was a 1.2 billion RMB (nearly US$200 million) project that was as much a coal-fired power plant as a source of fresh water for residents of Tianjin. The project had the capacity to produce 200 million cubic meters of water each year. The associated power plant that produced the energy to separate the salt and other minerals from the water produced 400 megawatts of electricity annually.[10] However, Tianjin said it didn't want the water from the desalination operation.[11] Tianjin residents balked at having to pay ten yuan (nearly US$2.00) per cubic meter to pipe water from the desalination plant. Residents had grown used to paying half that rate to tap into nearby rivers and lakes. City leaders also took issue with the electricity the plant generated.

The local power grid announced it could take no more than a third of the power generated by the coal-fired station, despite the city's growing energy requirements. Tianjin illustrated the paradox of China's model for urbanization: China needs the majority of its population to move to the cities to leverage economies of scale in resource usage. However, China's cities are the single greatest source of rapid increase in electricity use, and the most reliant on subsidized, cheap energy.

Building Sustainable Cities

By 2011 the urban population was nearly 700 million people, nearly double the figure in 1990.[12] About 70 percent of China's population will likely live in cities by 2035.[13] With urbanites in China consuming nearly quadruple the amount of energy of their countryside brethren,[14] Chinese cities consumed 75 percent of the energy its power stations generated in 2010. By 2030 cities could be siphoning nearly 85 percent of the energy the country produces.[15] Though the central government claimed to have achieved the energy efficiency goals of its 11th five-year plan of nearly 20 percent from 2005–2010; overall energy consumption may double from the current 1,000 gigawatts in 2010 to more than 2,000 gigawatts by 2020.[16] The leadership clearly understands that the more energy a society generates to meet its needs, the more its requirements will swell to even greater levels.

In an attempt to take a more holistic approach to energy efficiency and to reduce air pollution levels in cities, the National Development and Reform Commission (NDRC) launched a low-carbon pilot program in August 2010. The Commission identified five provinces and eight cities in China that were to lead the country in reducing energy consumption and carbon emissions as a proportion of local GDP. The program promised support of Guangdong, Liaoning, Hubei, Shaanxi, and Yunnan provinces and the cities of Tianjin, Chongqing, Shenzhen, Xiamen, Hangzhou, Nanchang, Guiyang, and Baoding. The cities were all charged with reducing their carbon "footprints" substantially before 2015 by drafting low-carbon development plans, establishing low-carbon industries, and promoting low-carbon lifestyles. A carbon footprint is the amount of carbon dioxide (CO_2) individuals, animals, and industries release into the atmosphere over a period of time. Carbon dioxide is a primary cause of climate change. Some of the cities were chosen because they were already industrial centers of cleantech, or had been ecologically focused for some time.

Hangzhou, for instance, is home to the famous tourist destination West Lake, about which Chinese philosophers and poets have waxed lyrical for more than a thousand years. Hangzhou is a two hour drive southwest of Shanghai. The West Lake Ecological District has been charged since 1992 with ensuring the air and water quality around the lake are high despite the rapid growth of the city. The municipality is also host to several economic development zones that pride themselves on promoting services and high-value manufacturing industries that produce little pollution.

In 2008 the Singaporean government and corporations invested in the Sino-Singapore Tianjin Eco-city. The Eco-city would be part of the Tianjin Binhai New Area, ostensibly a new city that will one day merge with the old Tianjin. The intention of the Eco-city was to integrate with the surrounding ecology. The new city sought to recycle waste, while a state-of-the-art public transport system would whisk residents throughout the area in lieu of automobiles.

I asked Richard Brubaker, an American professor at the China Europe International Business School (CEIBS) in Shanghai, if the efforts of cities like Hangzhou and Tianjin would actually create sustainable cities in China. Brubaker is a relaxed, thoughtful academic and industry consultant with an ironic sense of humor. Could there actually be such a thing as a sustainable city? I wondered. He told me:

> "Well, this is all about context really, and unfortunately, a 'sustainable city' is never really considered to be 'realistic,' because it is a city that does not offer 5% economic growth in perpetuity. It is a city that requires an investment, but also should be measured by returns other than simply economic output."
> He continued, "In the 'realistic' world though, I would say that the critical items I am looking at environmentally are buildings, transportation, food safety and water; socially I look at education, crime, and community service; and economically, it is about offering economic opportunity and a mixed economy that provides white and blue collar jobs."

Ultimately, however, the challenge of building new cities or retrofitting old ones for sustainability is successfully weaning residents and industries from the fossil fuel diets our modern societies are based on. Brubaker went on to say:

> "The reason the economy will move away from both is economic as inflationary pressures will force the prices of both up and industry will look to make demand side efficiency gains to reduce long term spend. The hurdle, at this moment, is that both

coal and oil are heavily subsidized resources, and there are two pressures on each: supply side pressures from finding/extracting/ transporting these resources is getting more difficult; and externalities are harder to keep off balance sheet. For instance, BP [British Petroleum] will have to pay the 'full cost' of their next platform upfront; also, coal mines are having to spend more to rehabilitate the land they destroy and are losing lawsuits. It seems to me there is a general trend in which externalities that were once so easy to pass on are growing more difficult to ignore."

Shanghai, in particular, as one of richest and fastest growing cities in China, is also one of the first to feel the weight of unsustainable economic and social development growth models.

Shanghai, compared to other metropolises in the world, is in a unique position to undertake sustainability initiatives. The centralized brand of governance backed by clear central government directives means the city could quickly undertake initiatives that other metropolises outside China may need years to start. Brubaker further explained:

> "Shanghai is deploying a varied strategy that looks to leverage economic incentives, new regulations, and government investments. Many will point to big ticket items like the metro system, and new water distribution investments. But the district of Minhang has put up 500,000 m^2 of green roofs, and is on track for another 500,000 m^2 by 2013. However, more fundamentally, the urban planning of Shanghai allows for a very efficient system that reduces many of the inefficiencies that dog western economies. Districts are integrated, communities are planned, and cars are largely unnecessary here."

However, an aspect of China's urban development model that is hemorrhaging energy involves one of its most fundamental assets: its buildings.

Building Energy Efficiency

Without fondness I recall standing in the middle of the living room of a Suzhou Chinese family's home, coat zipped up to my neck, cupping a glass of hot water. Still, my teeth chattered. Two of my hosts invited me to sit down on the worn, leather couch, stiffened by the pervasive cold. They stood with me. They themselves seemed as incapable as I of bending at the knees. We all tried to watch a little television while the mother of the family and her husband cleared the table away of the leavings of the Spring Festival meal. The apartment of the middle class family had no heat. Each room of the flat had boxy air conditioning units that could be used to heat spaces. However, it was clear the family wanted to save money by not turning on the units. Instead, they preferred bundling up in layers of long underwear and padded coats.

Increasingly, though, families and businesses are turning on their heating and cooling, if only during the coldest or hottest weather. In addition, new hotels, boutiques, spas, restaurants, and other amenities of modernity are sprouting everywhere in Chinese cities. Customers expect temperatures inside the establishments to be at comfortable levels. The number of apartments and businesses in China's cities is adding up to make the country the largest energy consumer in the world. Fuel bills are also revealing its buildings to be amongst the least energy efficient of any modern society.

Lighting, heating, and ventilating buildings are using more than a quarter of the power China generates, according to Li Bingren, chief economist of the Ministry of Housing and Urban-Rural Development.[17] The country uses an additional 15 percent of its energy on manufacturing and transporting building materials, and for constructing homes and offices, according to the Worldwatch Institute.[18] Li also acknowledged that daily energy consumption per capita in rural areas nearly doubled in the seven years since 2000.[19]

Li admitted that building efficiency was relatively low at 50 percent. "Even if the standard rises to 65 percent by 2020, the energy consumption for heating in China's buildings will still be 50 percent higher than the average in developed countries with the same climate," he said.[20]

Energy efficiency matters to a country that is one of the largest importers of coal and oil in the world. With its use of coal set to double within the next ten years as the size of its economy balloons, China already has the means of reducing its dependence on fossil fuels without the heavy layouts in alternative energy sources its leadership is promoting. As early as 2006 the central government was convinced it could not meet the energy demands of its buildings in 2020.[21] China's energy development plan as of 2011, with its emphasis on the supply side of the energy equation, was akin to pouring an increasing amount of water into a bucket full of holes while the bucket was getting larger. The Natural Resources Defense Council believed increased energy efficiency in China could cut the nation's growth in energy demand by half of current trends by 2030. Barbara Finamore, founder and director of the Natural Resources Defense Council China program, calculated that saving a kilowatt of power costs just a quarter of the amount used to generate a new kilowatt.[22]

China has the biggest construction volume in the world, though, with 2 billion square meters of floor area being constructed annually, according to Dr. Liu of the Energy Research Institute—a department in China's National Development and Reform Commission—at a talk he presented in Bangkok in 2010. Certainly, China's go-go approach to building construction does not lend construction efforts to considering energy efficiency, even when building designs required it. Energy conservation in some buildings actually dropped as much as 6 to 7 percent of the specifications in original designs, according to Qiu Baoxing, vice-minister of Housing and Urban-Rural Development.[23] Of course, unregulated property developers are in part to blame; however, prospective buyers themselves were loath to buy property that cost an extra 100 RMB to 150 RMB per square meter for things like additional insulation, properly installed heating and air conditioning (HVAC) conduits, and double-paned glass.[24] Even though salespeople could show potential customers that while energy efficient buildings may add 2 to 5 percent to a property's purchase price, the return on the investment could be as much as 10 times the difference spent when considered over a 20 year period.[25] Franz Lang, a German energy efficiency engineer in China, was not optimistic about the longevity of Chinese buildings, though.

I asked Lang what Beijing might do to completely restructure the energy efficiencies of the country's buildings. "In about five years," he said, only half-joking, "governments will realize the buildings won't be standing much longer [because of poor construction quality]. They'll acknowledge that their buildings are completely inefficient, tear them all down, and then start all over again." Nevertheless, Lang was excited to introduce me to an energy efficiency project in Suzhou, about an hour-and-a-half drive from Shanghai. Lang had advised on the implementation of energy-saving designs and technologies for a factory in the city limits. He insisted that many approaches to energy efficiency in urban settings in China were easily achievable, mostly common sense adjustments.

I met Austral Refrigeration's general manager, Johann Wiebe, on the sun-drenched third floor of the factory. Wiebe is a cherubic, good-natured man with nearly ten years' experience in China. He explained to me that local tax incentives encouraged the company to lease the three-story, 10,000 square meter facility. He told me that staff never had to turn on the lights in the open office space because a southern exposure pours through the large windows to keep the area brightly lit. "It was my belief from the beginning of this project that we were going to be energy efficient." Wiebe started the business in February 2010, and was in production by July of the same year. The factory shipped its first container of refrigeration units for supermarkets in Australia by the end of the summer of 2010, and by the end of the year saw its first profit. Since the company produced energy-efficient refrigeration units to keep meats, vegetables, milk and other dairy products cold, Wiebe believed it was important for the factory itself to be energy efficient. "My bosses in Australia would not have signed off on the investment in energy efficiency if the return was going to take more than a year," he added.

Lang attributed the company's rapid realization of its investment in operational efficiency to the processes the company put in place to make the business more self-contained and less dependent on electricity to generate its lighting, heating, and cooling. The company sourced all of its components and equipment from suppliers based in China, some of which were foreign-invested.

The key to the energy efficiency gains at the operation were more down to creating a "circulation" of thermal energy throughout the plant. They used very few hi-tech gadgets to achieve energy savings. Processes and alternative ways of looking at how consumers typically waste heat, in other words, were more important to establishing energy efficiency than new technologies. Wiebe showed me the nine solar water heaters arrayed in large gray square-meter tiles on the nearly flat roof, just opposite his office suite. "We can add more panels as we need," he explained. The panels took up a mere 5 percent of the space available on the rooftop.

If there was no sunshine for the panels to generate heat for use to mold large sheets of steel, then heat from the air compressors used to cool equipment was diverted to the jigs. The company also used heat recovery techniques to catch the heat radiated from ovens. The system distributed the heat from the ovens throughout the factory floor to heat the area during winter. The factory floor had dozens of large, 446-watt lights suspended from the dropped ceiling. They created a lower, false ceiling to trap heat closer to the ground to save on heating bills.

The weak link in the system, however, was the human factor. Wiebe explained to me that the Chinese staff was not interested in establishing habits and procedures that would save the operation a great deal of energy and money. So, management created a set of incentives and disincentives to let the staff know the company was serious about energy efficiency and to shape their habits. "Just switching off the lights as necessary required an education," Wiebe said. "We had to build bonuses and penalties around energy efficiency goals. Some staff didn't like the new system, so they left when we implemented it." However, the company was able to quickly replace staff who adapted to the mindset of the company. Educating consumers in Chinese society on sustainability issues, however, is far more challenging, as the owners of the green business Bambu discovered.

Green Shoots

Rachel Speth and Jeff Delkin started their sustainable business Bambu in the early 2000s. Bambu produces kitchenware made out of bamboo, coconut shells, husks, and cork. The products include bowls, plates and utensils, large and small. Styles are minimalistic, organic, painted in bold, energetic colors. Bambu takes bamboo materials from forests in China and Thailand and engage local communities that have little industry to hand-make and lacquer their beautiful kitchenware and accessories. Currently, according to Delkin, "sustainability is an option of the affluent" in China.

Businesses that work to be sustainable from the ground up are inevitably local in focus. They take it upon themselves to educate their local community of designers and craftspeople with the methods, requirements, and expectations of the international marketplace. They also work to keep alive and build on the traditional craft techniques of the local communities to maintain a competitive advantage that helps keep residents from suffering sub-standard qualities of life that are difficult to reverse once the traditions are lost forever. However, sometimes, the communities just don't understand commerce.

Speth explained to me how Bambu had worked closely with a village in Thailand that excelled in a special weave of bamboo into baskets. "No matter what we did and how we walked them through the production process, they just didn't get it." Especially problematic for the company was painting the baskets, which Western buyers preferred over the natural color of the baskets: spraying, catching and recycling paints that were inherently chemicals was problematic in the remote village. Eventually, Bambu gave up after more than two years of effort and retrenched in China. Another major challenge to their goal of developing a truly environmentally responsible business was addressing export markets.

Most of the customers for their products in 2011 were countries outside China. Speth told me, "We spend all this time and effort making 'green' products only to put them on stinky ships in the end." By "stinky" she meant the huge carbon footprints of diesel-powered cargo ships, as well as the waste crews dump overboard with each voyage. In 2012 they began changing their business model to develop what they called "local products for locals," to further reduce the carbon footprint of their products. In other words, products for the Asian market would be solely produced in Asia, while products for the American market would be produced in the United States. Packaging presented another obstacle to fully realizing their green credentials in China.

Chinese government regulations required a certain kind of plastic be included in the packaging of the wares they sold in the Chinese market. The plastic's manufacture is not based on a sustainability model, and it is not biodegradable. As a result, Speth and Delkin spent more time designing sustainable packaging than on actual product design.

Nevertheless, Bambu and other companies based on sustainability models found it important to their brands to educate buyers about the richness of craft traditions of the villages in which their products were made. Ultimately, what Bambu and other companies created was an *ecosystem* of local producers. Local companies became part of communities, contributing to the sustainability of the villages and their customs. Globalization, though, blows that model wide open.

Speth identified globalization as the Achilles Heel of sustainability models for societies. Nowadays consumers depend on the ready availability of products from around the world. Speth proposed, "Stop relying on other countries for what you've run out of." The proposal is based on a statement made by renowned architect William McDonough. McDonough's simple observation made a major impact on Speth's worldview: "There is no away."

"Dunno Where It Came From"

Globalization and urbanization have contributed to the rise in the wealth of developing countries in a way never before seen in human history. The Age of Cheap Stuff has provided all but those in abject poverty the opportunity to consume products that define "the good life" in higher-income societies they will never have the chance to visit, except through the sights and sounds and tastes they buy at their local shops. Globalization has provided the means by which so many dreams have come true that would have been impossible to realize before the turn of the new century. An axiom of modernization is that there is an infinite amount of resources with which to make stuff and an infinite amount of space in which to dispose of the waste.

Our consumer societies believe that when we "throw something away" it disappears from the Earth, vanishes from existence. McDonough's point is that the waste products—especially packaging—continue to live on, in some instances, for generations. The United States, with its relatively low population and great expanse of land in relation to China's, believes it can still afford unsustainable production and consumption patterns because, for the most part, the waste does not end up in "someone else's backyard" within the continental United States. The country is blessed with an abundance of land in relation to its relatively low population density. China, however, has four times as many people in about the same amount of area as the continental United States. America also has far more clean-water and clean-air resources than China. To its credit, the United States, since the 1970s, has worked to preserve its ecosystem and even reverse some of the adverse effects of past industrialization. Europe and Japan are certainly leaders in the area of environmental protection, since neither has the sort of space America does to dither with the issue. Further, the United States—and other Western countries—ships some of its most toxic waste to China.

Chinese buyers trade in disused computers, televisions, radios, and other electronic appliances that Westerners have disposed of. It is recycling at its crudest. Great hills of hardware dot China's east coast from which peasants and children—without protective gear—sift for parts that contain valuable metals and components that can be re-used in other manufactures. Toxins from decaying gadgets settle into the soil and enter the streams and water tables of the area. The toxins the derelict machines release are carcinogenic and are a leading cause of disabilities and deformities in the villages near where the mounds are excavated. This trade is one of the uglier faces of globalization. The effects of the dumps on the environment and local communities will never go away.

Globalization enables consumers to trump local constraints placed on supply and demand. Buyers can obtain material goods, food, and even energy from regions far from their homes. However, the traditional trading system is heavily subsidized by governments and their citizens. The subsidies provide food, energy, and water in abundance. Consumers do not realize the true price of the goods we are purchasing, though. A true price would consider the impact global supply chains are having on our natural resources and our environments locally and globally. Central to the concept of watergy is that societies may be able to import food and energy from abroad; however, they cannot economically import potable water in the quantities to which we have grown addicted. The misalignment between the globalization of trade in goods and the availability of water at a local level in China threatens to bring the society to a standstill.

I propose a corollary of "There is No Away" is "Dunno Where It Came From." Though the affluent might know their Louis Vuitton bags are "French" and their Ferragamo shoes are "Italian" and their iPads "American," consumers in a globalized world actually don't know where their wares were made. Plastic components may have been cast in Malaysia; leather shorn from cattle in America; labor supplied by Bangladeshi children; and products delivered on Chinese-made ships. There is no true accounting of the origins of the natural resources and energy inputs that go into many of our consumer products nowadays. Because we "dunno where it came from," we don't care where it came from, just as long as we can get it. With each acquisition we burden our local environments and resources further. We are spending our inheritance from the Earth with abandon.

The bill for basing modernization on an unsustainable Industrial Revolution model will come due one day, however. That is undeniable. One could say that, metaphorically, we all see the waiter coming to our table, flashing a ticket we all know will be far greater than what we brought along in our collective hip pocket. It's the price we'll all have to pay for presuming the Earth to be inexhaustible in its plentitude. However, the Earth is a closed system.

The Earth's ecosystem is closed to the extent that only sunlight is allowed to pour in. Everything else remains within its gravitational field. It doesn't have clean air or clean water pumped in from outer space. And the dirty air and dirty water are not pumped beyond the stratosphere, either. The lands upon which we live are the lands upon which we will pass away for the foreseeable future. There are no new spaces to which we can move away to escape our own waste. Policies that reshape our consumption behavior and re-establish our relationships with our environment are what we need to sustain modernity. Technology fixes are not sufficient, just as in the small laboratory of Austral Refrigeration in Suzhou.

Sustainability is a frame of mind; not just another marketplace in which to make profits. At the start of 2012 the European Union implemented a "carbon tax" on international flights into and out of the region. It was the sort of policy adjustment at the outset the world needed to ameliorate the effects of globalization on our home countries. The United States, China, and more than 20 other countries balked at the policy purely on the basis of traditional fossil fuel economics. The mantra of globalization has become a means of escaping our responsibility as stewards—and not masters—of the planet.

This is a revolutionary concept in China, which has always believed deeply in its responsibility to master its geography. Since the days thousands of years ago when Chinese engineers built dams, levees, and other great engineering controls to mollify the flooding of its great rivers, China has believed that the triumph of its masses over Nature took primacy. China's brand of rapid modernization, though, has tipped the global environment and national economies into a condition of instability perhaps never before seen in human history. Now, with the country coming against a hard ceiling to future growth and sustainability, it will have to develop new institutions and come to a new understanding with its environment. As drought, climate change, energy constraints, and a rapidly aging population change the complexion of the society, China may well come to sign a new social contract.

Chapter 10

Assembly Required

A s Chen Yulian waited for her husband at the high, wrought iron gate one summer day in 2010, she noticed six large men rounding the street corner, hulking toward her. Chen Yulian was a small, bird-like creature, so thin there seemed little insulating her sagging, aging skin from her brittle bones. At 58, she was far from feeling a need to look like the plump, well-coiffed wives of other government officials. A mere 5-feet 3-inches tall and weighing in at 82 pounds, she preferred wearing baggy pants and a simple smock when she went out-doors, especially in the searing heat of one of China's hot-pot cities, Wuhan. She noticed all but one of the men coming toward the gate at which she stood wore black clothing—ridiculous in the heat—and dark glasses. The one in the front—she guessed he was the leader—wore a black shirt and red shorts. She thought there must have been some altercation she had just missed. Perhaps there was a brawl they were joining. Their intention was clear, even to a blind man: they were going to injure someone—anyone, it seemed. She stepped closer to the gate to let them pass. She took out her mobile phone to call her husband to tell him she was waiting for him at the gate of his office at the Public Security Bureau (PSB).

The PSB was the last channel of adjudication for those with unresolved grievances. If a judge decided a case against an aggrieved party, the party could theoretically boot the case to a higher court. That seldom happened though, as complainants understood when decisions were stacked against them from the top-down. Petitioning, however, was a means as old as China itself for plaintiffs to circumvent the court system and go directly to the top officials of a city—even of the entire country—to get a hearing and, hopefully, a decision in their favor. Twenty years ago, and before that even, most complaints were disputes between people or families—civil cases; now, the vast majority of petitions are about illegal land seizures.

The group of men surrounded Chen Yulian. Wordlessly, they began pummeling her with their fists, feet, knees, and elbows. She did not immediately crumple to the ground, as there was a disconnect between her recognition of the bizarreness of the incident and the pain she was receiving at the end of each sharp blow. She was sure they were Black Society thugs—Chinese Mafia—mistakenly beating someone whom they believed owed them money or payment of some long overdue debt. One of the assailants grabbed her arms forcefully and swept her legs from beneath her like a Sumo wrestler. She fell to the pavement heavily.[1] Pain blasted through her from her hip. After some struggle, she stood to confront her attackers, but was repeatedly knocked to the ground. She could see between the legs of the men a crowd had formed around the assault. She heard someone shout, "Stop beating her! She's the wife of a high-ranking government official!" No one, however, dared intervene.

Doctors diagnosed Chen Yulian as having a concussion, soft tissue injury, a broken left foot, and nerve trauma. She vomited frequently and her body was covered in bruises. She stayed in the hospital for more than a month after the incident. She turned the event over in her mind as clarity gradually returned and she digested the horrific encounter. She did not know, though, whether she was more upset by the beating or by the revelation of who had assaulted her.

Actually, her assailants were not part of any mafia. They were plain-clothes police. The squad's duty was to disenchant potential petitioners from filing petitions of wrongdoing with the government. The day of the incident, the director of the PSB came to her bedside to apologize. He said, hat in hand, "When we heard about this incident we attached great importance to it. Look, I rushed over as soon as I had a moment! . . . It's a misunderstanding, merely a misunderstanding; we didn't know we had hit a big official's wife."[2]

Nevertheless, Chinese news articles, blogs, and forums dubbed the incident "Wrong Beating–Gate" (打错门). Chinese Internet users commented, "So long as it's no one important, beating is acceptable behavior?" One netizen questioned, referring to photos of a battered Ms. Chen lying in a hospital bed, "Is this democracy? Is this rule of law? Is this justice?"[3] *Shanghai Daily* newspaper columnist Wang Yong stated: "Instead of tossing out these bad apples [the police] one by one, it would be better to ask: Who hired them and enabled them to work against the people?"[4] The newspaper deleted the digital version of the column from its website soon after the publisher had posted it. Nevertheless, Ms. Chen was the unfortunate recipient of the backhand of 4,000 years of Chinese civilization, without the "civil."

Can't We Be Civil?

One of the most important innovations China will need to research, develop, and incorporate into the modern society its leadership is attempting to build and integrate with the rest of the world, are civil institutions. Civil institutions accept and even promote the reality that no government can address all the needs of its people. Indeed, the discouragement and, in some countries, the outlawing of non-governmental organizations is an indication of the degree of autocracy of the leadership. Autocratic governments insulate themselves from the needs of the people and the wider world, and the quality of life its citizens lead.

Civil societies are also indicative of the degree to which citizens can freely assemble, exchange information and ideas, and innovate. The existence of civil institutions does not imply the societies in which they exist are inherently innovative. Civil societies in which government has accepted the complementary role of civil institutions are mature, vibrant societies in which discourse is encouraged. Open societies nurture the creativity required to meet the society's spiritual and material requirements. So, though Europe, the United Kingdom, and the United States all support non-governmental organizations, charities, and a plethora of non-profit organizations, few dispute the fact that the United States as a society has a far more active culture of innovation than do its European and British counterparts. China is already meeting serious resource, environmental, and demographic challenges that are calling the viability of its social structure into question.

In time, China's government will be unable to meet the country's growing energy requirements. Authorities will one day have to ration natural resources—especially water. The great bulge of the population will age into retirement without sufficient government benefits and family members to support them. Chinese citizens will then have to learn how to help each other through institutions that complement and supplement government services. The central government will have to accept its limitations and begin to trust the self-organizing principals that citizens in Western countries develop to enrich their societies, not destabilize them. In modern history and throughout China's long history, however, an individual's and family's fealty went solely to the emperor and his representatives. To hold loyalty to other institutions—including one's own family—in equal proportion to that of the throne would mean death.

Chinese society throughout its imperial history has been a "doughnut" society: hollow in the middle except for the epicenter, where sits the emperor. The emperor seldom left his palace and never encountered the common man. The country was essentially administered by ministers who all passed the same civil service examination, no matter where in the country they took the grueling test. Not only was the examination a test of the degree to which potential administrators could memorize and regurgitate great swathes of poetry, philosophy, and history, but the examination served to ensure homogeneity of thought, belief, and response of imperial servants to dynastic edict, no matter where in China they hailed from. The 1,500 year old system was to serve as a means to align government administrators and to harmonize the disparate societies and geographies of China. Today, it is university graduates with connections in the Chinese Communist Party (CCP) who sit for rigorous government examinations. The exams test their understanding and expression in their lives of Marxist-Leninist-Mao Zedong Theory. The examinations are a continuation of a historic means of ensuring lock-step social harmonization through authoritarian rule.

Chinese citizens support each other outside government channels through concentric circles. The tightest circle is the extended family, headed by a patriarch. Beyond this innermost circle are circles of classmates and co-workers. The hometowns from which Chinese come make for the final circle on the periphery of social relationships Chinese have defined as paramount for their survival—especially when the government has let them down. At times in public spaces the circles of strangers come into contact. When the circles of strangers intersect during a moment of high tension the result is either extreme passivity or explosive aggression. Chinese seldom reach out to communicate or assist other Chinese not in one of these circles related to them personally; hence, no one dared come to Chen Yulian's aid. With the exception of her being a local, Ms. Chen did not come across the relationship "radar" of any of the onlookers. The idea of helping one's fellow man without commensurate payback in China—that is, *guanxi*—is inimical to Chinese social relations—unless the preservation of the family and the family's "face" is at stake. Of course, such a value system is contrary to the intent of institutions meant to help complete strangers who may not contribute a direct benefit to service providers.

Highly centralized governments have their limitations, however; especially with such a large and geographically dispersed group as the Chinese in Mainland China. Population explosions during the midlife of each dynasty stretched government resources beyond practicality. Floods and famines due to unsustainable pressures placed on the environment seized up the totalitarian model of governance. All that was left was for families and villages (often the same in historic China) to fend for themselves. Toward the end of the nineteenth century, villages sometimes had to defend themselves from marauding government soldiers, themselves unpaid for months and starving in some instances. Though the rich patrons of some Chinese towns did create benevolence societies to help the less fortunate in their towns, Chinese non-governmental organizations usually developed a violent response to the disintegration occurring around them. The Taiping Heavenly Kingdom in the mid-1800s was a direct response to the breakdown of the administration of Manchus who ruled China at the time.

The Taiping Rebellion was started by Hong Xiuquan. After he failed the government civil service examination several times in the early 1840s, the erstwhile student suffered feverish visions of himself as the younger brother of Jesus Christ. By 1850 he had 30 million adherents who marauded their way from south China to establish the capital of their Heavenly Kingdom in Nanjing. The Kingdom was a direct response to the decay that gripped the ailing dynasty. It provided a means for cult followers to take care of their own family and friends. Ironically, the final death toll after nearly 20 years of fighting was nearly 200 million people. The Boxer Rebellion of 1900 was a similar expression of citizen discontent with government administration and Western intrusion into Chinese society. The Boxers were unique in their belief that their kung fu made them invincible against bullets. They also believed the throne itself, in the person of the Empress Dowager, would defend them during the violent uprising against Westerners in 1900. The Falun Gong movement of the late 1990s was also a declaration of discontent with government social services— health in particular. Falun Gong, was a hybrid system of Buddhist beliefs, yoga-like exercises, and group-support mechanisms. Its membership ran into the millions. It raised a clear and present danger to Communist Party rule when thousands of exercisers gathered one morning outside the headquarters of the CCP itself in 1999 without the knowledge of the security apparatus. Nowhere in the mood to replay the sort of organized, concerted protests of the Taiping, the Boxers, or more recently Tiananmen Square protestors, the CCP dismantled the Falun Gong movement swiftly and violently. Remnants of the self-help group still exist in countries throughout the world, occasionally renewing its call for the CCP to allow them to practice freely in Mainland China. Despite China's violent history of imperial encounters with social and religious organizations, religion is thriving in China—albeit in a divided house.

"For We are Living in a Material World . . . "

Those with a religious bent believe that the root cause for dynastic meltdowns in China lays in the country's lack of freedom of religion. Actually, China, as a historically superstitious culture, has a plethora of religions and icons for individuals in need of supra-material orientation. In the 1980s the CCP revived Buddhism, Taoism, folk tales, Christianity, ancestor worship, Confucianism, and even Chinese civilization itself. The CCP realized it needed to provide society belief systems to replace the vacuum it left behind as it retreated from its *raison d'etre* as the standard bearer for communism in Asia.

Still, Brian Grim, Senior Research Fellow in Religion and World Affairs, reported in his article, "Religion in China on the Eve of the 2008 Beijing Olympics," that fewer than 1 out of 5 Chinese adults interviewed across six cities in China said they are religiously affiliated.[5] The United States, however, claimed 8 out of 10 adults as religious. However, in absolute terms the number of Chinese with religious inclinations is still enormous, with about the same number as the entire population of the United States at the time; that is, about 300 million.[6]

China Daily reported in 2007 that about 200 million Chinese followed in some way, shape, or form Buddhism, Taoism, or "legendary figures such as the Dragon King and God of Fortune."[7] Frankly, I believe every Chinese in China is a Buddhist at some level or other in his belief system; that is, most Chinese have no problems entering a Buddhist temple every few years, burning some incense and perhaps saying a few prayers for success in business or for the birthing of a son. The same Chinese would also have no problem negotiating with the Taoist bureaucratic hierarchy in Heaven for good luck in a business deal. Later, they may say a few Hail Mary's in Church, if they felt it would help serve their interests. Even the outlawed Falun Gong has made room for the Buddha and Jesus Christ, to help with protection against the Fox Spirits from Chinese countryside folklore.

Indeed, the Chinese government at the national and local levels have re-opened, renovated and even built new Buddhist and Taoist temples since the end of the Cultural Revolution in 1976. The small town of Anshan in Liaoning Province, a two hour drive south of the provincial capital of Shenyang, has outside its city limits a new Buddhist compound, the finishing touches of which were still underway when I visited in 2007. The centerpiece of the temple is a great monolith of stone, the Anshan Jade Buddha. The local government claims it is the largest Jade Buddha in the world at more than 250 tons. The Buddha image was found on the side of a mountain outside Anshan in 1960. Mao Zedong's right-hand man Premier Zhou Enlai declared the find a state treasure. In the 1990s a column of government trucks and army tanks from the People's Liberation Army moved the severed rock from the mountainside where it was discovered to its resting place. The government does not exert the same amount of constructive energy toward Christianity in the country.

Onward Christian Soldiers

Christianity had been flourishing in parts of Mainland China for centuries before the CCP outlawed it when the Party gained power in 1949. With a string of government policy failures from the 1950s through the 1970s, the Chinese were ripe for belief and value systems that seemed to have more durability than the flexible atheism of Party doctrine. In the 1980s Christianity became attractive in China as a value system that would help guide citizens through the vagaries of a time unlike any other in Chinese history. The ancient religion would also provide a channel through which adherents could develop their organizations for charity and altruism.

By 2006, according to the Chinese central government, about 21 million adults had claimed the Christian faith, a rise of 50 percent from 10 years before. Protestants outnumbered Catholics about three to one, with Protestantism having grown by more than 20 times since it first came to China in the early 19th century. Independent research institutions place the total number of Christians at anywhere from 50 million to 70 million associated with more than 300 house-church networks. House-church networks are small groups of family and friends who gather together in each other's residences to study the bible and discuss the gospels in private. They do not recognize the Communist Party as above their religious order. However, there does not seem to be the same level of animosity between house churches and the central government (or, even at the local level) as between Falun Gong and the government. Falun Gong adherents boasted that at its height in China the movement had tens of millions of followers. House churches, however, have been allowed to develop, presumably as long as they do not organize into a massive, major challenge to Communist Party hegemony, as Falun Gong had in 1999. At times, the local government seems absolutely apathetic to the activities of Christian worshippers.

While I attended a dinner banquet one evening with local Chinese lawyers and local Chinese government officials in a municipality in China, one of the lawyers freely discussed his and his wife's Christian beliefs at the table. I suppose he believed that as an American I too held the same beliefs, as he invited me that following weekend to a retreat he and fellow worshippers were having at a nearby civic center. I cut a glance at one of the government officials who sat at the large, round table, to see her reaction to the invitation. She had no response, which surprised me. Still, I declined the invitation as I never even participated in such groups back in the United States. Nevertheless, Christianity seems to supplement ancient Chinese values in an unexpected way.

Where Christianity seems fresh to Mainland Chinese is in the absolutism of its morality and its value system compared with relativistic Buddhism and Taoism. Also, the ease of access to and sharing of feelings within Christian study groups and confession booths gives Chinese a face-saving way to relieve pent up emotions. Channels of expression within the Church also mollify the riot of mixed feelings that naturally come from the frequent injustices they suffer in their crowded and capricious society. Buddhism, though, will always be part of the Chinese fabric of its world view and its perception of itself. Christianity, however, will continue to grow, albeit from a much lower base of adherents than China's classical belief systems. In contrast to China's other belief systems, though, Christianity in the country has provided social services sanctioned by the Ministry of Civil Affairs, which oversees the activities of charities in the country.

The Amity Foundation, for instance, is a Chinese Christian organization that received millions of dollars a year in funding from church groups around the world. The Catholic Church in China supported the Beifang Jinde, an outgrowth of a Catholic newspaper in Hebei

Province. The YMCA and YWCA also re-emerged in the 1980s. The "Y's" run neighborhood development programs that offer recreational facilities for young people, programs through which volunteers can befriend retirees, and training programs for laid-off workers.[8] An unexpected benefit of China's go-go economic development is a greater awareness at the grass-roots level that people must come together to help the less fortunate, whether or not it is sanctioned by the government.

A Charitable Streak

Grace was a young Shanghai resident who worked as a project manager for a British-based professional education company. She traveled frequently to Europe for her work. The day we met in Suzhou in an international five-star hotel she was wearing a pretty white blouse, low cut, a simple black skirt and colorful shoes made of textiles and colors one would find in a Tibetan wares shop. She had bought the shoes in Hong Kong, she told me. We drank bottled beers. She opted for a Guinness.

Grace was representative of Shanghai's new generation of 20-somethings who were university educated, had service-sector jobs, spoke English, were paid relatively well, and traveled frequently within China and abroad. I asked her about the religious disposition of this new generation, which was providing a model for other young Chinese in other large urban centers. "I've been to church in Prague, but didn't feel any pull toward joining." She paused in thought to scan her mental record of her friends. She finally said, "I don't know anyone who has become a Christian." I was a bit surprised by the answer. I had approached the topic of Christianity with the presumption it had gripped young professionals in China. Perhaps, I calculated, they felt their lives had little meaning or found themselves disoriented by all the changes happening around them. Indeed, Suzhou had four of its own churches, one of which had just been completed in the university town about a half hour drive from downtown Suzhou. Two years before the neighboring city of Kunshan, near Shanghai, completed construction of a huge post-modern Church funded by Taiwanese money. And Shanghai had preserved many of its churches, and was building new ones, too. Grace, though, was telling me she was unaware of any massive trend of Chinese people—young or old, rich, middle class or poor—toward Christianity. Indeed, she looked more perplexed than any other response to my pressing the question a second time.

Her face lit up when she told me she and a lot of her friends enjoyed doing charity work. She personally had done work for the American organization Up With People, in the Filipines countryside. She had helped build houses for the poor. "I lived with a Filipino family that every Sunday went to Church. They insisted I come with them, which I did—every Sunday. But I still never felt a need to join the Church." She and classmates had also traveled to one of the historically poorest provinces in China, Gansu, which has little agriculture, some mining and very little water. She and her classmates taught classes to some of the poorest children in China, many of whom would never make the state-mandated eight years of education for lack of teachers, school houses, materials, and tuition. "I first got involved with charity work in high school, cleaning rivers in Shanghai. I found the work so satisfying." She admitted that the first priority for many of her peers was making money. "But they're so busy; they don't have time for Church, even if they were interested."

With growing optimism in the charity sector, Grace hosted her own birthday party at a trendy gallery on Suzhou Creek in Shanghai in 2009. The email invitation said in English and Chinese that instead of receiving gifts, she would like celebrants to donate cash to her favorite charity. The party took place in the loft of the River South Art Center, on Suzhou Creek. The River South Art Center was historically a warehouse on a tributary feeding the Huangpu River. I was sure that without a lot of research I would find that little more than 100 years before, Western merchants had likely stored opium in the warehouse for transport and sale into the interior of China.

At the entrance to the loft was a sign-up counter and small wooden contribution chest for the Chinese charity, The One Egg Project. The One Egg Project involved donors making contributions that would help children in the poorest villages in China be able to afford to eat at least a single egg, daily. Apparently, such a simple unit-source of protein makes a quantum difference in the height, weight, and academic performance of children. I pitched in my 100 yuan donation. A young man in stylish eyeglasses gave me a colorful bookmark. "This is the child your donation will be supporting." My eggs would go to a little girl name Huang Ling, an eighth-grader in Wangmin Village, Xiji County, Ningxia Province.

A crowd of about 200 was already milling about inside the gallery, all young Chinese professionals evenly split between men and women. Some were dressed in jeans with laptop computer bags slung over their shoulders, while others were stylishly dressed in evening attire that gave the event an almost chic feel. During breaks in programming, chill-out music filled the space and made everyone feel "cool." There were very few Westerners at the party. I saw only one young businessman still cosseted in his dark suit, and a small group of French standing together, talking behind one of the charity displays.

Within the loft itself an array of other charities displayed their causes at tables, counters, and video displays: Raleigh, outdoor leadership adventures that contribute to charities; Shanghai Young Bakers, which takes teenage orphans and provides free training as bakers in Western (predominantly French) bakeries, restaurants, and hotels; Shokay, which sells wares made of yak wool from Mongolia; The Zhejiang Xinhua Compassion Education Foundation; The Xingeng Workshop, a volunteer organization that helps stricken villages get back on their feet.

Just inside the wide entrance, off to the side of a central dais, stood a large screen where some of the charities displayed videos of the results of their efforts throughout some of the poorest parts of China. A master-of-ceremonies introduced in Chinese each of the charities in attendance. Members of the charity groups took a few minutes to deliver professionally produced video- and slide-presentations of their mandates in action. At the end of the evening Grace announced that over 300 guests had contributed more than 38,000 RMB (nearly US$5,550) to The One Egg project. Grace's admirable efforts, however, took place in a national policy gray area.

From the 1950s to the 1970s the CCP regarded charity work as "a decoration of the ruling class used to cheat the people." The government-run China Charity Federation (CCF), the largest official charity in the country, maintained that China had more than 100 registered charities since the central government legalized the institutions in 1994. In the 20 years since then, the official charities raised about US$700 million.[9] One of the reasons for the relatively low level of donations had to do with China's tax code for donors: individuals are actually taxed for donations. Donors may pursue a labyrinthine application procedure for tax-free donation status, however. Claiming exemptions is an even more grueling procedure. In 2008, the central government amended China's corporate tax law to provide a tax deduction of up to 13 percent of the tax bill, up from 3 percent. Still, government minders believed most Chinese companies and individuals would use any exemptions to escape paying tax. Hence, policy development is slow.[10]

In 2002, philanthropic giving through "un-registered," private channels in China totaled 2.2 billion yuan (US$323 million). When private foundations could legally register in China in 2004 total receipts exceeded 100 billion yuan (US$14.6 billion) annually. By 2010 there were around 1,500 private foundations doing needed work across the country. One of the private foundations that has benefited through the liberalization of the charity policy in China is Jet Li, kung-fu movie star and founder of the Chinese charity the One Foundation. He cited his organization had over a million pledged volunteers at the time. Established in 2007, he was aiming to create a new model of "social entrepreneurship," in which individuals with the means reached out to other individuals to help the less fortunate in China and around the world. The One Foundation since its establishment has contributed to the relief of twelve national and international disasters, including the Sichuan earthquake in 2008. The Foundation received donations from close to 1 million individuals who used their mobile telephones and the Internet to contribute to disaster relief.[11] However, by and large, citizens have a great distrust of official charities.

For instance, during the summer of 2011 the Chinese Internet and Twitter-like service Weibo were alight with the photos and personal information of a 20-year-old woman who promoted herself as the Business General Manager of Red Cross Society. China's Red Cross Society has no relation with the international organization. The young lady, named Guo Meimei, posted photos of herself leaning against an expensive sports car and living in a luxury villa. Two years before she had been a model who had undergone plastic surgery. The scandal drew in a Vice President of the Chinese Red Cross, Guo Changjiang, who was Guo Meimei's benefactor. Chinese netizens accused Guo Changjiang of embezzling funds from the charity and doling the money out to sycophants. Some local governments and citizens, however, understand that the challenges confronting the nation will require more than nepotism and cynicism.

The Final Innovation

Through Grace I was able to meet the executive staff of the Non-Profit Incubator (NPI) in Shanghai in the summer of 2011. NPI was a social experiment with the full backing of the Shanghai government and funding from some of the largest multinational companies in the world. The intention of NPI was to help cultivate organizations with mandates to help communities become self-sufficient. The downtown site was located in a renovated factory of an extinct State-owned Enterprise. To step into the building was to feel oneself a child again, the high, vaulted ceiling uplifting one's spirits while the walls with colorful, child-like murals animated one's heart.

I met the deputy manager of NPI, Ms. Ding Li, in the lively cafeteria, on the ground floor opposite the main entrance. Employees with a variety of handicaps were cleaning the dining area and serving counter after lunch. One of the workers smiled at me and said "hello" loudly. The Executive Director explained to me that NPI had originally been launched in 2006 in Shanghai with the intention of addressing some of the social issues that had begun to press on the city. Some of those issues involved taking care of a demographic in Shanghai that was aging ahead of the rest of China.

I recalled a conversation I had with Richard Brubaker, a Professor at the China Europe International School (CEIBS), a few weeks before my visit to NPI. Brubaker had told me some districts of Shanghai in 2011 already had populations in which 30 percent of the residents were over the age of 60. Local governments were already beginning to feel the burden of supporting a social welfare fund into which a diminishing number of workers were contributing funds into the retirement pool. Shanghai also has a substantial portion of its population who are disabled: autistic, deaf, mute, or with limbs that have not fully functioned from birth.

The NPI facility in which I was standing was the Shanghai Social Innovation Park. The site incubated businesses to provide the special-needs demographic with opportunities to help themselves by helping others. NPI, however, was also much more than a business incubator.

NPI's venture philanthropy provided small- and medium-sized non-profit organizations with seed funding, management, and techni-cal support. NPI also supported what it called a Community Service Platform (CSP), which managed public facilities in communities in the Pudong district of the city. The CSP also trained social workers to better serve communities and organized various community pro-grams. The CSP was so successful in Shanghai that NPI rolled it out to Sichuan province, to help rebuild communities destroyed dur-ing the 2008 earthquake that killed nearly 100,000 people. NPI also provided Corporate Social Responsibility (CSR) consulting services to large companies such as Motorola, Novartis, Lenovo, Cannon, Nokia, Intel, and others, to help them develop community-based programs in China. NPI was also approved by the Shanghai Civil Affairs Bureau to create a public charity called the Shanghai United Foundation. The Foundation raised and disbursed funds for a variety of non-profit organizations and social enterprises. I marveled most, however, at the refurbished factory I was in, which housed the social business incubator.

Ding Li introduced me to Frank Wu, who actually managed the incubator. Frank was an enthusiastic man in his mid-thirties with a light frosting of white at the tips of his otherwise black hair. Otherwise an unassuming fellow, it was clear as he took me through the facility he deeply appreciated the efforts of the organization to better a society beset with huge challenges. On our way to the exposed stairway that connected the ground floor with the second floor he explained that participants in the program for the autistic had painted the colorful murals. On the second floor he introduced me to facilities where the blind were taught massage skills. When they graduated from the program they would get jobs as professional masseuses at the company that spon-sored the training. Within a large, glass-encased workshop area a young

Chinese woman led a group of a dozen or so chatty participants with learning disabilities through a session on how to make teddy bears. As we rounded the corner to pass down a corridor a young woman with Down's syndrome brightly said "hello" to me—twice, in case I didn't hear her the first time—and waved at me.

In a large office area segregated with low-walled cubicles Frank explained the space actually housed several businesses. One was Heifer International, which donated calves to poor rural families and taught them how to nurse the calves so they could pass on offspring and teach other families. Another was a graphic design business for physically handicapped professionals who had received formal training in their craft but who could not find jobs because they were disabled— not because they cannot perform their jobs. The for-profit business prepares the designers to market themselves and manage professional portfolios that leave little doubt in the minds of potential customers as to the abilities of the designers. Another section of the space was set aside for a call center business manned by staff with physical disabilities. None of the staff was there when I visited; however, Frank explained that each staff was capable of making 400 to 800 sales calls each day. The tour left me feeling optimistic about the positive, constructive possibilities in which modern Chinese society could develop—the CCP willing, of course.

Hot House Innovation

The CCP believes it can have its innovation cake and eat it too. That is, it believes it can command large swathes of its economy to become technologically innovative while maintaining iron-fisted control of the society. It bases its approach on a post-Soviet model of governance that even the Soviets eventually found wanting. Innovation with Chinese characteristics seems more about showing the world how brilliant Chinese citizens can and have always been, when foreigners are not intruding into their country, rather than about addressing the very real problems confronting its society. As the CEIBS Professor Rich Brubaker told me during one of our conversations, "Innovation is not about intelligence; it's about incubation."

Increasing pollution, environmental degradation, natural resource depletion, and public health issues are eroding its social gains as quickly as it modernizes. China's leadership believes that through systematically acquiring technology from abroad, localizing it to address domestic issues, re-packaging it in cheap-labor wrapping, and then selling it on to other countries China will become a sustainable superpower.

The leadership has it wrong. Many of the social controls it places on its citizens, families, companies, and neighborhoods need to be dramatically revised. Otherwise, people and companies will not feel safe enough to take the risks "Big-I," disruptive, world-beating innovation requires to erupt. In other words, all the technology in the world is not going to solve the country's greatest vulnerability: a lack of civil society. Its own citizens do not feel liberated enough to reach out within their own communities to work together, to help each other, to assemble so they can exchange ideas and swap thoughts and try on different futures. Whether it's the ubiquitous stinky public bathroom in China that no one wants to clean specifically because it is in the public domain; or the crumbling stairways and disused garden plots of apartment buildings for which no one wants to take personal responsibility, Chinese society needs to see that far more can be gained working with strangers toward a common good than not.

In the instance of the police beating up the hapless Ms. Chen, the political system saw even the most remote indication of assembly and dissent as punishable by death—or near-death, in her case. Onlookers were too afraid or too disinterested to get involved in what was clearly wrong. Even if Ms. Chen had been an accused serial killer certain rights should have been accorded her in a civil society so justice could be properly carried out. And, though Ms. Chen herself was clearly wronged, she believed that as the wife of a government official she was immune from the sort of day-to-day indignities served up to so many of the country's citizens with lower socioeconomic status. Within the Chinese system, Ms. Chen herself likely would not have intervened if she had seen a half-dozen thugs kicking in the rib cage of a little old lady in broad daylight. And nor would anyone have thought to ring the police if Science Cop Fang Shimin had been caught by the thugs intent on breaking his bones on a public street. Yet, the very essence of scientific and technological revolution is about dissent; it is about questioning results; it is about pushing the envelope of inquiry and authority. China cannot have true in-your-face world-shaking "Capital-I" Innovation until its society and its governance structure accept and assimilate that axiom.

Innovation is dissent. It is about breaking molds and taking risks and the desire to disrupt the current workings of the society through creative destruction. Efforts like the Social Innovation Park are easy for Westerners to sneer at or to look down upon as naive, or even as a government public relations stunt. Everyone I met at the Park, however—*especially the students and entrepreneurs and future teachers and skilled professionals with their disabilities and sunny dispositions*—did not find the park a Potemkin initiative, all smoke-and-mirrors, no back-end substance. With locations that have sprouted like strawberries in Shenzhen, Beijing, and Chengdu, NPI has great potential to serve as a model for social, educational, and scientific communities in China.

The NPI model placed emphasis on sharing across domains of experience and ability. It implied learning through creative projects, instead of just by rote, as is the traditional Chinese way. The approach expanded one's awareness of one's environment through experimentation and observation instead of just through brute ideology. The work environment encouraged participants to take care of one another with the profound understanding that we're all on this planet together: Chinese, American, European, South American, Muslim, Jew, Christian, and the rest.

As the old saying goes, "Just because the hole is on your side of the boat, doesn't mean it's just you who will drown." The goal of the kinds of innovations incumbent on all our societies to foster is not to make winners of the ones who die with the most stuff. Instead, the aim should be to work together to build social and technology ecosystems through which modern society may be able to thrive in a way that is truly in harmony with Nature—in an environment in which each of us is afforded the opportunity to leave the world just a little better than when we'd come into it.

Afterword

The Curse of Steve Jobs

T he world is in no doubt about the contributions to personal technology innovation that Steve Jobs, former CEO of Apple Computer, made to modern society. The iPad, for instance, finally pried open the market for notepads after decades of promise. The device gave me handy and timely access to news, information, and entertainment that was otherwise very difficult to access on the wrong side of the Great Firewall of China. With Jobs's passing, thousands of Chinese laid wreaths at Apple shops in China and passed their condolences on to store staff. Some fans openly wept. Millions of others lamented through "tweets" on the Chinese online Weibo service that China had no Steve Jobs to offer the world.

The chairman of the Chinese Museum of Finance, Wang Wei, responded bluntly in the wake of Jobs's death in 2011: "In a society with an authoritarian political system, monopolistic business environment, backward-looking culture, and prevalent technology theft, talking about a master of innovation? Not a chance! Don't even think about it."[1] However, creating a social, political, and economic environment that could foster individuals with the vision of a Steve Jobs may be misdirected. Serious challenges lay ahead in the continued development of China's society and for post-industrial society at large. Jobs preached and practiced money-spinning gadget-innovation. This approach to invention is not the right sort to resolve the pressing issues of ecological degradation and dwindling natural resources.

Tyler Cowen in *The Great Stagnation: How America Ate All the Low-Hanging Fruit of Modern History, Got Sick and Will (Eventually) Feel Better* makes the argument that America—and, by extension, the West—has reached an innovation plateau upon which it has become increasingly more expensive to deliver the sorts of innovations of a hundred years ago. A century before, inventions changed the living standards of entire societies within decades. My grandparents—or at least the generation born at the turn of the twentieth century—saw cars, televisions, radios, washing machines, electric lighting, airplanes, nuclear weapons, and other fateful creations. For most middle-aged residents in rich countries nowadays, the basic material goods in their lives haven't changed much.

The average rate of innovation peaked in 1873, Cowen writes. The year marks the height of the Industrial Revolution. It also signaled the beginning of the era of technological disruption my grandparents would eventually come to know. "Recent and current innovation is more geared to private goods than to public goods," he writes. The focus on innovation of private goods meets the requirements and expectations of a consumer society and services economy that has migrated from labor-intensive agriculture and manufacturing as primary sources of national income. Societies reward R&D focus on upscale "designer" solutions, whether they be drugs, Gucci bags, iPods, or basketball players. The economic framework for the last 30 years has evolved into a winner-take-all climate, in which the gap between the superstars and the rest has been increasing at a blistering pace.

The designer approach to innovation, however, has seen little new wealth created since the early 1970s, and instead has been a channel for wealth redistribution. Statistics on the extent to which the rich have gotten richer in the West while the middle class has shrunk and the poor have grown poorer are abundant. The size of the labor force required to research, develop and produce designer consumption products and services has been shrinking steadily since the 1980s. The armies of the unemployed, underemployed, and those who have simply given up looking for work have mushroomed in the West.

The Chinese of Mainland China have seen their lives change in the past 30 years to the same dramatic extent as my forebears 100 years ago. Now, the country is coming up on the innovation plateau the West encountered in the 1970s. The Chinese leadership is fully aware that for the last 30 years the country has picked most of the low-hanging, Industrial Revolution fruit that has nourished its economic development. Conditions in China for the past three decades favored foreign direct investment. Globalization presented international consumer markets willing and able to buy Chinese-made products. A bulge of able-bodied youngsters who found working at factory machines around the clock preferable to life on the farm also came. In its efforts to catch up with the West, a country that had little in the way of infrastructure plowed more than half its new-found wealth into the development of roads, bridges, airports, and real estate. Disintegration of technological barriers in the vein of what Thomas Friedman writes in *The World is Flat* facilitated the transfer of any real wealth remaining in the West overwhelmingly to China. "Innovative" financial products provided the West the illusion its societies could "manufacture" wealth *ad infinitum*. China has been the single greatest beneficiary of the meltdown of the West's financial system and of the innovation plateau upon which the West has constrained invention. Now China is working to co-opt more technology from beyond its borders into its laboratories and markets to continue its social development.

Indigenous, Not Ingenious

China now wants to pick up the West's own technologies and approaches to protecting ideas, then make them its own through an initiative it calls "indigenous innovation." The country wants to become an innovation powerhouse in its own right. Beijing has centrally planned to become an innovation society. Universities, laboratories, and businesses are under heavy pressure to "manufacture" patents. Meeting patent goals means promotions and ever-closer orbit to the center of power in Beijing. Central planning goals, however, seem to prefer to obviate international standards of academic and research integrity as well as measures of the degree of inventiveness of patents. The CCP's approach to innovation has called into question the extent to which China is merely tweaking technology imported from other countries and re-hashing standing patents. The number of research papers published by institutes within China, as measured by the number of scientific papers published that international scholars reference, is negligible. China has become over-reliant on importing technologies—and overseas Chinese—to claim the mantle of "innovation nation."

China's political environment stresses harmonization of thought, creativity, and action of its citizens—no matter the education level. The leadership's belief that homogenization will cultivate the kind of maverick, breakthrough thinking that disruptive scientific discoveries require, is chimeric. Instead, it is more realistic to envision the CCP sponsoring Manhattan Project-sorts of efforts, populated by armies of pliant researchers. The majority of the most important research projects in China are likely military-related. Military projects take place in political and perhaps geographic silos. A commissar sees to it that his project cleaves to the wishes and intentions of the Communist Party. The largest Internet companies in China have just such political "blinders" of creativity placed on them to ensure the harmonized experience of Internet users in China.

As Cowen notes in *The Great Stagnation*, the only significant innovation for public consumption that has come along in the past 30 years involves the digitization and commoditization of information. Music, books, newspapers, magazines, and computer databases are now readily available to modern and rural societies around the world. The global delivery platform has placed at our fingertips the sum knowledge and experience of humankind. It has the power to shape worldviews and the possible futures of individuals in ways far greater than even the pamphlet, the book, the radio, and the television ever could.

However, China's leadership has invested a great deal of resources into cleaving China-based Internet providers from international channels. Government censors are then better able to filter the kind of information that flows to Chinese netizens. State interests are also able to cordon off a domestic market in which it is able to cultivate champions locals hope will become global brands in their own right. Chinese Internet companies like Baidu.com, SinaWeibo, and RenRen are unashamed knock-offs of Google.com, Twitter, and Facebook, respectively. These and other Internet services have variations that meet specific Chinese tastes and practices—no different in degree of localization than most other countries. However, none have been able to become the globe-straddling titans their Western forebears have. China-based software designers and programmers are finding themselves in an Internet space increasingly insulated from the international sphere. They will find it more difficult to obtain the concepts, hands-on experience, and training they require to expand on the full capabilities of a digital toolbox. The inward focus on the domestic market will be good for business at home, but awful for impressing the rest of the world's users. Meanwhile, China's services outsourcing industries, which depend heavily on digital infrastructures, will find it difficult to reach beyond the shadow of Indian providers. India's service vendors have long-established the installed international customer base, credibility, and English-language training Western buyers seek.

India's services outsourcing sector has reached middle age, however. Chinese vendors do actually have an opportunity to grab market share from Indian providers. Chinese vendors need only come up with an earth-shaking service innovation or acquire the experience levels and language skills of their Indian counterparts overnight. Unfortunately, Chinese service providers have been finding it difficult to break out of the orbit of service sector support for Japanese and South Korean corporations. The East Asian market provides little opportunity for creative expression and increasingly sophisticated output. Back-office operations support in China has become a victim of export manufacturing success. Inflows of hot money into the country have lifted operational costs, especially salaries in services outsourcing hubs like Shanghai, Dalian, and Hangzhou. The only real competitive advantage the Chinese have in their competition with the Indians is lower costs. However, that edge is fast eroding. Eventually services outsourcing in China will become a stunted, domestic exercise. The sector will have employed far fewer able bodies than central planners had calculated.

Digital technologies are such great enablers of productivity that fewer staff are required at even the largest Internet companies. Beijing will need to continue to support state-owned enterprises involved in heavy metal manufacturing to gainfully employ millions of citizens.

China's grand plans to achieve innovation stardom include adopting state-of-the art technology from foreign companies involved in capital intensive manufacturing. Central planners see adapting rail, automotive, shipping, and other heavy metal industries to meet local requirements, and then exporting the technologies as their own. The tragic accident on a high-speed rail line during the summer of 2011 shook the Chinese people's faith in the implementation of the plan and the integrity of the government. Corruption on an epic scale involving billions of dollars was a major contributor. The faulty understanding and implementation of the "black boxes" foreign vendors used to obscure the technology they had licensed to Chinese engineering firms exacerbated systemic problems. The accident was a turning point in the Chinese leadership's relationship with its people. The CCP accepted online criticism from millions of Chinese Internet users. Government censors did not shut down the services that supported the messaging systems. Authorities did not resort to heavy-handed, wholesale retribution, either.

Officials instead recalled new rail cars intended to ply the high-profile Beijing-Shanghai line. The recall was a huge loss of face for a government that only weeks before had been volleying international criticism leveled against it, that it was driving its trains too hard and too fast. Suddenly, international interest from regions ranging from the United States through South America and the Middle East in purchasing entire high-speed, low-cost railway "kits" evaporated. The central government by the end of 2011 had to bail out once high-flying State-owned railway companies whose fortunes had sunk on international bourses. China's domestic automotive industry suffered a similar image problem concerning the quality of its products in its own market and in international markets.

Chinese buyers flocked to imported car brands in 2011 once government subsidies to support domestic brands ended in 2010. Meanwhile, the European Union market—especially Germany—continued to resist having Chinese automobiles travel its roads because of safety, quality, and maintenance issues revealed in exhaustive tests. American buyers kept Chinese autos at arm's length for the same reasons, despite price points that were substantially lower than other brands. Overproduction of Chinese brands began to erode margins in the domestic market. It became increasingly difficult for makers to invest in the sort of technology R&D and brand differentiation to ensure survival in uncertain global markets. The central government's plans to dominate world shipping lines with great cargo- and oil-carriers made in China began to sink its industry at the end of 2011 for much the same reasons as its automotive market: over-capacity. The global economic downturns of 2008 and 2011 saw economic reality bite, as central planning approaches to filling quotas clashed with market fundamentals. Shipping rates plummeted so dramatically during the three-year period that it was going to take ship buyers and leasing arrangements decades instead of years to see a profit from their investments in new ships. China's domestic investment in heavy metal technologies and plans to flood international markets with low-cost, questionable-quality products produced by the State only reinforced the world's impression of Brand China.

In 2010 Chinese leadership would have had international buyers believe that China's miracle economic development was built on the backs of an industrious people wisely led by the brains and ingenuity of a few billionaire mavericks. The largest Chinese companies on the Global 500 list of the world's biggest corporations, however, are State-owned Enterprises (SOEs) or companies with indirect links to State sponsorship. Nevertheless, private, domestic companies in China, with less tenuous relations with the central and local governments, still fought for global market share. Their most challenging work involved gaining global recognition for "hard" innovations involved in production. However, it was "soft" innovations in their company image, operations, management, and strategy that would make the sales in the international arena.

The extent to which a company is able to produce innovative products that disrupt—not replicate—other industries comes down to incubating talent, not stamping intelligence. China's family, education, and political systems place primacy on homogenizing individual initiative and creativity out of youngsters and adults. Social conditioning tends toward following the nearest strong man without question. The sort of flatter, flexible multinationals with greater frontline decision making power are nearly nonexistent in China's corporate genes. However, the country's new-found image as the largest energy consumer and polluter in the world is not as easy to innovate away as its leadership would like.

The Scramble for Energy

If there is any challenge facing China and the world it is energy consumption and resource usage. With another 100 million individuals slated to move into cities, the country's leadership expects China will double energy consumption by 2020 to 2,000 gigawatts of electricity. Coal is still the overwhelming fuel of choice in powering generators, taking up on average over 70 percent of China's energy portfolio. So great is China's dependency on fossil fuel that wind-, solar-, nuclear-, and hydroelectric-power sources are at best complementary solutions—not viable alternatives for the foreseeable future.

China has been able to point out on a score card of the international community's own making that from 2007 to 2010 the nation developed the largest capacity of wind power in the world. The nation also became the largest manufacturing base for solar power panels on the planet. Little is advertised, though, about the abysmal failure rate of wind turbines and the lack of *installed* capacity for solar panels domestically. Though policy directions seem in favor of pushing complementary energy sources, implementations at the local level leave much to be desired. Central planning has sanctioned wind turbine and solar panel makers absorbing and regurgitating technology innovations from abroad. Export of the energy products at low prices and in great quantities—with questionable quality—has raised the hackles of the international markets. Competitors mobilized in 2011 to bring attention to government subsidies of the technologies. A toxic clean-tech supply chain further called into question the country's green credentials and intentions for a cleaner, energy-efficient society.

China considers the unfiltered use of fossil fuels as detrimental to the environment. Coal-powered plants and gasoline-guzzling automobiles are main culprits for fouling the air. The country, however, can do more to curb rampant air pollution by tightening exhaust emissions standards for car makers. Authorities can enforce regulations on power plant carbon emissions. Electric vehicles are a wonderful vision of a clean-air future. However, the implementation itself will only be as clean as the coal-powered electricity generators from which the e-vehicles draw their energy. China's construction industry presents just as much of a challenge to the country's rampant use of fossil fuels.

Chinese homes are built of cement and steel without the least bit of insulation. Great draughts of air pass through window and door seals no matter the season. By the mid-2020s China will have to undertake a major re-construction of the vast majority of its residential and commercial property to make the structures energy efficient. The gargantuan effort itself will require at least as much in the way of resources and energy as in the past ten years of construction activity. Beijing will be certain in the new round of construction to enforce energy efficiency standards in the building of commercial and residential property.

In the final analysis, sustainability as China is practicing it is illusory. Economic growth models and measures of economic "wealth" are based on Industrial Revolution models. The industrial revolution is firmly rooted in fossil fuel energy sources (heavily subsidized, at that), centuries-old production technologies, and exploitative thinking about the relationship between human beings and nature. The trajectory of social development along which China and other developed countries are traveling motivated the oil conglomerate Shell, in 2010, to explore energy-related scenarios for the future.

The two scenarios upon which Shell settled for examination were called Scramble and Blueprint. Scramble involves countries becoming further enmeshed in a mad scramble for energy and other natural resources. Territorial disputes erupt. Resource-related conflicts between China and its neighbors in the South China Sea and the Sea of Japan become clear and present flashpoints in this vision. Water rights in the Himalayas, which feed China and its neighbors in the south, provide another flash point. Wars are fought that, eventually, bring about the realization that collaboration across borders is more constructive than deploying troops and firing missiles. The Blueprint scenario sees countries coming to their senses about collaborating on energy and resource issues without resorting to their militaries. Shell saw a relatively narrow window of opportunity in the current decade where the Blueprint scenario could become the new norm.

It is the urgency of environmental- and resource-related constraints and the potential for wide-ranging conflicts that should be driving innovation in China—not dictating the injection-molding of armies of Steve Jobs with Chinese characteristics. Nevertheless, social harmonization is a prime tenet of the CCP's philosophy of governance. Its iron grip on the reins of power will continue to trump the assembly of people and ideas that incubate great invention. Cultivating a civil society may see the creation of innovations that can disrupt the society in the way the Renaissance changed the European worldview 500 years ago.

Free Exchange

Even the advent of spontaneous, legalized volunteer corps to help the elderly, the infirm, and the disenfranchised throughout China are monumental contributions to the nation. Hundreds of millions of country folk will be filtering into cities over the next decades without the twenty-first-century knowledge skills they will require to work in a services economy. They will need community support networks and charities that will help keep the society from fracturing into factions of the discontented. However, in an energy-constrained and resource-constricted world, mutual support that can be had without bureaucratic interference will become paramount for social stability. Local environments that foster and even encourage spontaneous assembly without government interference will provide fertile ground for freer exchanges of informal information and ideas.

Steven Johnson writes in his book *Where Good Ideas Come From: The Natural History of Innovation* that throughout world history the greatest innovations were born in environments in which people, hunches, and ideas were allowed to collide. Whether the 1400s in Venice, the 17th and 18th centuries in England, or the 1920s in Europe and America, dialog across disciplines was alive. Writers, scientists, poets, and even clergymen at times engaged, exchanged thoughts and worldviews, and disengaged and re-engaged with other mixed creative communities. These were all times when new geographies were being discovered. Explorers were stumbling across new cultures and different ways of relating with the world. Understanding the jumble of new experience required paradigms divorced from that over which the church had presided for nearly 1500 years. Modern societies have a new frontier to engage in the twenty-first century.

Pollution, climate change, natural resource depletion, population pressures, and energy production constraints are presenting China and the West with a hard ceiling against which their social development is pressing. Ian Morris, in his book *Why the West Rules . . . for Now*, defined social development as the sum of a society's ability to get things done, and to shape its physical, economic, social, and intellectual environments to its own ends. China will require new scientific, communications, and creative paradigms to keep its society from collapsing back to simpler times, and to continue to advance the interests of its people and culture. What China needs is a scientific revolution on the order of the Renaissance to resolve the global challenges confronting it—not variations of the iPad. A Steve Jobs with Chinese characteristics is not sufficient to meet oncoming challenges of global proportions. Another Leonardo DaVinci, on the other hand, and the culture of creativity and experimentation he represented, is in order.

Oops!

Tim Harford writes in *Adapt: Why Success Always Starts with Failure* that experimentation requires that mistakes be made, recognized as such, and rewarded for narrowing the field of possibilities of what actually works in the new condition. The level of creativity needed to meet oncoming environmental and resource challenges, though, will have to be epic in its reach. Modern society will have to foster the sorts of discoveries and inventions that can turn the global thermometer back to the temperature it was at the start of the nineteenth century. New thinking will have to replenish the oceans. Great inspiration will have to dissolve the toxins that have leeched into so much of the soil and water in China. Intensely disruptive innovation will have to create clean, cheap renewable energy for all.

Science needs paradigms that are up to resolving the new-century challenges the Industrial Revolution and consumer culture have created for modern society. The paradigms that are relevant and may resolve the challenges a society faces often run counter to the prevailing political and scientific climate of the time, as Thomas Kuhn wrote in *The Structure of Scientific Revolutions*, his seminal study of the work of scientists. This was certainly the case with Galileo and his astronomic observations and interpretations, for which he was imprisoned by the Church hierarchy in seventeenth-century Italy. However, the implications of his discoveries and those of his maverick contemporaries changed the way scientists of the time worked. His sacrifices contributed to the transformation of the nature of inquiry itself. His creativity, within decades of his death, helped construct the worldview of a clockwork universe that ushered in the Industrial Revolution. The Industrial Revolution incubated the tools the West would use to broach the hard ceiling to social development both Europe and China was pressing against at the time.

Since 1980 China has grasped those same centuries-old tools to develop its own society. Its rapid social development has created a tipping point of social, economic, and ecological instability on a global scale. The new and frightening context requires an entirely new way to design and manage modern society, use energy, and consume natural resources. However, China cannot manage all this itself; nor can any single country. Instead, new questions, new challenges, and the development of radically new solutions require new ways of connecting, of creating the sort of liquid networks currently dammed up by patent licensing practices, scientific paper citations, and political ideologies.

Michael Nielsen presents in his book *Reinventing Discovery: The New Era of Networked Science* that societies are able to accelerate scientific revolution. Nielsen is a physicist who has worked on quantum computing research. He believes humanity can solve incredibly complex problems by sharing data in banks available to scientists around the world—and even to the public. He laments that while in the United States much of research is publicly funded, results are locked away on the computer storage media of individual scientists. Many researchers hope for commercialization of their work or citations for published papers that take a year or more for publication. Even after publication, data in most instances is still inaccessible to interested parties.

Nielsen argues, however, that the way science is done can change more in the next 30 years than the way it has been done in the previous 300. Much of that has to do with the Internet. Cyberspace is as much an ecosystem of ideas as a medium for entertainment. Nielsen offers the example of the HapMap, a chart of how and where human beings can differ in their genetic code. The variations flagged in the chart offer researchers opportunities to find correlations between victims of disease and control groups. The map was the combined work of scores of scientists around the world, who each deposited a chunk of genetic data into an online databank as the decoding occurred. International collaborations are currently building enormous online databases that map the world's species, climate, its oceans, and even human languages. A new generation of science is developing with a different set of reward structures for scientists. No single individual, group, or country has the capacity or resources to gain the insights and discoveries that cross-border virtual collaboration can. And therein lays the ultimate challenge for China: Can it learn to share?

A New Dialog of Discovery

The immediate answer is no. China's leadership has been re-innovating traditional Western scientific and research institutions to meet domestic political expediencies. Corruption and nepotism have forced further limitations on the free-flow and expression of data and ideas. Beijing maintains a blueprint of indigenous innovation that expropriates technologies and discoveries, tinkers with them, and then calls them their own without honoring provenance.

Understandably, other countries, researchers, institutions, and even corporations are inclined to share less than the state-of-the-art with China. Nevertheless, the CCP severely restricts the free assembly of people and the clash of ideas in the public arena. There can be little traffic in the hunches, intuitions, and leaps of faith that characterize true scientific revolution. Official censorship of the Internet fractures the society from the insights of the international community. Chinese researchers and potential innovators are growing increasingly isolated from the banks of data and the flows of inspiration dozens of countries are working in concert to mobilize. China's society is not developing as an incubator for innovation or fresh discovery. Social and political strictures in the country limit the kind and quality of information exchanges, risk taking, and out-and-out mistakes upon which disruptive discovery and innovation thrives. China needs to remove the constraints before it can cultivate the kinds of individuals and teams its society requires to contribute to a rising international dialog of discovery. The possibility exists of the country contributing to new paradigms of inquiry that can resolve the rapidly evolving issues modern society's accelerated social development has spawned.

The alternative is that current-day China, within a few decades, risks becoming annotated as just another dynasty in a long history of cyclical feudalism, albeit one with digital characteristics. The Digital Dynasty may well become known to future historians as the epoch that had the capital with which to fund grand initiatives. Its society had the technologies within its reach upon which to build a new understanding of Nature. Its researchers received the invitation to collaborate with the rest of the world in earth-shaking ways to solve humanity's most pressing problems. Instead, historians may lament, its leaders chose to collapse the society in on itself out of pride and arrogance. China, however—now at the leading edge of history—merely presages the way for all human civilization.

The West and the rest can help China help us all through leading by example. For those of us fortunate enough to live in democratic civil societies we can begin to ameliorate the effects of long-term negligence of our environment and our natural resources. We can begin to communicate globally, but buy locally to practice sustainability. Governments should phase in an end to subsidies for fossil fuels and water, and implement taxes that reflect the true costs of consumption of limited natural resources. Private citizens whose taxes pay for research should demand from their governments that results remain in the public domain for the betterment of all humanity—not just to profit a few. Citizens should vote with their tax dollars on the type of reward systems that promote data and research sharing based on public largesse. And voters should push for an international patent system that disregards inconsequential tweaks of current technology. Instead, inventions that can be applied to the public good should belong to the public domain, and any innovations drawn from that domain should not become the sole purview of privateers.

The stakes for human civilization are high during the twenty-first century. The 20 percent of the world that led the Industrial Revolution needs the help of the 20 percent that is China to overcome some of the greatest challenges the world has ever faced. The remaining 60 percent of the Earth's population needs also to contribute to efforts through any multilateral channel available. Humanity needs to creatively and constructively address the sustainability of a modern world as we would *all* like to envision it: a beautiful blue-green pearl of magnificent, networked intelligence proudly pirouetting in the vastness of space.

Notes

Chapter 1   Innovation Nation

1. Malcolm Moore, "Celebrity Chinese Monk on the Run from the Authorities," *The Telegraph*, September 3, 2010.

2. Evan Osnos, "'Science Cop' Mugged," *The New Yorker*, August 31, 2010.

3. The currency of the People's Republic of China is the renminbi, which means the "people's currency." It is comparable to the United Kingdom's sterling. The yuan is the primary unit of measurement of the renminbi and comparable to the pound or the dollar.

4. "Details of the Fang Zhouzi Attack Emerging," *China's Scientific & Academic Integrity Watch*, accessed January 20, 2011. Available online at http://fang zhouzi-xys.blogspot.com/2010/09/details-of-fang-zhouzi-attack-emerging .html.

5. Josh Chin, "A Bad Week for an Antifraud Activist," *Wall Street Journal*, China Realtime Report, October 31, 2011. Available online at http://blogs .wsj.com/chinarealtime/2010/10/14/a-bad-week-for-an-antifraud-activist.

6. Andrew Jacobs, "Rampant Fraud Threat to China's Brisk Ascent," *New York Times*, October 6, 2010.

7. Ibid.

8. Ibid.

9. Sam Geall, "Who Tried to Kill Fang Xuancheng?" *Foreign Policy*, July 6, 2010. Available online at www.foreignpolicy.com/articles/2010/07/06/why_was_china_afraid_of_a_science_journalist?page=0,1.

10. Ibid.

11. Anil Gupta and Haiyan Wang, "Chinese Innovation is a Paper Tiger," *Wall Street Journal*, July 28, 2011. Available online at http://online.wsj.com/article/SB10001424053111904800304576472034085730262.html.

12. David Tyfield, JIN Jun, and Tyler Rooker, "Game-Changing China," *Nesta*, June 2010. www.nesta.org.uk/publications/reports/assets/features/game-changing_china.

13. Steve Lohr, "When Innovation Too, Is Made in China," *New York Times*, January 1, 2011.

14. Anil Gupta and Haiyan Wang, "Chinese Innovation Is a Paper Tiger," *Wall Street Journal*, July 28, 2011. Available online at http://online.wsj.com/article/SB10001424053111904800304576472034085730262.html.

15. Ibid.

16. Ibid.

17. Ibid.

18. "50 SOEs to Go Worldwide," *Shanghai Business Review*, December 27, 2010.

19. "The Boot Is on the Other Foot," *The Economist*, March 30, 2006.

20. Li Yuan, "China's Internet: Why China Has No Steve Jobs," *Wall Street Journal*, October 7, 2011. Available online at http://blogs.wsj.com/chinarealtime/2011/10/07/chinas-internet-why-china-has-no-steve-jobs/?KEYWORDS=steve+jobs+china.

21. Anil Gupta and Haiyan Wang, "Beijing is Stifling Chinese Innovation," *Wall Street Journal*, September 1, 2011. Available online at http://online.wsj.com/article/SB10001424053111904800304576472034085730262.html.

22. Ibid.

23. David Barboza, "Entrepreneur's Rival in China: The State," *New York Times*, December 7, 2011. Available online at www.nytimes.com/2011/12/08/business/an-entrepeneurs-rival-in-china-the-state.html?_r=1&hp=&pagewanted=all.

24. Ibid.

25. Ibid.

26. Ibid.

27. Ibid.

28. Ibid.

29. Ibid.

Chapter 2   The Fractured Web

1. "Trouble on the China Express," *Wall Street Journal*, August 1, 2011. Available online at http://online.wsj.com/article/SB10001424053111904800304576474373989319028.html.

2. "China's E-commerce Scale Increased by 20% in 2008," China Tech News. com, Jan 7, 2009. Available online at www.chinatechnews.com/2009/01/07/8432-chinas-ecommerce-scale-increased-20-in-2008.

3. Yang Wanli and Chen Limin, "A Taxing Issue for Online Shops," *China Daily*, July 12, 2011. Available online at www.chinadaily.com.cn/bizchina/2011–07/12/content_12882261.htm.

4. Ibid.

5. Nick Mackie, "Online Shopping Is Growing Rapidly in China," BBC, August 29, 2011. Available online at http://online.wsj.com/article/SB10001424053111904491704576570612044417314.html.

6. Jeremy Page, "Why China Is Trying to Censor Talk about Jiang Zemin," *Wall Street Journal*, July 7, 2011. Available online at http://blogs.wsj.com/chinarealtime/2011/07/07/why-china-is-trying-to-censor-talk-about-jiang-zemin/.

7. Michael Wines and Sharon LaFraniere, "In Baring Train Crash Facts, Blogs Erode China Censorship," *New York Times*, July 29, 2011. Available online at www.nytimes.com/2011/07/29/world/asia/29china.html?_r=1&hp=&pagewanted=all.

8. "Baidu and Microsoft Tie-up for English Search in China," BBC, July 5, 2011.

9. "Microsoft, Baidu to Expand Web-Search Partnership in China," *Bloomberg*, July 4, 2011.

10. Ibid.

11. "How Chinese Users Search Online," iMedia Connection report, July 28, 2009. Available online at www.imediaconnection.com/con tent/23899.asp.

12. Eliot Gao, "Alibaba-Yahoo Fight Highlights Threat to China Internet Control," *Wall Street Journal*, July 4, 2011. Available online at http://blogs.wsj.com/chinarealtime/2011/07/04/researchers-alibaba-yahoo-fight-highlights-threat-to-china-internet-control/.

13. Loretta Chao and Laurie Burkitt, "Chinese Online Retailer Hopes to Raise Up to $5 Billion in U.S." *Wall Street Journal*, September 16, 2011. Available online at http://online.wsj.com/article/SB1000142405311190449170457657061204417314.html.

14. Lee Chyen Yee and Argin Chang, "eBay Eyes up to 40 Percent Jump in China Sales," *Reuters*, August 30, 2011. Available online at www.reuters.com/article/2011/08/30/us-ebay-idUSTRE77T68120110830.

15. Nick Mackie, "Online Shopping is Growing Rapidly in China," BBC, August 29, 2011. Available online at http://online.wsj.com/article/SB10001 424053111904491704576570612044417314.html.

16. Ibid.

17. Kathrin Hille, "China's State Broadcaster Attacks Baidu," *The Financial Times*, August 17, 2011.

18. Ibid.

19. Ibid.

20. Eliot Gao, "Alibaba–Yahoo Fight Highlights Threat to China Internet Control," *Wall Street Journal*, July 4, 2011. Available online at http:// blogs.wsj.com/chinarealtime/2011/07/04/researchers-alibaba-yahoo-fight-highlights-threat-to-china-internet-control/.

21. Ibid.

22. Ibid.

23. "Flatter World and Thicker Walls? Blogs, Censorship and Civic Discourse in China," *Public Choice*, August 9, 2007.

Chapter 3   The Silicon Paddies of China

1. "Global Outsourcing Market to Be Worth US$1,430bn by 2009," *Computer Business Review*, August 2007. Available online at http://cbr.co.za/article .aspx?pklarticleid=4714.

2. Tian Chengping, "Labour and Social Security Development in China," speech, September 14, 2006.

3. Ron Gluckman, "China's VanceInfo Technologies Tries to Outdo Indian Outsourcers," *Forbes Magazine*, October 26, 2011. Available online at www .forbes.com/global/2011/1107/companies-people-technology-service-provider-chen-outsourcing-india-gluckman.html.

4. Ibid.

Chapter 4   Heavy Metal

1. Edward Wong, "China's Railway Minister Loses Post in Corruption Inquiry," *New York Times*, February 12, 2011. Available online at www.nytimes .com/2011/02/13/world/asia/13china.html.

2. Simon Rabinovitch, "Crash Threatens China's High-speed Ambitions," *The Financial Times*, July 24, 2011. Available online at www.ft.com/intl/.cms/s/0/ f978586e-b5e3–11e0–8bed-00144feabdc0.html#axzz1TBZrNeHZ.

3. Jonathan Shieber, "New Revelations in China's Railway Corruption Scandal," *Wall Street Journal*, China Realtime, March 23, 2011. Available

online at http://blogs.wsj.com/chinarealtime/2011/03/23/new- revelations-in-chinas-railway-corruption-scandal/.

4. Li Jing, "Relatives Sorrow Amid Claims and Doubts," *Xinhua*, July 28, 2011. Available online at www.ecns.cn/2011/07–28/1154.shtml.

5. James T. Areddy and Norihiko Shirouzu, "China Bullet Trains Trip on Technology," *Wall Street Journal*, October 3, 2011. Available online at http://online.wsj.com/article/SB1000142405311190435350457656898365856132.html.

6. Shelly Zhao, "The Politics of China-Africa Oil," *The China Briefing*, April 13, 2011. Available online at www.china-briefing.com/news/2011/04/13/the-geopolitics-of-china-african-oil.html.

7. Sam Chambers and Paul French, *Oil on Water* (London: Zed Books, 2010), 60.

8. Ibid, 39.

9. Ibid.

10. Robert Wright and Simon Rabinovitch, "China Vows to Turn Tide on Flood of Ships," *The Financial Times*, November 3, 2011.

11. "Heavy Duty: China's Next Wave of Exports," *Economist Intelligence Unit Whitepaper*, August 2011, 6.

12. "China Cars Face Hurdles to Sell Abroad," *China Daily*, April 18, 2007.

13. Qiang Xiaoji, "China's Automobiles Struggling to Enter EU Market," *China Daily*, December 12, 2009.

14. Xu Xiao, "Auto Exports Rise, but Numbers Still Modest," *China Daily*, August 22, 2011. Available online at www.chinadaily.com.cn/bizchina/2011–08/22/content_13164406.htm.

15. Wang Chao, "European Cars Boost Sales in Sluggish Chinese Market," *China Daily*, July 15, 2011. Available online at http://europe.chinadaily.com.cn/epaper/2011–07/15/content_12910598.htm.

16. Brian Spegle, "Train Spat With China Heats Up," *Wall Street Journal*, July 11, 2011. Available online at http://blogs.wsj.com/chinarealtime/2011/07/08/train-spat-with-japan-heats-up/?mod=WSJBlog&mod=chinablog.

17. Jonathan Soble, "Japanese Rail Chief Hits at Beijing," *The Financial Times*, April 5, 2010. Available online at www.ft.com/cms/s/0/b2ebd992–40dd-11df-94c2–00144feabdc0.html#ixzz1VuqszJyh.

18. James T. Areddy and Norihiko Shirouzu, "China Bullet Trains Trip on Technology," *Wall Street Journal*, October 3, 2011. Available online at http://online.wsj.com/article/SB1000142405311190435350457656898365856132.html.

19. Yuriko Koike, "Unsafe at Any Speed," *TODAYOnline*, July 29, 2011. Available online at www.todayonline.com/Commentary/EDC110729–0000049/Unsafe-at-any-speed.

20. Ibid.

21. Brian Spegle, "Train Spat with China Heats Up," *Wall Street Journal*, July 11, 2011. Available online at http://blogs.wsj.com/chinarealtime/2011/07/08/train-spat-with-japan-heats-up/?mod=WSJBlog&mod=chinablog.

22. Jason Dean and Jeremy Page, "Trouble on the China Express," *Wall Street Journal*, August 1, 2011. Available online at http://online.wsj.com/article/SB10001424053111904800304576474373989319028.html.

23. Simon Rabinovitch, "Crash Threatens China's High-Speed Ambitions," *The Financial Times*, July 24, 2011.

24. Keith Bradsher, "China Is Eager to Bring High-Speed Rail Expertise to the U.S.," *New York Times*, April 7, 2010. Available online at www.nytimes.com/2010/04/08/business/global/08rail.html.

25. Michael Wines and Keith Bradsher, "China Rail Chief's Firing Hints at Trouble," *New York Times*, February 17, 2011. Available online at www.nytimes.com/2011/02/18/world/asia/18rail.html?_r=1&pagewanted=all.

26. John Garnaut, "China Inc Goes Off the Rails in Saudi Arabia While Building Mecca Monorail," November 16, 2010. Available online at www.smh.com.au/business/china-inc-goes-off-the-rails-in-saudi-arabia-while-building-mecca-monorail-20101115-17ud1.html.

27. "China Coming Down the Tracks," *The Economist*, January 28, 2011. Available online at www.economist.com/node/17965601.

28. Simon Rabinovitch, "Crash Threatens China's High-speed Ambitions," *The Financial Times*, July 24, 2011. Available online at www.ft.com/intl/cms/s/0/f978586e-b5e3-11e0-8bed-00144feabdc0.html#axzz1TBZrNeHZ.

29. Keith Bradsher, "China Is Eager to Bring High-Speed Rail Expertise to the U.S.," *New York Times*, April 7, 2010. www.nytimes.com/2010/04/08/business/global/08rail.html.

30. "Heavy Duty: China's Next Wave of Exports," *Economist Intelligence Unit Whitepaper*, August 2011, 6.

Chapter 5 Brand China

1. Andrew Hupert, "China's Other Branding Problem," *China Economic Review*, January 24, 2011. Available online at www.chinaeconomicreview.com/today-in-china/2011_01_24/Chinas_other_branding_problem.html.

2. John G. Spooner and Michael Kanellos, "IBM Sells PC Group to Lenovo," *CNET News*, December 8, 2004. Available online at http://news.cnet.com/IBM-sells-PC-group-to-Lenovo/2100-1042_3-5482284.html.

3. Xiao Geng, Xiuke Yang, and Anna Janus, *China's New Place in a World in Crisis*, Australia National University, 160.

4. "Red Flag Raises," *The Economist*, July 7, 2011. Available online at www
   .economist.com/node/18929130.

5. Ibid.

6. "When It Matters," *The Economist*, August 20, 2011. Available online at www
   .economist.com/node/21526407.

Chapter 6   Declaration of Energy Independence

1. Lin Boqiang, "Powering Future Development," *China Daily*, January 20, 2012.
   Available online at www.chinadaily.com.cn/usa/business/2012–01/20/con-
   tent_14480632.htm.

2. Richard Lester and Edward Cunningham, "*Greener Plants, Grayer Skies:
   A Report from the Front Lines of China's Energy Sector*," MIT Industrial
   Performance Center, August 2008.

3. Ibid.

4. Leslie Hook, "China Denies IEA Claim on Energy Use," *The Financial Times*,
   July 20, 2010.

5. British Petroleum's Energy Outlook 2030.

6. Michelle Price, "A Consumption Conundrum," *Wall Street Journal*, December
   6, 2011. Available online at http://online.wsj.com/article/SB1000142405297
   020434610457663856134092500 4.html.

7. Daniel H. Rosen and Trevor Houser, "China Energy: A Guide for the Perplexed," 9. A part of the China Balance Sheet, a joint project by the Center
   for Strategic and International Studies and the Peterson Institute for
   International Economics, 9.

8. Ibid, 9.

9. "Crisis Prevention," *The Economist*, February 24, 2011.

10. Deborah Seligsohn, Robert Heilmayr, Xioamei Tan, and Lutz Weischer.
    "China, the United States, and the Climate Change Challenge (Washington,
    DC: World Resources Institute, 2009). Available online at www.wri.org/
    publication/china–united-states–climate-change-challenge.

11. Institute for Energy Research Testimony Before the Select Committee
    on Energy Independence and Global Warming Hearing on the Global
    Clean Energy Race, September 22, 2010. Available online at www.insti-
    tuteforenergyresearch.org/2010/09/22/ier-testimony-on-the-hearing-on-
    the-global-clean-energy-race/.

12. James Kynge, *China Shakes the World: A Titan's Rise and Troubled Future—and
    the Challenge for America* (New York: Houghton Mifflin Company, 2007).

13. "Engine Trouble," *The Economist*, October 23, 2010, 81.

14. Daniel Rosen and Trevor Houser, *China Energy: A Guide for the Perplexed* (Washington, DC: Center for Strategic International Studies and the Peterson Institute for International Economics, May 2007), 6.

15. Ibid.

16. British Petroleum's Energy Outlook 2030.

17. Jonathan Watts, "China's Coal Addiction," *Foreign Policy*, December 2, 2010. Available online at www.foreignpolicy.com/articles/2010/12/02/china_s_addiction_to_coal?page=0,2.

18. Elisabeth Rosenthal, "Nations That Debate Coal Use Export It to Feed China's Need," *New York Times*, November 21, 2010. Available online at www.nytimes.com/2010/11/22/science/earth/22fossil.html?_r=1&ref=todayspaper.

19. Ibid.

20. Ibid.

21. Jonathan Watts, "China's Coal Addiction," *Foreign Policy*, December 2, 2010. Available online at www.foreignpolicy.com/articles/2010/12/02/china_s_addiction_to_coal?page=0,2.

22. British Petroleum's Energy Outlook 2030.

23. Clifford Kraus, "Breaking Away from Coal," *New York Times*, November 29, 2010.

24. Mary Kay Magistad, "China's Search for Cleaner Coal," *The World*, December 1, 2010. Available online at www.theworld.org/2010/12/01/china-clean-coal-greenhouse-climate/.

25. U.S.–China Energy Center website. Available online at www.nrac.wvu.edu/projects/sheia/index.html.

26. Annette Cary, "Researchers Look to China for Help with Projects," *News Tribune*, December 12, 2010. Available online at www.thenewstribune.com/2010/12/12/1462000/richland-researchers-look-to-china.html.

27. "Chinese Power Plants Have Been Staging Brown Outs, with Some Functioning Only Days of Coal Inventory," *MyChinaViews*, December 31, 2010. Available online at http://mychinaviews.com/2010/12/pricing-fracas-leads-to-coal-shortage/.

28. Sephen Kurczy, "China to Mold Future World Energy Use: IEA," *Christian Science Monitor*, November 10, 2010. Available online at www.csmonitor.com/World/Global-Issues/2010/1110/China-to-mold-future-world-energy-use-IEA.

29. Wang Guanqun, "Driving Mad! 4 Million Cars Clog Beijing Roads," *Global Times*, December 21, 2009. Available online at news.xinhuanet.com/english/2009–12/21/content_12681158.htm.

30. "Huge Source of Oil, Gas Found in South China Sea," *India Talkies*, January 17, 2011. Available online at www.indiatalkies.com/2011/01/huge-source-oil-gas-south-china-sea.html.

31. "Natural Gas Demand to Soar." Available online at http://europe.chinadaily .com.cn/business/2011–01/29/content_11940148.htm.

32. "China's Natural Gas Approach: Pipelines are Best Way to Resolve Shortages." Available online at www.chinasignpost.com/2010/12/china%E2%80%99s-natural-gas-approach-pipelines-are-best-way-to-resolve-shortages/.

33. "Natural Gas Demand to Soar." Available online at http://europe.chinadaily .com.cn/business/2011–01/29/content_11940148.htm.

34. Ibid.

35. "National Gas Consumption to Increase." Available online at www.china-daily.com.cn/usa/business/2011–01/21/content_11898239.htm.

36. "China First-Quarter Gas Imports More Than Double, NDRC Says." Available online at www.bloomberg.com/news/2011–04–15/china-first-quarter-gas-imports-more-than-double-ndrc-says-1-.html.

37. Ibid.

38. "National Gas Consumption to Increase." Available online at www.china-daily.com.cn/usa/business/2011–01/21/content_11898239.htm.

39. Gordon Feller, "China's Energy Demand—Improving Energy Intensity is Proving a Daunting Task in the World's Most Populous Nation," *EcoWorld*, May 20, 2007. Available online at www.ecoworld.com/energy-fuels/chinas-energy-demand.html.

40. "China 2008 Power Consumption Up 5.23 pct, Lowest Rise in 10 Years," *Reuters*, January 5, 2009. Available online at www.forbes.com/feeds/ afx/2009/01/05/afx5882229.html.

Chapter 7   Consider the Alternatives

1. "China Surpassed US on Wind Power Capacity," *Shanghai Business Review*, January 17, 2011.

2. "China Showing Signs of Solar Cell Oversupply," Interfax, September 29, 2010. Available online at www.interfax.cn/news/15299.

3. Keith Bradsher, "On Clean Energy, China Skirts the Rules," *New York Times*, September 8, 2010. Available online at www.nytimes.com/2010/09/09/ business/global/09trade.html?_r=2&pagewanted=all.

4. Ibid.

5. "The Sun Also Rises," China Economic Review, July 2010. Available online at www.chinaeconomicreview.com/industry-focus/in-the-magazine/article/ 2010–07–01/The_sun_also_rises.html.

6. "Solar Energy, New Times Online." Available online at www.nytimes.com/ info/solar-energy/?inline=nyt-classifier.

7. Recharge News, December 28, 2010. Available online at www.rechargenews. com/energy/solar/article239439.ece?WT.mc_id=rechargenews_rss.

8. "China Seen Quickening Hydropower Approvals," *China Daily*, July 28, 2010.

9. Ai Yang, "Cambodia: China Not Behind Mekong Floods," *China Daily*, November 19, 2010.

10. "Tibet's Hydropower Station Won't Affect Water Flows," *Xinhua*, November 18, 2010.

11. "'Tibet Dam is First in Series," *Hindustan Times*, November 19, 2011.

12. "European Pressurized Reactor," Wikipedia. Available online at http://en.wikipedia.org/wiki/European_Pressurized_Reactor.

13. Dinakar Sethuraman and Rakteem Katakey, "Nuclear Plant to be Built in Shandong," March 24, 2011. Available online at http://europe.chinadaily.com.cn/business/2011–03/24/content_12221281.htm.

14. Leslie Hook, "China Nuclear Protest Builds Steam," *The Financial Times*, February 28, 2012.

15. Brian Dumaine, "China Charges into Electric Cars," October 19, 2010.

Chapter 8 Errors of Emission

1. Ariana Eunjung Cha, "Solar Energy Firms Leave Waste Behind in China," *The Washington Post*, March 9, 2008.

2. Ibid.

3. "Toward a Just and Sustainable Solar Industry, A Silicon Valley Toxics Coalition Whitepaper," January 14, 2009.

4. Ariana Eunjung Cha, "Solar Energy Firms Leave Waste Behind in China," *The Washington Post*, March 9, 2008.

5. Ibid.

6. Austin Ramsey, "On the Streets of China, Electric Bikes Are Swarming," *Time Magazine*, June 14, 2009. Available online at www.time.com/time/world/article/0,8599,1904334,00.html#ixzz1aLgPp54y.

7. "China Drives Electric Bike, Scooter Boom," MSNBC, July 27, 2009. Available online at www.msnbc.msn.com/id/32172301/ns/world_news-world_environment/t/china-drives-electric-bike-scooter-boom/#.TpJey3JqnIV.

8. Ibid.

9. Ibid.

10. Ibid.

11. Jane Spencer and Nicholas Casey, "Toy Recall Shows Challenge China Poses to Partners," August 3, 2007. Available online at http://online.wsj.com/article/SB118607762324386327.html.

12. Hu Yongqi, "Lead Poison Factory 'Tipped Off' about Green Checks," *China Daily*, January 13, 2010. Available online at www.chinadaily.com.cn/china/2010–01/13/content_9311412.htm.

13. James T. Areddy, "Shanghai Closes Plants Using Lead," *Wall Street Journal*, October 5, 2011. Available online at http://online.wsj.com/article/SB100014 24052970203791904576610230760888692.html.

14. "24 Children Hospitalized for Lead Poisoning in E China," *China Daily*, January 6, 2011. Available online at www.chinadaily.com.cn/china/ 2011–01/06/content_11800307.htm.

15. Hu Yongqi, "Lead Poison Factory 'Tipped Off' about Green Checks," *China Daily*, January 13, 2010. Available online at www.chinadaily.com.cn/china/2010–01/13/content_9311412.htm.

16. "Lead Poisoning Sickens 16 Children in Central China," *China Daily*, June 12, 2010. Available online at www.chinadaily.com.cn/2010–06/12/content_9968401.htm.

17. "Battery Plant Blamed for Lead Poisoning," *China Daily*, January 6, 2011. Available online at www.chinadaily.com.cn/bizchina/2011–01/06/content_11805198.htm.

18. "China Shuts Battery Factories Due to Lead Poisoning," BBC, May 30, 2011. Available online at www.bbc.co.uk/news/business-13594890.

19. "Battery Plant Blamed for Lead Poisoning," *China Daily*, January 6, 2011. Available online at www.chinadaily.com.cn/bizchina/2011–01/06/content_1 1805198.htm.

20. Hu Yongqi, "Lead Poison Factory 'Tipped Off' about Green Checks," *China Daily*, January 13, 2010. Available online at www.chinadaily.com.cn/china/2010–01/13/content_9311412.htm.

21. Sharon LaFraniere, "Lead Poisoning in China: The Hidden Scourge," *New York Times*, June 15, 2011. Available online at www.nytimes.com/2011/06/15/world/asia/15lead.html?pagewanted=all.

22. Ibid.

23. Ibid.

24. James T. Areddy, "Shanghai Closes Plants Using Lead," *Wall Street Journal*, October 5, 2011. Available online at http://online.wsj.com/article/SB100014 24052970203791904576610230760888692.html.

25. Michael Montgomery, "Rare Earths: Common Applications," *Rare Earth Investing News*, August 3, 2010. Available online at http://rareearthinvesting-news.com/investing-in-rare-earths/rare-earths-common-applications/.

26. Suzanne Goldenberg, "Rare Earth Metals Mine is Key to US Control over Hi-Tech Future," The Guardian, December 26, 2010. Available online at www.guardian.co.uk/environment/2010/dec/26/rare-earth-metals-us.

27. Ibid.

28. Keith Bradsher, "Main Victims of Mines Run by Gangsters Are Peasants," *New York Times*, December 30, 2010. Available online at www.nytimes.com/2010/12/30/business/global/30smugglebar.html?ref=global.

29. Ibid.

30. Simon Perry and Ed Douglas, "In China, the True Cost of Britain's Clean, Green Wind Power Experiment: Pollution on a Disastrous Scale," *Daily Mail*, January 29, 2011. Available online at www.dailymail.co.uk/home/moslive/article-1350811/In-China-true-cost-Britains-clean-green-wind-power-experiment-Pollution-disastrous-scale.html#ixzz1acZ2q0Z8ii.

Chapter 9   Dragon on a Diet

1. Sun Wukong, "Thirsty China Launches Water Saving Plan," *Asia Times*, March 7, 2007. Available online at www.atimes.com/atimes/China_Business/IC07Cb03.html.

2. Jonathan Watts, "Can the Sea Solve China's Water Crisis?" *The Guardian*, January 24, 2011.

3. Sun Wukong, "Thirsty China Launches Water Saving Plan," *Asia Times*, March 7, 2007. Available online at www.atimes.com/atimes/China_Business/IC07Cb03.html.

4. Ibid.

5. Mao Yushi, Sheng Hong, and Yang Fuqiang, *The True Cost of Coal*, September 2008.

6. Ibid.

7. Ibid.

8. Bill Dodson, *China Inside Out: 10 Irreversible Trends Reshaping China and its Relationship with the World* (Singapore: John Wiley & Sons, 2011), 93.

9. Zhang Qi, "Is it the End-of-the-Line for Coal-to-Oil in China?" *China Daily*, October 9, 2008. Available online at www.chinadaily.com.cn/bizchina/2008–10/09/content_7090441.htm.

10. Jonathan Watts, "Can the Sea Solve China's Water Crisis?" *The Guardian*, January 24, 2011. Available online at www.guardian.co.uk/environment/2011/jan/24/china-water-crisis?CMP=twt_fd.

11. Ibid.

12. Jamil Anderlini, "China's Rapid Urbanization Could Prove Illusory," *The Financial Times*, July 20, 2011. Available online at www.ft.com/intl/cms/s/0/6bca8058-b2d4–11e0-bc28–00144feabdc0.html#axzz1o9D6y89R.

13. Wang Hongyi, "Builders Follow Environmental Approach," *China Daily*, January 9, 2012. Available online at www.chinadaily.com.cn/usa/business/2012–01/09/content_14404733.htm.

14. Lin Boqiang, "Powering Future Development," *China Daily*, January 20, 2012. Available online at www.chinadaily.com.cn/usa/business/2012–01/20/content_14480632.htm.

15. "China Clean Revolution Report III: Low Carbon Development in Cities," The Climate Group, December 2010.

16. "Country Analysis Briefs: China," United States Energy Information Administration, November 2010, 17.

17. Jin Zhu, "Rising to the Challenge of Conserving Energy," *China Daily*, September 21, 2010. Available online at www.chinadaily.com.cn/cndy/2010–09/21/content_11331549.htm.

18. "China Pushing for Energy-Efficient Buildings," World Watch Institute, January 2010.

19. Jin Zhu, "Rising to the Challenge of Conserving Energy," *China Daily*, September 21, 2010. Available online at www.chinadaily.com.cn/cndy/2010–09/21/content_11331549.htm.

20. Ibid.

21. "China Launches Massive Reconstruction of Buildings for Energy Saving," *Xinhua*, March 29, 2006. Available online at http://english.people.com.cn/200603/29/eng20060329_254429.html.

22. Li Xing, "Keeping in Step to Cut Carbon Footprint," *China Daily*, January 18, 2011. Available online at www.chinadaily.com.cn/usa/2011–01/18/content_11873641.htm.

23. Jin Zhu, "Rising to the Challenge of Conserving Energy," *China Daily*, September 21, 2010. Available online at www.chinadaily.com.cn/cndy/2010–09/21/content_11331549.htm.

24. "执行新的建筑节能标准不会引起房地产市场波动," *People's Daily*, January 18, 2010. Available online at http://env.people.com.cn/GB/5300758.html.

25. "China Pushing for Energy-Efficient Buildings," World Watch Institute, January 2010.

Chapter 10   Assembly Required

1. Elaine Chow, "If You're Beating a Petitioner, Make Sure It's Not an Official's Wife," *Shanghaiist*, July 21, 2010. Available online at http://shanghaiist.com/2010/07/21/if_youre_beating_a_petitioner_make.php.

2. Ibid.

3. Christopher Carothers, "Outrage as 'Wrong-Beating Gate Scandal' Breaks," *Wall Street Journal*, July 22, 2011. Available online at http://blogs.wsj.com/chinarealtime/2010/07/22/outrage-as-wrong-beating-gate-scandal-breaks/.

4. Ibid.

5. "Religion in China on the Eve of the 2008 Beijing Olympics," *Pew Forum on Religion & Public Life*, May 7, 2008. Available online at http://pewresearch .org/pubs/827/china-religion-olympics.

6. Ibid.

7. "Religious Believers Thrice the Estimate," *China Daily*, Feb 7, 2007. Available online at www.chinadaily.com.cn/china/2007–02/07/con tent_802994.htm.

8. Nick Young, "Three 'C's': Civil Society, Corporate Social Responsibility and China," *China Business Review*, January–February 2002. Available online at www.chinabusinessreview.com/public/0201/young.html.

9. "Underpinning Charity Work," *Beijing Review*, Nov 23 2007.

10. "Now Is the Time to Begin Charity at Home," *China Daily*, Oct 31, 2007.

11. "The Celebrity, Jet Li," *Forbes Magazine*, Sep 28, 2009.

Afterword   The Curse of Steve Jobs

1. Li Yuan, "China's Internet: Why China Has No Steve Jobs," *Wall Street Journal*, October 7, 2011. Available online at http://blogs.wsj.com/chinareal time/2011/10/07/chinas-internet-why-china-has-no-steve-jobs/?KEYWO RDS=steve+jobs+china.

About the Author

Bill Dodson is the author of *China Inside Out: 10 Irreversible Trends Re-shaping China and Its Relationship with the World* (John Wiley & Sons, 2011).

Bill has been writing and advising on China's business and economics issues and managing companies in China, since 2002. He has been quoted on China-related topics on Bloomberg.com, and in *Newsweek* magazine, *The Economist*, National Public Radio, *China Economic Review*, *Shanghai Business Review*, *China International Business Magazine*, *The China Economic Quarterly*, *Monocle*, and others.

He has published nearly 100 articles in international magazines on China's industry and consumer trends.

A graduate of Cornell University, he has served as a columnist for the *China Economic Review*, and produced a monthly China business management column for *Eurobiz Magazine*, a publication of various European companies invested in China. A former senior consultant with PricewaterhouseCoopers, he has also served as a senior adviser to Bearing Point. He is a frequent speaker on economics and investment trends in China. He has advised executive management teams at Global 500 companies such as Ford Motor Company, Electrolux, and TOTAL—the French energy group—on China economic and consumer trends. He also regularly lectures at executive MBA programs from around the world on the trends shaping China's economy and business climate.

He lives in greater Shanghai.

Bibliography

Brynjolfsson, Erik, and Andrew McAfee. *Race Against the Machine: How the Digital Revolution is Accelerating Innovation, Driving Productivity, and Irreversibly Transforming Employment and the Economy.* Lexington, MA: Digital Frontier Press, 2011.

Cowen, Tyler. *The Great Stagnation: How America Ate All the Low-Hanging Fruit of Modern History, Got Sick, and Will (Eventually) Feel Better.* New York: Dutton, 2010.

Diamond, Jared. *Collapse: How Societies Choose to Fail or Succeed.* New York: Viking, 2005.

Diamond, Jared. *Guns, Germs and Steel: The Fates of Human Societies.* New York: W. W. Norton & Company, 2005.

Economy, Elizabeth. *The River Runs Black: The Environmental Challenge to China's Future.* Ithaca and London: Cornell University Press, 2010.

Fenby, Jonathan. *The Penguin History of Modern History: The Fall and Rise of a Great Power, 1850–2009.* London: Penguin Books, 2009.

Fishman, Ted C. *China, Inc.: How the Rise of the Next Superpower Challenges America and the World.* New York: Scribner, 2005.

French, Paul, and Sam Chambers. *Oil on Water.* London: Zed Books, 2010.

Friedman, Thomas L. *Hot, Flat and Crowded: Why the World Needs a Green Revolution— and How We Can Renew Our Global Future.* London: Allen Lane, 2008.

Friedman, Thomas L. *The World is Flat: The Globalized World in the Twenty-First Century.* London: Penguin Books, 2006.

Fukuyama, Francis. *The Origins of Political Order: From Pre-historic Times to the French Revolution*. New York: Farrar, Straus and Giroux, 2011.

Gifford, Rob. *China Road: A Journey into the Future of a Rising Power*. New York: Random House, 2007.

Harford, Tim. *Adapt: Why Success Always Starts With Failure*. New York: Farrar, Straus and Giroux, 2011.

Harney, Alexandra. *The China Price: The True Cost of Chinese Competitive Advantage*. New York: The Penguin Press, 2008.

Hewitt, Duncan. *Getting Rich First: Life in a Changing China*. London: Vintage, 2007.

Johnson, Steven. *Where Good Ideas Come From: The Natural History of Innovation*. New York: Riverhead Books, 2010.

Kuhn, Thomas S. *The Structure of Scientific Revolutions*. Chicago: University of Chicago Press, 1996.

Kynge, James. *China Shakes the World: A Titan's Rise and Troubled Future—and the Challenge for America*. New York: Mariner Books, 2007.

Leeb, Stephen. *The Coming Economic Collapse: How You Can Thrive When Oil Costs $200 a Barrel*. New York: Warner Books, 2006.

Mertha, Andrew C. *China's Water Warriors: Citizen Action and Policy Change*. Ithaca and London: Cornell University Press, 2008.

McGregor, Richard. *The Party: The Secret World of China's Communist Rulers*. New York: HarperCollins, 2010.

Nielsen, Michael. *Reinventing Discovery: The New Era of Networked Science*. Princeton: Princeton University Press, 2012.

Prestowitz, Clyde. *Three Billion New Capitalists: The Great Shift of Wealth and Power to the East*. New York: Basic Books, 2005.

Ross, Andrew. *Fast Boat to China: High-Tech Outsourcing and the Consequences of Free Trade—Lessons from Shanghai*. New York: Vintage Books, 2007.

Shenkar, Oded. *The Chinese Century, The Rising Chinese Economy and Its Impact of the Global Economy, the Balance of Power, and Your Job*. Upper Saddle River, NJ: Wharton School Publishing, 2005.

Strahan, David. *The Last Oil Shock: A Survival Guide to the Imminent Extinction of Petroleum Man*. London: John Murray, 2007.

Tainter, Joseph A. *The Collapse of Complex Societies. New Studies in Archaeology*. Cambridge, UK: Cambridge University Press, 1988.

Watts, Jonathan. *When a Billion Chinese Jump: How China Will Save Mankind—Or Destroy It*. London: Faber and Faber, 2010.

Zakaria, Fareed. *The Post-American World*. New York: Norton, 2008.

Index

223